CANADA

LECTOR HOUSE PUBLIC DOMAIN WORKS

CANADA

BECKLES WILLSON,
JOHN LANG

ISBN: 978-93-5614-604-4

Published: 1907

LECTOR HOUSE LLP
E-MAIL: info@lectorhouse.com

Landing of the Loyalists, 1783

(*Page 132*)

ROMANCE OF EMPIRE

CANADA

BY

BECKLES WILLSON

AUTHOR OF 'THE GREAT FUR COMPANY,' 'LEDGER AND SWORD,' ETC.

EDITED BY
JOHN LANG

WITH TWELVE REPRODUCTIONS FROM
ORIGINAL COLOURED DRAWINGS BY
HENRY SANDHAM

1907

TO
MY SON
GORDON

PREFACE

In the following pages is told the history of my native land, as a sagamore of the olden time might tell the legends of the past to the young braves of his tribe gathered round the lodge fire. Though primarily intended for youth, yet there is scarce any one of intelligence and spirit who may not find some entertainment in hearing of the doings of the valiant heroes, the bloodthirsty villains, the virtuous ladies who played their part in the Canadian drama, and then passed for ever away.

Elsewhere I have given the story of Hudson's Bay,[1] and what is recounted here of fur-traders and fur-trading forts owes much, as the reader will expect, to my former book.

---

[1] *The Great Fur Company* 1899.

CONTENTS

LIST OF ILLUSTRATIONS

THE ROMANCE OF CANADA

CHAPTER I

CARTIER UNFURLS THE FLAG OF THE LILIES

Nearly four centuries ago, in the spring of the year, the banks of the river Thames from Windsor to Greenwich were lined with a multitude of gaily-dressed lieges. Artisans and their wives, tradesmen and apprentices, farmers in smock frocks, gentlemen in doublets and hose, and ladies in farthingales, all came out to snatch a peep of a brave spectacle. From lip to lip ran the news that at last the royal barge in its crimson and gold trappings had set out from Windsor. Bluff "King Hal," as the people affectionately termed their monarch, and his new queen, Anne Boleyn, were that day making their first voyage together down the Thames to the royal palace at Greenwich.

Glance at this spectacle but a moment, for, if an English reader and more familiar with English than with Canadian history, it will serve to fix the date of my story's opening firmly in your mind. The banks are re-echoing with loyal cheers, the State bargemen are plying their oars and the State trumpeters their trumpets, while poor Anne Boleyn, little dreaming of the fate awaiting her, smiles and nods merrily at the crowds who wave their silken kerchiefs in the sunshine. So this first water pageant of the season passes along.

Now, History borrowing something of Romance, has so ordered it that on this self-same day, the 20th of April 1534, when the English King was setting out on the river journey with his new queen, on the other side of the English Channel another and very different embarkation was taking place, and a very different voyage was begun.

The object of this enterprise was far indeed from pleasure, and its consequences were very important and far-reaching, not only to the King of France, but to King Henry the Eighth's successors, the English people and the British Empire of our own day. Different as it was, there was here, too, cheering and waving of caps and cries of "Vive le Roi!" as the soldiers, sailors, and townsfolk on the dock at St. Malo bade lion-hearted Jacques Cartier godspeed on his adventurous voyage to the New World.

At this time, you must bear in mind, more than forty years had elapsed since Christopher Columbus had returned to Spain with tidings of his glorious discovery on the other side of the Atlantic. When Jacques Cartier, son of a Breton mariner, was born, all Europe was still ringing with the news. As the child grew up he heard tales of how often famous mariners had in turn sailed boldly to the west and claimed for Spain, Portugal, and England the lands which might lead to India and serve as gateway to the Spice Islands of the East. Amongst these sailors were John Cabot and his son Sebastian, who, although themselves Venetians, sailed from the port of Bristol and flew the English flag. In 1498 the Cabots explored the whole coast of North America from Labrador to South Carolina, and were the first Europeans actually to land in the country we to-day know as Canada. After the Cabots, who claimed the whole northern lands for England, came, a quarter of a century later, a Florentine navigator, named Verrazano, who declared the entire region annexed to the French Crown. And now, because of Verrazano's claim, King Francis of France was sending Jacques Cartier forth from St. Malo with two little ships and 120 men to explore inland and set up the French flag and a French colony in a New France beyond the sea. So this Frenchman, valiant, lean, and rugged, with his little band of compatriots, sailed away on that April day while Bluff King Hal of England was merrymaking on the Thames, well content with his little isle of England, giving no thought to Empire or distant deeds of discovery and conquest amongst the savage nations of the earth.

Straight towards the setting sun steered Cartier and his men. As they were not buffeted greatly by the waves, in twenty days' time, on the 10th of May, they reached the straits which led to the gulf and river of St. Lawrence. How their hearts leapt when they sighted land! On their left they saw the great island of Newfoundland and on the right Labrador's bleak shores stretched before them. "Surely," cried Cartier, "this is Cain's portion of the earth!" But their spirits rose when they sailed into the Gulf and came to rich forests of pine, maple, and ash, with abundance of blossom and wild berries on every hand. They had been afraid that the interior was as desolate as their first glimpse of Labrador. The few Indians on the banks gazed upon them with a wondering but friendly eye. The explorers were unprepared, too, for the great heat which overtook them. By day the land was bathed in intense sunshine, and at night a gorgeous moon lit up the broad waters, while owls and bats wheeled in air heavily perfumed with wild shrubs and flowers. A bay in which he anchored Cartier called Baie des Chaleurs. Sailing on, he came to a promontory, which he christened Cape Gaspé, where he landed and set up a cross 30 feet high. On its front was a shield with the arms of France. As you travel through Eastern Canada to-day you will frequently come upon crosses by the wayside, where the country folk kneel and say their prayers. This at Gaspé was the first cross erected in New France. While the pious sailors were erecting it a number of red-men flocked near and surveyed the proceeding jealously, as if the white newcomers were about to charm away their land; but Cartier explained as best he could to their medicine-men and distributed amongst them some knives and trinkets, of which he had brought out hither a goodly store.

Having quieted their suspicions, Cartier lured two of the young red-men into his ship, wishing to show them, on his return, to the King. Cartier had meant to continue his voyage much farther westward, but adverse winds met him, wherefore, abandoning this resolution, and taking counsel with his officers and pilots, he decided to set sail for France. As truly as Columbus he had discovered a new world, and from the two natives whom he bore away Jacques Cartier had learnt of the existence of the great river St. Lawrence. So much interest was awakened in France by Cartier's narrative of his voyage, that there was no difficulty about procuring the money for another expedition. The French Court and people were filled with enthusiasm about Canada, and so they continued to be for more than two centuries. How their hope and confidence were rewarded we shall see in due time.

When Jacques Cartier again took his departure from St. Malo, in May 1535, he commanded three ships and 110 sailors. A number of nobles and gentlemen, moreover, belonging to some of the proudest families in France, went with him, eager for adventure. They thought, as marine adventurers often thought in those days, that this time surely they would find the gateway to the passage of Cathay and win wealth untold. But they were not so lucky as at first; the winds were so bad that seven weeks elapsed before Cartier reached the Straits of Belle Isle. From this point the squadron steered for the Gulf St. Lawrence, so named by Cartier in honour of the saint upon whose day it was discovered. Keeping on, as his Indian interpreters bade him do, he sailed up that stream which the Indians called "The Great River of Canada."

Can you wonder at Cartier and his attendant nobles feeling a thrill of excitement as the landscape no white man had ever seen before slowly unfolded itself to view? Opposite the great mouth of the mysterious Saguenay red-men in birch bark canoes came to greet them. Their two interpreters could exchange language with these, although their many months' residence in France had made them very different in appearance from their brother savages of Canada. They wore now slashed crimson doublets and brilliant striped hose, while the massive feathers in their heads caused the Canadian Indians to regard them as chiefs of great renown. Cartier led his ships on to what the natives called "The Kingdom of Canada," which stretched along the St. Lawrence as far as the Island of Montreal, where the King of Hochelaga held his sway. To the fertile Isle of Orleans, which Cartier reached on the 9th of September, he gave the name of Isle of Bacchus, on account of the abundant grape vines growing upon it. From here the explorer could see on the north bank of the great river a towering promontory lit up by the morning sun. This was Cape Diamond, at whose base there crouched the Indian village of Stadacona. Cartier anchored here his little fleet, and the chief of the neighbouring tribe, Donacona, came to greet him, with twelve canoes full of warriors. After a speech of welcome, the women of the tribe, or squaws, danced and sang without ceasing, standing in water up to their knees.

Jacques Cartier was delighted with the country he had discovered, and lost no time in deciding to proceed up the river as far as Hochelaga. Donacona and the other chiefs, on hearing this, did their utmost to dissuade him by inventing stories about the dangers of the river. Perceiving these made little impression on the sturdy sailor, three Indians were forthwith dressed as devils, "with faces painted as black as coal, with horns as long as the arm, and covered with the skins of black and white dogs." Cartier was told that these devils were the servants of the Indian god at Hochelaga, who warned the European strangers that "there was so much snow and ice that all would die." To their astonishment, however, Cartier only laughed at such tricks, and told them that "their god was a mere fool, and that Jesus would preserve them from all danger if they would believe in Him." Wishing also to impress upon them his own great power, he ordered several pieces of artillery to be discharged in the presence of the chief and his warriors; whereupon they became filled with astonishment and dread. Never before had they heard such terrible sounds. What were these strangers who could produce thunder at will? To reassure them, the "pale-face" chief distributed trinkets, small crosses, beads, pieces of glass, and other trifles amongst them and sailed on boldly up the river.

Jacques Cartier and the Red-skins

In a fortnight a town, consisting of about fifty large huts or cabins surrounded by wooden palisades, came into view; 1200 souls belonging to a tribe called the Algonquins dwelt here in Hochelaga. The whole population assembled on the banks and gave the visitors friendly welcome. All that night the savages remained on the shore, burning bonfires, dancing, and crying out "Aguaze!" which was their word for welcome and joy. The poor Indians took Cartier and his men for gods. He distributed gifts amongst them and professed to heal their ailments.

Near the town of Hochelaga was a mountain, to which the Indians conducted their visitors. From the summit this first band of Europeans in Canada gazed down at the wonderful panorama spread before their eyes, glistening rivers, green meadows, and forests of maple brilliant in autumn scarlets and yellows. Naming this lofty eminence Mount Royal, Jacques Cartier and his companions returned to Stadacona. Having decided to spend the winter in Canada, a fort was forthwith built on the shore, but before the little colony could be more than half prepared, a fierce Canadian blizzard was upon them. Never had they known such cold and such tempests. From their lack of fresh food, scurvy rioted amongst them, and out of 110 men 25 died. When the disease was at its height an Indian told them that they could be cured by the juice of a spruce tree. Out of their fort they ran with the axes, and so quickly did they drink the juice that in six days the whole of a great tree had been consumed.

Thus was the little colony made well again. Lest the Indians should know how weak they were during that terrible winter, they continued to dread; but no attack was made upon them, and in the spring Cartier made ready to return to France. This time Donacona and four other chiefs were seized by stratagem and taken on board ship. A cross 30 feet high, with the fleur-de-lys fastened to it, was set up on the shore, and in the middle of May the waters of the St. Lawrence began to bear them down to the Gulf and the open Atlantic. Exactly one month later Cartier was being greeted by the cheers of the people of his native St. Malo.

Alas! Donacona and the other Indian braves whom the French had borne away never returned to Stadacona and their forest haunts. Before Cartier was ready to make another voyage to Canada, five years later, all had pined away and died. It was then that the Sieur de Roberval, a nobleman of Picardy, was appointed by King Francis as lieutenant, with the high-sounding titles of Governor of Canada, Hochelaga, Saguenay, Newfoundland, Belle Isle, Carpunt, Labrador, the Great Bay, and of Baccalaos, as well as Lord of Norembaga, which latter country existed only in imagination. Roberval meant to have gone out with Cartier, but was detained until the following year. On his third voyage Jacques Cartier visited Hochelaga and tried to pass up the river beyond the village, but the dangerous rapids of Lachine caused him to pause. When he returned to France a year later, he took with him some small transparent stones which he supposed were diamonds, but which were really only quartz crystals; he also carried away what he deemed to be gold ore, but which turned out to be merely mica. On the way back he met the Sieur de Roberval, who afterwards built a fort on the St. Lawrence and explored the surrounding country. But Roberval wrought nothing, and famine at length reduced the survivors to a state of abject dependence upon the natives. In vain

Roberval entreated the King to come to his rescue with supplies of colonists, food, and ammunition. Instead of acceding to this petition, King Francis despatched orders for his lieutenant to return home to France. Roberval reluctantly obeyed, and thus this first attempt to establish a French colony on the banks of the St. Lawrence ended in failure.

Cartier was allowed by the King to bear always the title of "Captain." He undertook no more voyages into unknown lands, but died about 1577 in his own manor-house close to St. Malo. While he was thus spending his later years in an enforced retirement, eating his heart out for want of adventure, a daring Spaniard, De Soto, was facing dangers at the other and southern end of the Continent, close to the triple mouths of the Mississippi, which he had discovered.

King Francis of France, years before, had been stricken by death, and thereupon his country became plunged in unhappy civil war. Catholic and Huguenot dipped their blades in each other's blood; but in the midst of the long and deadly strife Canada was not wholly forgotten. Frenchmen still spoke with pride of the valiant Cartier and the flag of the lilies which he had unfurled in the Western world.

CHAPTER II

POUTRAINCOURT GOES FORTH TO ACADIA

It was a terrible era for France. Catholics and Huguenots made fierce war upon one another, and in the midst of all the fighting and murders and massacres such as that of St. Bartholomew, which you may read about in French history, conquest and discovery languished. Although the King, the Court, and the Cardinals had no time to spare to Canada, yet you must not suppose that for the next fifty years there was no connection at all between the New World and France. The red-men, paddling up and down the mighty St. Lawrence, very often met with pale-face mariners eager to exchange guns and hatchets and beads for the furs of the animals trapped in the northern wilderness. Many European ships—often over a hundred sail—came every year to Newfoundland to the cod-fisheries off that coast, and some of these sailed onward into the Gulf and on to Tadoussac, and even as far as Three Rivers. At these places fur-trading stations were set up, and hither repaired each season the hardy mariners, who were not slow to discover more profit in Europe out of sable and beaver skins than out of cod-fish. Those wild animals, whose fur was esteemed in France and other lands, were so plentiful in Canada that in course of time the peltry trade, as it was called, grew to be the principal business of the country. As each spring came round the savage tribes, whose hunting-grounds were far in the interior, would pack their furs in canoes and paddle hundreds of miles down the lakes and rivers to the post where the white trader was awaiting them. When the Indian had bartered his furs, back he paddled again to his own hunting-grounds, and the trader in turn sailed back to France, to return the next season.

Meanwhile, too, English sailors, lieges to the great Elizabeth, had been visiting the New World which Cabot had claimed for England. First there came Martin Frobisher in 1576, who, looking for a short route to India, set foot on the shores of Labrador. Again, on the other side of the continent, Sir Francis Drake, sailing round the world, sighted the snowy peaks on the borders of British Columbia, which afterwards became a part of the Canadian Dominion. Then came Sir Humphrey Gilbert, half-brother of Sir Walter Raleigh, with 260 men and several ships, to plant a colony in Newfoundland. Sir Humphrey's sovereign mistress, Elizabeth, had graciously granted him a charter of 600 miles in every direction from St. John's, whereby he became lord and master of what we know to-day as Nova Scotia, New Brunswick, Prince Edward Island, and parts of Labrador and Quebec. It was on a serene August morning that the fleet reached harbour. Donning his most gorgeous doublet of lace and velvet, and surrounded by his stalwart retainers, Sir Humphrey landed at St. John's and took possession of Newfoundland in Elizabeth's name. When he had reconnoitred the coast, our courtier resolved to return with his people to England for provisions and reinforcements. Nowadays many of our bravest sailors would be afraid to trust themselves in the little ships that formed his fleet. They were very short, curved, and blunt, and, compared to our modern floating castles, were only giant cockle-shells. A few days out a hurricane arose, and in the midst of the raging seas Sir Humphrey's ship, the *Squirrel,* was doomed. But not even his dreadful fate, when it loomed around him, could fill the brave commander's soul with fear. With waves careering mast-high he sat placidly on deck with a Bible on his lap. "Cheer up, lads," cried he to his sailors, "we are as near heaven on sea as on land." And so the cruel billows rolled over the *Squirrel,* and it and the brave souls it bore were lost for ever. The expedition from which so much had been hoped in England was an utter failure. It was the sons of France who were destined to found and people Canada, and to perform such deeds of daring valour and endurance as are not to be surpassed in the history of our own island motherland. Englishmen, it is true, were to have all Canada at last, but nearly two hundred years were to roll by before their soldiers could wrest the mainland from their hereditary rivals.

Fifteen years had passed since Sir Humphrey Gilbert went down in the little *Squirrel,* when a French noble, the Marquis de la Roche, received a commission from King Henry the Fourth of France to colonise Canada. With the commission in his pocket the Marquis knew not which way to turn. It was not easy in those days to find Frenchmen ready to live in a country supposed to be ice and snow the whole year round. But "where there's a will there's a way," and the Marquis at last chose fifty sturdy convicts from the prisons and galleys, and, embarking with his retinue, set sail for the West. A long low sandbank called Sable Island guards the entrance to St. Lawrence Gulf, and here the Viceroy set forty of his convicts ashore while he explored the waters roundabout. At first the marooned convicts were delighted with their freedom. They roamed hither and thither, finding a lagoon of fresh water, frequented by wild cattle and coveys of wild ducks. Sweet berries flourished in abundance. During all that summer the convicts amused themselves, keeping a sharp look-out for the return of their lord and master, the Marquis, who had gone to find them a haven to settle in and build their dwellings. Day succeeded day, week followed week, but the Marquis never came back. A violent storm had arisen which drove his vessel eastward across the wide Atlantic to the very shores of France, where the hapless nobleman was seized by a powerful enemy and cast into prison. Can you not picture the rage and despair of the unhappy men on Sable Island when they realised their plight? Winter was fast approaching, and they had neither proper food, fuel, nor raiment. Quarrelling fiercely, they slew one another, while those who were left, huddled together in rude huts formed of wreckage, lived on raw flesh and dressed themselves in the hides of wild cattle. They gave themselves up for lost, but at length the Marquis de la Roche, far away in France, was able to tell the King of the predicament of the abandoned convicts. A ship was sent out to rescue them, and, like so many wild animals, with long matted hair and beards, they grovelled at the feet of their deliverers. After such hardships as they had undergone, King Henry was not the one to send them back to prison; he pardoned them instead, and all who had survived went back to their homes. De la Roche, broken in health and fortune, died soon after, so this project for starting a colony was, as you see, not a whit luckier than Cartier's or Roberval's or Sir Humphrey Gilbert's had been. Was the next attempt to reap greater success?

In that summer of 1599, when the convicts were still on Sable Island, to the north of them, in the Gulf of St. Lawrence, fur-trading ships pressed forward under full canvas to the westward. These ships were owned by two men of King Henry's Huguenot subjects, named Pontgravé and Chauvin, who had formed themselves into a partnership to buy and sell furs. No trader could lift a finger in those days without a royal charter or patent, and these men were influential enough to get a charter from the King bestowing upon them the exclusive right to the fur trade of Canada. It was hardly likely they could really make good such a right, or that the other Frenchmen who had been buying furs from the Indians would thereafter stop buying them on account of it. But it was a safe precaution, and made their rivals' operations illegal. On their part Pontgravé and Chauvin promised the King that they would settle in Canada 500 colonists. In this they were promising more than they could perform; the most they actually did do was to induce sixteen men to remain all winter at Tadoussac, with insufficient food, clothing, and shelter. Alas! when the ships from France appeared in the St. Lawrence next year, the last year of the sixteenth century, they found most of the sixteen dead. Their surviving companions had married native wives and gone to live in the wigwams of the Indians. Once more you see this enterprise had not fared any better than those which had gone before, and, like the others, Chauvin died recognising bitterly that his scheme was a failure.

How was it with his partner, Pontgravé? Pontgravé was only a trader, but he was of dogged tenacity. He saw that if Canada could be colonised by his countrymen, there was a great fortune to be made out of the fur trade, and the way to do it, he reasoned, was to bring his chief rivals together to form a company, so that, instead of being enemies, all would work together to keep out the smaller traders or "pirates," and gradually establish proper trading-posts in Canada. An influential and wealthy old soldier named Aymar de Chastes, Governor of Rouen, interested himself in the scheme, and, being high in favour with the King of France, he procured a charter and set about seeing if he and his friends could not succeed where the others had been so signally defeated.

We have now reached the point in our story at which Samuel de Champlain, the real founder of New France, enters upon the scene. For Aymar de Chastes, casting about for an experienced and adventurous spirit to help in the new enterprise, bethought him of a valorous naval captain who had recently returned from Mexico and the Spanish main, ready for anything which would fill his purse or increase his renown. Captain de Champlain was a truly great man, no mere hot-blooded, roystering swashbuckler, as many adventurers were in those days, but romantic, pious, and humane. He was then about thirty-six years old. Offering with alacrity his sword and his skill on an exploring expedition up the St. Lawrence, Champlain went, in company with Pontgravé and another adventure-loving nobleman of the Court, Pierre du Gast, better known as the Sieur de Monts.

When these pioneers reached Tadoussac they left their ships and ascended the river in boats to the farthest point yet reached, the Rapids, just above Hochelaga, now the city of Montreal. Just as Jacques Cartier had done nearly seventy years before, Champlain toiled up the forest-clad slopes of Mount Royal in order to obtain a good view of the surrounding country. He, too, was charmed with all that met his eye, and having drawn up a map and written down a narrative of all he had seen, Champlain and his companions re-embarked in the autumn, when the Canadian woods were brilliant in their browns and purples, yellow and crimson foliage, and sailed back across the salt seas to France. What was their mortification to discover that during their absence their patron, De Chastes, had died, and the company he had exerted himself to make prosperous was all but broken up. But Champlain was not to be beaten. He showed his narrative and his maps to the good and wise King Henry, who was perfectly satisfied of his good faith, and agreed to allow De Monts and his friends to continue the work of colonising Canada and organising the fur trade. De Monts, who was a Huguenot, was forthwith appointed the King's Viceroy in New France, on condition that he and the others bore all the cost of the expedition, and by and by, in the spring of 1604, four vessels once more sailed away. It was arranged that two of the ships should engage in the fur trade on the St. Lawrence, while the other two were to carry out the colonists, soldiers, work-people, priests, gentlemen, and, as always happened, as always must happen, a few rogues, to whichever spot De Monts selected for the purpose. The little fleet steered farther south than was done in the last voyage, and thus it came to pass that it finally reached that part of New France then called Acadia, and to-day marked Nova Scotia on the map. How it came by its name of Nova Scotia you shall hear later on. One day, just before De Monts and his heterogeneous crew landed, they anchored in a harbour where one of their sheep (*moutons*) jumped overboard. So De Monts, who was not without a vein of humour in these matters, christened the harbour Port Mouton. All were delighted with the beauty of the landscape, the grassy meadows, the silvery streams replete with fish, the wooded mountains.

Besides De Monts and Champlain there was a third leader of the expedition, a certain rich nobleman of Picardy named Baron de Poutraincourt. It was Poutraincourt who named the place where he wished to found a colony Port Royal. It was, wrote Champlain afterwards, "the most commodious, pleasant place that we had yet seen in this country." Unhappily the leaders could not instantly make up their minds, and the landing and settlement actually took place many leagues farther along on the banks of a river which now forms the boundary between the two great countries of America and Canada, which river was then, and ever since has been, called the Holy Cross (Ste. Croix) River. What a scene of joyous bustle ensued! Eighty people disembarked from the ships, and were soon hard at work building the little fort and houses of the first French settlement on the coast of the North-American Continent. While the colony was thus industriously making ready for the winter, Champlain, thinking he might be better employed, went off exploring the coast in his ship, sailing up and down what was destined to become long before he died the territory of New England.

Great trials were in store for the little colony. Very quickly the settlers found that Holy Cross River was a very uncomfortable place, lacking sufficient shelter, with little or no fuel handy. What was far worse than the winter's cold, scurvy broke out amongst them, and by the time the leaves were putting forth their first blossoms thirty-six persons had perished of this disease. Poutraincourt's choice, Port Royal, after all, was best, and there in late spring they began to construct a town near what is now called Annapolis. De Monts and Poutraincourt returned in the autumn to France, and after much labour and trouble managed to induce a large number of mechanics and workers to come out to Acadia. It must be confessed that there were on board Poutraincourt's ship, the *Jonas*, which sailed from Rochelle in May 1600, some very reckless, unruly characters. But their leader felt convinced that they would make good colonists, if they were only shown the way. Amongst those to help him he had brought a very clever man, Lescarbot, a lawyer and poet, full of enthusiasm for the new project.

In the meantime what of the founders and original settlers of Port Royal? Thinking they had been deserted by their leaders, and lacking provisions and clothing, they became almost as discouraged as the poor convicts had been on Sable Island.

As the summer season wore on they constructed two little craft—the very first ships ever built in Canada—and straightway sailed for the Newfoundland fishery banks to seek some of their countrymen, leaving two only of their number and a wise old Indian chief, named Meinbertou, to greet the newcomers on board the *Jonas*. A peal of a cannon from the little fort testified to the joy of its inmates that the long-expected succour was at last at hand. A party was sent to overtake the little Port Royal ship to bring back the colonists. No sooner were they landed than Poutraincourt broached a hogshead of wine, and Port Royal became a scene of mirth and festivity. When Champlain and Poutraincourt went off to make further exploration, Lescarbot was left in charge of the colony. He set briskly to work to show the people how they should become prosperous. He ordered crops of wheat, rye, and barley to be sown in the rich meadows and gardens to be planted. Some he cheered, others he shamed into industry, never sparing himself, so that by and by it was not wonderful that everybody loved the merry, witty, bustling Lescarbot. Not a day passed but he set going some new and useful work. Until now the people had ground their corn with hand-mills, as their fathers and grandfathers had done for hundreds of years; Lescarbot showed them how to make a water-mill. He also taught them how to make fire-bricks and a furnace, and how to turn the sap of the trees into tar and turpentine. No wonder the Indians, astonished to see so many novel industries growing up before their eyes, cried out, "How many things these Normans know!" When the explorers returned to Port Royal, rather dispirited, Lescarbot arranged a masquerade to welcome them back, and all the ensuing winter, which was extremely mild, was given up to content and good cheer. Then it was that Champlain started his famous "Order of a Good Time," of which many stories have come down to us. The members of this order were the fifteen leading men of Port Royal. They met in Poutraincourt's great hall, where the great log fire roared merrily. For a single day each of the members was saluted by the rest as Grand Master and wore round his neck the splendid collar of office, while he busied himself with the duty of providing dinner and entertainment. One and all declared the fish and game were better than in Paris, and plenty of wine there was to toast the King and one another in turn. At the right hand of the Grand Master sat the guest of honour, the wrinkled sagamore, Membertou, nearly one hundred years old, his eyes gleaming with amusement as toast, song, and tale followed one another. On the floor squatted other Indians who joined in the gay revels. As a final item on the programme, the pipe of peace, with its huge lobster-like bowl, went round, and all smoked it in turn until the tobacco in its fiery oven was exhausted. Then, and not till then, the long winter evening was over.

What jolly times those were! If only they could have lasted! Port Royal might have become a great city and Acadia a populous province. But bad tidings for Port Royal came from France. The next ship that sailed into the harbour brought word that De Monts' charter had been revoked by the King, and his friends would support his scheme with no more money. So there appeared nothing to do but to bid good-bye to Port Royal and their Indian friends, who watched them depart with sadness, promising to look after the fort and its belongings until the white men should return from over the wide sea.

Champlain had already in his heart chosen another field—the lands far inland on the St. Lawrence; but as for Poutraincourt, he swore to deal a blow at his enemies in France and come back to take deep root in the fertile Acadian soil. While, therefore, Champlain was with his followers founding Quebec, and De Monts, discouraged, had lost all interest in Acadia, Poutraincourt busied himself to such purpose that three years later (1610), in spite of all the baffling obstacles he met with, he set out again for his promised land with a fresh shipload of settlers.

At this time King Henry the Fourth was surrounded by members of the Society of Jesus (called Jesuits), who had made themselves already very powerful in the politics of Europe. The King ordered Poutraincourt to take out a Jesuit priest to Acadia, but Poutraincourt, distrusting the Jesuits, evaded the priest who had been chosen to accompany him at Bordeaux, and took out one of his own choosing instead, Father La Flèche. What was their joy when they landed in midsummer to find everything at Port Royal just as they had left it! One may be sure the Indians gave their pale-face friends a cordial greeting. Old Membertou, still alive, embraced Poutraincourt and declared that now he was ready to be baptized a Christian. The christening duly took place, and the ancient sagamore was renamed Henri, after the King, and his chief squaw was christened Marie, after the Queen. There were numerous other Indian converts, and great celebrations took place, for the colonists were religious enthusiasts and believed such doings would give great satisfaction to the King.

But, alas, the King was never to hear of it! Even while all this was happening, while the future of the colony promised so well, a terrible blow had fallen upon it and the realm of France. The brave and humane Henry the Fourth had been stabbed to death by the dagger of the assassin Ravaillac. The new King, Louis the Thirteenth, being only a little boy, all the power and influence of the Court fell into the hands of the Queen Dowager, Marie de Medici, a false and cruel woman. Her closest friends and advisers were the Jesuit priests. Now these Jesuits, although professing Christianity and brotherly love, held in horror anybody who did not think exactly as they did. They wanted especially, by whatever means, to make converts of the Canadian savages. They wanted too, being very ambitious, to get the direction of the affairs of the New World into their own hands.

'The Order of a Good Time' 1606

Yet ignorant of the royal tragedy, Poutraincourt sent his son, Biencourt, a fine youth of eighteen, back in the ship to France, to report to his Majesty the success at Port Royal in converting the natives. Whereupon the Jesuits decided that the time had come to supplant Poutraincourt. They announced that they would send back two of their priests with young Biencourt. A number of rich and pious Catholic ladies of the Court, headed by Madame de Guercheville, interested themselves so far in the work as to buy up all the rights of Poutraincourt's friends and partners, including De Monts, as proprietors of Acadia. Henceforward Poutraincourt was to be under the dependence of the Jesuits. That was the unwelcome news his son sailed back to tell him. The two priests whom he was obliged to receive—Biard and Ennemond Massé—were the very first members of their famous order to engage in the work of converting the North-American Indians. You will see as our story progresses what a terrible and dangerous task this was, and how it demanded men of boundless zeal and courage to undertake it.

Under the circumstance, quarrels were to be expected; and quarrels enough came. The Jesuits at Court, finding Poutraincourt insubordinate, seized the trading vessels destined for Port Royal on one pretext or another, and brought about so many imprisonments and lawsuits, that at last Poutraincourt was ruined. No longer could he send out supplies of provisions, and his people at Port Royal had to subsist through a whole winter upon acorns, beech-nuts, and wild roots. When Madame de Guercheville and her Jesuit friends had thus crippled poor Poutraincourt, she withdrew the priests to other localities named in her charter, over which she really supposed she had control. As for the sturdy old sagamore, Membertou or Chief Henri, he soon breathed his last. On his deathbed he prayed to be buried with his forefathers, but of course the priests overcame his scruples, and his wrinkled body was laid in the little cemetery at Port Royal.

You may be interested to know what were the French Jesuit rights in North-America. The charter the young king, or rather the Queen Dowager, gave to Madame de Guercheville actually included nearly all the territory from the St. Lawrence River to Florida. Was there no one at hand to remind the crafty Marie that the continent she thus complacently handed over was not hers or her son's to bestow; that the English had a far better right than the French to its possession; that in that very year an English colony had been settled in Virginia, chartered by King James the First of England? Curious to relate, the land which the English king granted was as wide in extent, in truth it was almost the very same region as that claimed by the French. So here we have the cause and beginning of a quarrel which occasioned seas of bloodshed, and was to last, very nearly without interruption, for just a century and a half, between the French and the English colonists in North-America.

In the spring of 1613 the Jesuits despatched a new expedition under a courtier named La Saussaye, who, having landed at Port Royal to take on board the two priests there, sailed on and founded a new colony at Mount Desert, now in the American State of Maine. They had just commenced to erect buildings and put up the walls of a fort, when, greatly to their surprise, a strange war-ship appeared in the little harbour. It drew nearer, and they saw, with misgivings, the blood-red cross of St. George floating from the mast-head. The captain of the war-ship turned out to be Samuel Argall, a young and daring English mariner, who had joined his fortunes to those of Virginia. While he was cruising with sixty men off the coast of Maine on the lookout for codfish, some friendly Indians boarded the ship and told him that French intruders were hard by, building a fort. By no means a kind, indulgent young man was Argall, and his eyes kindled angrily.

"Oho!" he exclaimed, with an oath, "how dare these rascals venture into King James, my master's territory!" Whereupon, stimulated by hopes of plunder, he unmuzzled his fourteen cannon and assaulted and sacked the yet defenceless French settlement, killing several, including one of the priests, and making prisoners of the rest. This done, he destroyed every trace of the colony. Fifteen Frenchmen, including La Saussaye, he turned adrift in an open boat, while the others he took back with him to Virginia. Those whom Argall abandoned to their fate would surely have perished had it not been for friendly Indians, who gave them food and helped them on their way north. There they eventually met a trading vessel and were carried back to France. As to the prisoners, on landing at Jamestown they were treated as pirates by the English settlers there. Although afterwards released, the Virginian governor, Sir Thomas Dale, was so incensed at hearing from one of them about Port Royal, that he bade Argall return, with three armed ships, and sweep every Frenchman out of Acadia. Argall carried out his instructions only too well; he set fire to the fort and settlement of Port Royal, and in a few hours the entire place, the gallant Poutraincourt's hope and pride, was a mass of smoking ruins. Luckily for themselves, most of the French happened to be away in the forest at the time, and so saved their lives. Some took permanent refuge with the Indians, and amongst these was young Biencourt. Others found their way to the colony which, as we shall now narrate, Champlain had by this time formed far away at Quebec. But it was all over with Port Royal, at least for the present. With a heavy heart Poutraincourt sailed away to France, and soon afterwards in battle laid down his life for his sovereign.

So ends the first chapter in the story of that part of Canada then called Acadia. We will return to it again, for the adventurous young Biencourt is still there roaming in the woods with a handful of faithful followers, ready to found Port Royal anew. In the meantime what was happening to Champlain, who a few years before had sailed a thousand miles up the mighty St. Lawrence to found a colony? It is high time that we should now turn to his adventures.

CHAPTER III

OF THE DOINGS OF GALLANT CHAMPLAIN

When the Sieur de Monts abandoned Acadia, thinking, as indeed it seemed, an evil spell had been cast upon it, he turned his attention to Quebec and the river St. Lawrence. Here, far inland, was a fair region which promised wealth and glory, and over this region he appointed Champlain his lieutenant. Of the two ships which De Monts fitted out one was for the fur trade, of which King Henry, ere his heart was pierced by the dagger of Ravaillac, gave him a monopoly for one year; the other was to carry colonists to found a new French settlement. You have seen how one after another the French colonies had, from this cause or that, come to destruction; but with such a wise and strong head as Samuel de Champlain, one now was expected to bear better and more lasting fruit. Truly, whatever their faults, the founders of New France were very determined men, arising fresh after each disaster, resolved to people with their countrymen the great Western wilderness. When Champlain's ships, once safely through the Straits of Belle Isle, reached Tadoussac, Champlain left there his associate Pontgravé to barter for furs with the Indians. He himself continued his voyage up the river until he came to the spot where Jacques Cartier had passed the winter of 1535, and with his men consumed a whole spruce-tree in order to drive away the scurvy.

It was at Quebec (a word meaning in the Indian language a strait) that on the third day of July 1607 Champlain gave orders to disembark. In the shadow of the towering rock of Cape Diamond, the first thing to be done was to clear a site and erect cabins for shelter. As his men toiled on unceasingly the natives gathered round in wonder and admiration. They were unaccustomed to much manual work themselves, their squaws doing most of the labour. They saw in a few short weeks the bastions of a fort and cannon set up. Scarcely had the workmen completed their task and got all snug and tidy for the winter than a plot was formed amongst some of Champlain's followers to kill him. The leader of the plot was a Norman locksmith, Jean Duval, a brave and violent fellow who had served with Champlain in Acadia, and was impatient under any kind of authority. According to the plan the conspirators drew up, their leader was to be shot, the stores pillaged, and then they were all to fly to Spain with the booty. Lucky it was for the great and good pioneer that one of the plotters, filled with remorse, went to Champlain a few days before the mutiny was to be carried out and confessed all. Champlain with great promptitude seized Duval and hanged him to the nearest tree, but the rest he only sent back to France, where the good King, at his request, pardoned them. Meanwhile Pontgravé had collected and sailed away with his cargo of furs. Spring came; the snows melted and were replaced by green meadows and blossoming trees; everywhere the birds sang. Champlain, without waiting for Pontgravé's return, set off up the river and soon met again friendly Indian chiefs of the Algonquin and Huron tribes, who told him terrible tales of their sufferings at the hands of their enemies the Iroquois or the Five Nations. In their despair these chiefs sought out the Man-with-the-Iron-Breast, as they called Champlain, on account of the steel breast-plate he wore, and asked his help against the blood-thirsty Iroquois. These men of the Five Nations, Mohawks, Senecas, Cayugas, Onondagas, and Oneidas, lived in the forests south of Lake Ontario, and were perhaps at once the most intelligent and the most cruel of all the Indians on the continent. It was the Iroquois who had destroyed the old Huron towns of Stadacona and Hochelaga which Cartier had seen and described, and as they bore the Hurons and Algonquins an implacable enmity, it was natural that they would extend this enmity to the pale-faces who had now come to dwell in the Huron country. They might, it is true, have been propitiated; but Champlain did not stop to consider any questions of policy: he favoured at once the idea of alliance with the surrounding red-men, an alliance which was to cost him and his new colony a bloody and fearful price. Champlain, then, made three warlike expeditions into the country of the Iroquois during the next six years. In the first he paddled in canoes up the Richelieu River and came to a beautiful lake, to which he gave his own name ("Lake Champlain"). Meeting a party of Iroquois of the Mohawk nation or tribe, he fell upon them suddenly. The Mohawks fancied at first that they had only to do with Algonquins, and felt confident of victory, until the Frenchmen's muskets rang out; then not fast enough could they flee in panic from the magic bullets, leaving many slain, including their bravest chiefs. Champlain had only 60 Frenchmen and Indians, while the Mohawks numbered 200; but his victory was complete; not one of his force was killed, and the town of the enemy was wiped from the face of the earth. Notwithstanding Champlain's protests, the Algonquins insisted on torturing one of their Iroquois captives to death by every device of savage cruelty. Mercy was not in their code; they neither gave it, nor, when captured, expected it.

During the next three years Champlain was kept very busy in explorations, in attacking the Iroquois, and in protecting his colony. During this time he returned to France, and was favourably received at Fontainebleau by King Henry, who listened with interest to Champlain's tale of his adventures in "New France." But in spite of royal favour, Champlain had so many rivals and enemies that, like Poutraincourt in Acadia, he found it impossible to get the charter renewed, and so his friend and patron, De Monts, was obliged to try and get along without it. Equipping two more ships, he sent Champlain back with them to Canada.

The great ambition of Champlain's soul was to find a passage through the continent to China. At last it seemed to him that the friendliness of the Hurons and Algonquins would furnish him with the means of attaining this desire. He had just made arrangements with the chiefs, when the news came to him of King Henry's assassination, and he felt it was necessary for him to return without delay again to France. De Monts, his patron, still enjoyed the title of Lieutenant-General of New France, but his resources and influence had been sadly crippled by the King's death, and the cost of keeping up Quebec, Tadoussac, and Acadia was very great. He had no longer the monopoly, that is to say, the sole right of buying and selling Canadian furs—it was a right thrown open to other traders; and when Champlain on his next voyage back from France once more sailed up the St. Lawrence, he found many strange fur-traders trafficking with the savages.

The leader had now more to do and think about than ever; he wished, moreover, to prepare a fitting home for a fair and youthful partner who was ever in his thoughts. During his absence in Paris he had espoused a charming Huguenot girl named Helen Bouillé, daughter of the murdered King's private secretary. Her name survives to-day in "Helen's Island" in the river opposite Montreal. So many traders did Champlain find in the vicinity of this island, that he built a fort there and resolved to turn the site of Hochelaga into a trading station. Two uneventful years passed by, and then, in the very year Argall was destroying hapless Port Royal (1613), Champlain's imagination was kindled by the astonishing tale of a certain Nicholas Vignau. This adventurer had passed a winter amongst the red-men of the upper Ottawa River. Vignau told his chief that, in company with some Algonquins, he had once arrived at a remote sea-shore, where his eyes had beheld the fragments of a wrecked English ship. Champlain's heart bounded with joy; he thought his hopes were now about to be realised. Taking Vignau, two white followers, and an Indian guide, the explorer passed the dangerous rapids of the Ottawa and made the acquaintance, one after another, of its lakes, cataracts, and islands. He pressed on, passed the Rideau (Curtain) Falls, so named because of the resemblance of this sheet of water to a great white curtain. He and his awe-struck companions stared at the raging, foaming cauldron of the Chaudière, close to where the city of Ottawa, capital of the Canadian Dominion, now stands, while the Indians cast into the waters gifts of tobacco and other things to propitiate the angry god of the waters. At last the party reached Allumette Island. Here dwelt a friendly Algonquin chief named Tessouat, who received the Frenchmen hospitably and invited them to a banquet. Tessouat knew Vignau; he knew also how he had passed his time amongst the men of his tribe. So when Champlain related at the feast what Vignau had told him of his journey to the sea-shore, Tessouat bluntly told his guest that Vignau, though a pale-face, was a liar, and that he had never been on such a journey. For a while the shock of this discovery overwhelmed Champlain with rage and sorrow. Tessouat was so indignant at the way the French leader had been deceived, that he wanted Vignau to be put to death, but Champlain was of too noble and forgiving a nature for that, and contented himself with rebuking the offender. At the same time, although Vignau confessed his falsehood, we are able to see to-day a certain foundation for his story which was obscured from Canada's founder. We happen to know now what Champlain centuries ago did not dream of: that only three hundred miles separate Allumette Island from the southern end of the great inland sea, Hudson's Bay. This body of water two or three brief seasons before had been discovered by an Englishman, who, like Champlain, had tried to find a short route to China and the East Indies.

In 1610 Henry Hudson, in the pay of the Dutch, sailed up the river which now bears his name, and paved the way for the Dutch colony, afterwards called the

New Netherlands. A year later, in the service of England, he sailed northwards in the *Half Moon*, passed through the narrow Hudson's Straits, and so on into the ice-bound inland sea. There his terrified crew mutinied, turning their brave commander adrift in an open boat, together with his son and two of his faithful companions. Thus perished Henry Hudson, who was never heard of again. As for the craven mutineers, when they stole back guiltily to England, they were seized and made to pay the penalty of their crime. Three ships were sent out to search for Hudson, but, alas, it was then too late.

Of this inland sea Vignau may have heard stories from the Indians. It may be that those who told him had really seen the wreck of poor Henry Hudson's boat on the shores, but this we shall never really know until the great Day of Judgment comes, when the sea gives up its dead and all secrets of the deep are known.

In the discovery of Lake Ontario, two years later, Champlain found some compensation for his disappointment. He was the first European to visit the "freshwater sea," as he called it. He penned a description of all he had seen, and carried it to France, where it was eagerly read. One of Champlain's mottoes was that "the salvation of a single soul was worth more than the conquest of an Empire." Up to now Quebec had been wholly without priests, but when Champlain returned to the colony he brought out four priests of the Order of the Recollets, pious men who had taken vows of poverty and self-denial. These set about converting the savages to Christianity. One of them, Joseph Le Caron, went forward to the distant Huron country, which had not yet been visited by any European. Champlain himself accompanied the priest from Quebec. On reaching the rapids just above Montreal, the Governor held a conference with the Hurons, who had come from their homes in the West to meet him and induce him to fulfil his pledge to attack the Iroquois. This expedition was one of the most fateful episodes in Champlain's life. He knew nothing about Iroquois history or character. If he had had any suspicion of what his present action was to cost his countrymen in Canada, he would rather have died than provoke the enmity of so terrible a foe. Champlain chose this time to take a most round-about route, measuring full 300 leagues, he and his men often carrying on their backs the canoes and baggage, living on coarse food, and suffering many hardships. Even the priest was obliged to take his share of the hardest work, paddling his oar until the sweat mantled his brow, staggering through the forest with a load such as a mule might carry, and with it all obliged, with the whole party, to hasten at full speed for fear of falling behind into the hands of Iroquois. In those days when there were no roads and hardly even any long paths, travellers made their way by following the rivers and lakes in canoes. When they came to the end of one waterway and wished to reach the beginning of another, they followed what were called the portages or carrying-places, paths in the woods, sometimes only a few yards long and sometimes as long as nine or ten miles.

For many weeks did Champlain sojourn in the Huron country, and then, in early autumn, he departed from their chief town, Carhagonha, on Lake Simcoe, with several hundred red warriors, to inflict chastisement on the painted warriors of the Five Nations.

Crossing Lake Simcoe, Champlain and his followers travelled slowly and with much hardship through the country north of Lake Ontario, until by this very roundabout route the whole party came in a month's time to the fort of the Onondagas, which they intended to attack. As they drew near, the French and Indians fell in with outlying bands of this tribe, capturing many prisoners. Champlain strove unceasingly to induce his Huron allies to show mercy to the captives, but the Indian warrior always deemed mercy a pitiful sign of weakness. He wanted not only to cut off the hands and feet of the male prisoners, gouge out their eyes and burn them alive, but to torture the women and children as well. Only was it when Champlain threatened to withdraw his French soldiers altogether that the Huron chiefs consented to confine their barbarities to the men alone. When the allies got closer to the Onondaga fort they found it was much more strongly defended than they had supposed. It consisted of four rows of strong stakes, and a thick wall made of heavy branches of trees. On the top of this wall were gutters of wood to conduct water to any part which the enemy should set on fire. The water was drawn from a small pond inside the fortification, where all the Onondagas were assembled in little houses, having a large store of bows and arrows, stones and hatchets. Provisions, too, were plentiful, for the Indian harvest was just over. Champlain saw at once that to take such a fort was not an easy task, and advised his Indian allies to be prudent. But the young Hurons were foolhardy and rushed at the four-fold palisade with ear-splitting war-whoops, flourishing their tomahawks. The consequence was as Champlain foresaw: they were shot down or killed by a shower of stones by the enemy. After a time, when they had lost heavily, the Hurons were ready to listen to reason. A plan was devised. In the night-time Champlain had a high wooden platform built; upon it he placed several of his musketeers so that they could fire into the fort, while 300 Hurons were stationed close by to set fire to the palisade. These measures might have succeeded, but the wind unluckily was in the wrong direction and blew the flames of the Huron torches away from the fort. Champlain himself, while trying to make the unruly Hurons obey his orders, was twice wounded, and many of his followers were killed. Then it was that the foolish Huron chiefs became disheartened. They lost faith in the "Man -with -the -Iron -Breast" and decided to give up the attempt and retreat homewards before the winter set in. In vain Champlain besought them; they were obdurate. As it was, when they got to the place, eighty miles away, where their canoes had been left, high winds and snowstorms had begun, and their wounded, including Champlain, suffered much. Solemnly had they promised the French leader that after the attack on the Iroquois they would carry him down the St. Lawrence to Hochelaga, but now they became traitors to their word and refused him even two guides for such a journey. There was nothing else to do: Champlain was obliged to go back with them and spend the whole of the succeeding winter in their lodges. On the way they made many halts to allow the Hurons time to procure stores of fish and game, which were very plentiful in the region north of Lake Ontario. Not until two days before Christmas was the journey ended.

Champlain was not idle that winter, for when his wounds had healed he moved amongst the tribes, making himself acquainted with the country and the language. The woods were filled with June flowers ere he returned to Quebec, where he had been mourned as one dead. You can imagine how rejoiced were the band of martial pioneers there to see their leader once more alive and well. They cheered and sang songs and waved flags in his honour, and even discharged the great cannon, whose echoes startled the Indians prowling afar on the green banks of the St. Lawrence.

Verily the part which Samuel de Champlain and his little band of Frenchmen had played in giving armed assistance to the Hurons and Algonquins was to have terrible results. It threw the Iroquois into friendship with the Dutch and other enemies of the French, who supplied them with firearms. It caused them to bear a hate to Champlain and all his countrymen almost as great as the hate they bore to the dusky Hurons.

All this time Champlain, great as was his ambition, can only be regarded as the agent or manager of a company of men in France whose first wish was to make money out of the fur trade. These men in their hearts had very little sympathy for Champlain's schemes of colonisation and conversion of the savages, and, becoming dissatisfied with the profits Champlain was making for them, they tried repeatedly to procure his recall. In order to baffle the intrigues against him and explain to the King himself the importance of Canada to the kingdom of France, Champlain sailed away yet again for home, leaving sixty men, the entire French population of Canada, behind him in Quebec. By his zeal and eloquence he was able to obtain some fresh supplies for his colony, and also some more soldiers and workers. Amongst these was an apothecary named Louis Hébert, who is often spoken of as the first emigrant to Canada, because he took with him his wife and two children, intending to settle as a farmer on the land. Direct descendants of Hébert are alive in Canada to this day. Two years later Champlain managed to bring a body of eighty colonists out to New France, and the next year (1620) his own wife, Helen de Champlain, accompanied him for the first time to the colony. This time he had triumphed over those who wished to depose him, and was now confirmed in his title of Viceroy of New France, and all seemed in the general rejoicings on his return to promise well for his enterprise. Not only the French in Quebec, but the Indians were delighted at the beauty and manners of the Governor's wife, then only twenty-two years of age. They tell of her that she wore always a small mirror suspended from her neck, according to the custom of the ladies in those days. When the red-men who drew near her looked in the little mirror they saw each, to his astonishment, his own face reflected there, and went about telling one another that the beautiful wife of the white chief cherished an image of each in her heart.

Once in Quebec, Champlain lost no time in laying the foundation of a Government House, since known as the Château of St. Louis, reared on the heights of the rock. This building came to be the residence of every succeeding Governor of Canada for two hundred years, until one night it was wholly destroyed by fire and never rebuilt. In the year it was begun, too, the Recollet priests began to build their convent, and other large buildings arose.

So now you see quite a flourishing little town was fast growing up in the midst of the Canadian wilderness. But with the advancement of his schemes came many new troubles for the lion-hearted Champlain. In the first place, the Indians had acquired a passion for strong drink—"fire-water" they called it,—and although people of their fierce, reckless disposition should never have been allowed to touch a drop, yet the fur-traders were so callous and greedy as to be always ready to supply them with gallons and hogsheads of the fatal brandy. The consequences were what might have been expected, and Champlain was very angry as he looked upon the scenes of riot and bloodshed. But his efforts to keep liquor from the Indians only made the traders hate him more bitterly. To this source of anxiety was added another: the bloodthirsty feud between the Iroquois and the Algonquins and Hurons, which occasioned constant bloody massacres and made the life of the French colonists at Quebec, Three Rivers, and Tadoussac one of never-ending danger. On a certain night a band crept down the St. Lawrence silently to Quebec, having sworn an oath to wipe the city of the pale-faces from the face of the earth. But the stone buildings, the cannon and muskets in the hands of the determined Frenchmen daunted them and they beat a retreat. Not to be wholly balked of blood, they fell upon the Algonquins, who were bringing furs to Quebec, slaughtering them without mercy. Then there were plots against Quebec, even amongst the tribes which Champlain considered friendly, for savages were, and ever will be, fickle, and often the most trifling incident will tempt them to treachery.

Meantime Champlain's friends in France, the associated merchants, had lost their fur-trading monopoly because they had failed to fulfil their pledges. In consequence of this, the monopoly was handed over by the King to two Huguenot gentlemen, William and Emery de Caen, an uncle and nephew. The uncle was a merchant and the nephew was a sea captain, and, although Protestants themselves, they were charged not to settle any but Catholics in the colony. This arrangement turned out a very bad one. The Huguenots and Catholics quarrelled in New France, as they had been quarrelling in Old France, and finally, so violent grew the disputes, that the King joined the two associations into one under the title of "the Company of Montmorency," with Champlain still as Viceroy. Matters thereafter went so much more smoothly that Champlain decided to take the opportunity of paying another visit to his native country. With him he took his beautiful young wife, Helen de Champlain, who had had nearly five years amongst the Indians and the rough fur-traders, and had endured many hardships and faced many dangers. You must bear in mind that when she sailed away she left behind only fifty of her fellow-countrymen in Quebec. This is a very small number, but they were for the most part very much in earnest, very hardy and rugged, and inspired by Champlain in a strong belief in the future of the country. Before we have finished our history you will see whether that belief was justified or not.

CHAPTER IV

ROMANCE OF THE TWO DE LA TOURS

Two years did the doughty hero Champlain linger in Old France. To everybody he met, king, courtier, priest, and peasant, he had but one subject: Canada, never ceasing all this while to urge the needs of the colony across the sea and to further its interests by tongue and pen. It needed all his influence. The Duke of Montmorency, becoming disgusted by the perpetual squabbles of the merchants, sold his rights as patron of Canada to the Duke de Ventadour, a religious enthusiast, whose passion was not trade nor settlement, but saving human souls. Although bred a soldier, he had actually entered a monkish order, vowing to spend the rest of his days in religious exercises, and it was this nobleman who now sent out to Quebec the first little body of Jesuit priests, five in all, that arrived in that colony. Now these Jesuits were the very last people either Champlain or the Huguenots wanted in Canada. They belonged to a very powerful, crafty order. They could sway both king, queen, and minister to their wishes. De Caen and the Huguenot traders received the five priests when they arrived at Quebec as coldly as Poutraincourt had done in Acadia, but the Recollets generously gave them shelter in their convent until they could build one for themselves. This they soon did on the very spot where, ninety years before, Jacques Cartier had laid out his little fort. These five priests were destined to have some thrilling experiences and to meet with terrible ends, all of which you shall hear in due time.

Meanwhile Champlain at home in France saw with eagle eye that Huguenot and Catholic could never live together in peace across the wide waste of waters. They were always quarrelling. The colony did not grow as it should, in spite of the fact that in a single year 22,000 beaver skins were sent by the De Caens to France. Nor was religion attended to as devoutly as he thought the Huguenots ought to attend to it. But perhaps this was because the Huguenots did not acknowledge the authority of the Pope. So he wrote strongly to De Caen about it, and the letter fell into the hands of the most powerful, most crafty man of that era, far more powerful than King Louis the Thirteenth himself. Cardinal Richelieu was the King's Prime Minister. Having at length accomplished great things for his master in France, Richelieu now turned his attention to Canada. With a stroke of the pen he abolished the monopoly of the De Caens and founded the "Company of the Hundred Associates," with himself at the head. Thence-forward no Huguenot was to be permitted to enter the colony under any conditions. The new Company was given a perpetual monopoly of the fur trade and control of other commerce, besides being made lord of an enormous territory extending from the Arctic Ocean to Florida. Moreover, the Company was bound to send out at once a number of labourers and mechanics and 4000 other colonists. Champlain was made one of the Associates, and continued in his command of Quebec. Canada was now to be governed directly by the King, just as if it were one of the provinces of Old France, and nobles were to be created who would take their titles from their estates.

All then seemed bright and rosy for the colony on the St. Lawrence. But the best-laid plans, you know, "gang aft agley"; Richelieu, with all his strength and cunning, had no power over English ships, and English sailors would only laugh at his pretensions. At the very moment when Champlain saw all his hopes about to be realised, the most cruel blow that had yet fallen fell upon him. War had been declared between France and England, and King Charles of England, seeing his American colonies already prosperous, wished to extend his royal sway over the whole continent. Thus, while the little band of Frenchmen in Quebec were nearly starving, owing to supplies running short during the winter of 1628, and were straining their eyes for the arrival of the great fleet of eighteen ships sent out by Richelieu, an English admiral sailed coolly up the St. Lawrence. Sir David Kirke commanded a stout little fleet for King Charles, and it occurred to him that it would be very good policy to capture Quebec. Imagine the dismay of Champlain, the priests, the traders, farmers, and soldiers of the colony when, having waited for succour until long past midsummer, the oncoming ships turned out to be English, and they received a summons from the English admiral to surrender! How weak his fort was Champlain well knew, but that did not prevent him from replying firmly and with dignity to the summons, saying that he would defend his post until death. Secretly he hoped that the French fleet he expected would come in time. Although he intended to take Quebec, Kirke did not press his advantage just then. He had now a far better plan: to lie and wait for this same French fleet, and cripple the colony in that way. His reward duly came. Off Gaspé, Kirke met the squadron from France, and after a fierce struggle captured all the ships but one, together with much booty.

What a plight was the brave Champlain now in! Cut off from all communication with France, for at least ten months must his forlorn band wait before assistance could arrive. He set to work to grapple with the difficulty by sending all his men farming, and hunting, and fishing. Very little land was cleared as yet; it hardly seemed worth while clearing it as long as the dreaded Iroquois were allowed to shoot the farmers as they worked, and afterwards to swoop down and burn up the crops. Worst of all to Champlain's mind, the Hurons and Algonquins whom he had befriended chose such a time as this to manifest their enmity to him. Instead of helping, they refused him succour. But food of some sort must be got. He set his people digging up wild roots in the woods, and despatched a boat down the river to search the gulf for a friendly trader or fisherman who would give them dried codfish. At the end of a long year of hardship, when no French ship came to his relief, Champlain was ready, in sheer desperation, to march his hungry little garrison against the Iroquois, capture one of their towns, and pillage it of corn. But before he could really carry out this dangerous scheme the English admiral once more showed his face in the St. Lawrence. This time it seemed far better to surrender to such an enemy as the English than to perish miserably from starvation in the wilderness. Kirke offered honourable terms, and Champlain, perceiving how utterly useless was resistance, gave up for a time the fort, magazine, and dwellings of Quebec. On the 24th July 1629 Champlain and ten priests and a number of others embarked on board one of the English ships to be carried to England, and from thence to France. For the first time in its history, the flag of England was hoisted, amidst great cheering on the part of the lusty English mariners, over Quebec.

You must not suppose the English abused their victory. All the settlers who chose were allowed to remain on their property. Lewis Kirke was installed as English Governor, and treated all with kindness, giving them bounteous provisions.

On the way down the river the ship bearing away Champlain met, near Tadoussac, Emery de Caen, returning with supplies for Quebec. Too late! Kirke turned his guns on the Frenchmen, and De Caen was forced at the cannon's mouth to surrender. But although he did so, young De Caen told the Englishman that which completely spoilt Kirke's rest that night. "I have heard," quoth De Caen, "that peace hath been declared between the two Crowns, and that when you captured Quebec and the sixteen French ships, King Louis and King Charles had been friends for a good two months. You have, therefore, done a gross and unlawful thing."

De Caen spoke not falsely, for so it turned out to be. When Kirke anchored in Plymouth harbour he learnt, to his chagrin, that peace had really been made some time before, and that all conquests from France must be restored. The doughty, scarred old Governor, Champlain, posted in hot haste to London, and unfolded the tale of Quebec's surrender to King Louis' ambassador. But, strange as it may appear, King Louis was in no hurry to get back Quebec into his hands again. It seemed to His Majesty, fond of his ease and pleasure, that all Canada was far more trouble than it was worth. The capture of Quebec did not mean the loss of the whole of New France. Several places in Acadia still belonged to King Louis, besides the Island of Cape Breton. But even these possessions only seemed to promise more expense and bloodshed and wrangling.

In the meanwhile another personage—a Scotsman—had appeared on the scene and laid claim to a large part of the country. Sir William Alexander was a man of letters and a successful courtier. Being a great favourite of old King James the First, as long ago as 1621 that monarch had listened graciously to Alexander when he averred that, by reason of Cabot's discoveries, the whole North-American Continent belonged to England by right. "As there is already a New England, your Majesty should go further and found a New Scotland." King James desired nothing better. He gave Sir William a grant of the Acadian Peninsula and a great deal of the adjoining mainland for his ambitious and patriotic purpose. As the King was fond of Latin, instead of New Scotland the country was christened Nova Scotia. The English set out modestly at first to people the country. As Sir William was satisfied for some years in sending out a trading ship each year to Nova Scotia and in exploring the region, there was no fighting, or even ill-feeling, between the French and the English. When in 1625 King James died, King Charles not only confirmed Alexander's charter, but actually allowed his enterprising subject to establish an Order of Knights-Baronets of Nova Scotia. Any wealthy and respectable person could, by paying a certain sum towards the funds of the new colony, obtain an estate of 18 square miles and become a baronet; and over one hundred persons did this, and some of their descendants are baronets in Great Britain to this day.

Sir William had no desire to drive away the French settlers in Acadia, which, you remember, was more or less in the hands of Biencourt, son of Poutraincourt. Besides Biencourt there lived in Acadia at this time the two La Tours, father and son. Claude de la Tour, the father, was a brave and courtly Huguenot. He occupied a trading post on the borders of what is now Maine; while Charles, his son, held a strong little fort called St. Louis, near Cape Sable. When Biencourt died he bequeathed his title and all his interests in Acadia to young Charles, because he had been his friend and companion from boyhood.

You have seen that soon after this a war broke out between France and England—the war in which Admiral Kirke captured the French fleet and summoned Quebec to surrender. On board one of the captured ships of the French fleet was the hope of Acadia, in the person of Claude de la Tour. He had gone home to France, and was now bringing out men and arms and provisions to make Port Royal strong enough to resist the new English pretensions to this fair region. While the valiant Champlain saw himself shut up starving in Quebec, Claude de la Tour was buffeting the waves on the way to England as Kirke's prisoner of war. De la Tour, being a Protestant of noble birth and of charming manners, was well received in London, and made much of. The very best people were anxious to make his acquaintance. He, on his side, found the English most agreeable, and ended by courting one of the Maids of Honour of Queen Henrietta Maria and marrying her. Sir William Alexander quickly saw how useful he would be, and soon had him created a baronet of Nova Scotia. After this La Tour took service in the English Royal Navy, and having obtained a grant of territory in Nova Scotia, undertook to found there an English settlement. Not only this, but he promised to bring his son into the English service. Sir William Alexander readily agreed to the plan of making La Tour's son, Charles, a baronet also, and this was accordingly brought about.

All this while young Charles de la Tour, rightful lord of Acadia under Poutraincourt's charter, knew nothing of his good fortune or of these proceedings on the part of his father. It remained for the elder De la Tour to break the glad news to his son. Two ships of war were put under his orders, and in these, with his pretty young English bride and many Scotch colonists, the old man set sail. His task turned out to be a far harder one than he had thought. When he got to his destination on the other side of the Atlantic he demanded an interview of his son, who was, surprising to relate, most ungrateful. What astonished him most was to find his father in command of an English ship, and wearing the dress of an English Admiral. Claude began by telling his son Charles of the flattering reception he had met with in London, and the honours that had been heaped upon him.

"I am an English Baronet," he exclaimed, embracing the youth, "and, what is more, so also are you. Rejoice, therefore, at the good fortune that has befallen us, and fly the proud blood-red cross of St. George from yonder staff."

De la Tour refuses to yield his Allegiance. 1630

But Charles, far from showing joy, seemed thunderstruck. Disengaging himself from his sire's embraces, he replied haughtily that "if those who sent you on this errand think me capable of betraying my country, even at the solicitation of a parent, they have greatly mistaken me. I am not disposed to purchase the honours now offered me by committing a crime. I do not undervalue the proffer of the King of England; but the Prince in whose service I am is quite able to reward me; and whether he do so or not, the inward consciousness of my fidelity to him will be in itself a recompense to me. The King of France has confided the defence of this place to me. I shall maintain it, if attacked, till my latest breath."

After this, what could the disappointed father do but return crestfallen to his ship? After writing his son a letter urging him to obedience, Sir Claude bethought him of the effect of cannon and muskets as arguments. He would bring the ungrateful youth to reason by force. Thrice he landed his soldiers and sailors and tried to storm Fort St. Louis; but in vain. His men were repulsed, and soon became disgusted with the whole enterprise. Eventually they all repaired to Port Royal and took up settlement with the other Scotch colonists there. It might be supposed that in this extremity the young English girl to whom Sir Claude had promised power and luxury on his Nova Scotian estates would now desire to return to England, and he begged her to do so. But she refused.

"I have shared your prosperity, Sir Claude," she said gently, "I will now share your evil fortunes."

And evil, indeed, they turned out to be.

In 1632 came the shameful treaty of St. Germain-en-Laye, by which Canada and Nova Scotia were ceded back to France by King Charles, who was afraid that by his refusal he would not receive from King Louis the wedding dowry promised to his sister, Queen Henrietta Maria of England. This treaty made a great difference to the fortunes of the Frenchmen in the New World—to Champlain and the De la Tours. It deprived Sir Claude of his hopes, even of his refuge at Port Royal. Not daring or wishing to return either to France or England, he was obliged to throw himself on his son's protection. Charles gave him and his pretty stepmother a house hard by Fort St. Louis. He was rewarded. The story of Charles de la Tour's loyalty reached the ears of his monarch, who graciously made him a Lieutenant-Governor, and sent out men, stores, and ammunition of war to uphold his faithful subject in the lands and forts he had guarded so zealously.

We must now, for a little while, leave Charles de la Tour and his fortunes. We will return to them anon, but meanwhile it behoves us to see what was happening to Champlain and Quebec. You will remember that the great Cardinal Richelieu had placed himself at the head of the Company of the Hundred Associates. He had made Canada a royal province, with a nobility of its own and with Champlain as Viceroy. The war with England and the captures of Kirke brought this great scheme to a halt for some years, but the treaty of St. Germain-en-Laye was signed at last, and the Hundred Associates were ready to begin their operations. By the end of May 1633 Champlain was back again in his fort on Cape Diamond. This time he had with him two hundred persons and great equipments. In his Company also were a number of Jesuits, to take the place of the Recollets. With such zeal did they administer their charge that life at Quebec became pious and orderly, and many Indian conversions to Christianity were made. A new fort was built at the old trading station of Three Rivers, at the mouth of St. Maurice River, as a protection against the Iroquois, but otherwise not very much happened worth describing here during the last two years of Champlain's life. The veteran was now but two years short of the allotted span, and could survey the fruits of his long labours in Canada with satisfaction. He had not, it was true, made Canada full of towns and cities and filled her countryside with prosperous farms and peasantry. But he had trod out a path through the forest and had sown the seed of future greatness. If only he had not also sown the seed of future hatred—if only he had made the Iroquois a friend instead of a foe! Nevertheless, when he fell sick on Christmas Day 1635 and his heroic spirit passed away for ever from the land he loved, Samuel de Champlain had well earned the name by which he is to-day called on the banks of the St. Lawrence, the "Father of Canada."

In his prime Champlain had a handsome countenance, a noble and soldierly bearing, and an iron constitution. In an age when fifty miles was considered a great journey, he travelled many thousands by sea and by land, crossing the ocean at least twenty times to defend or promote the colony's interests in Old France. His wife survived him nearly twenty years, and having founded a convent at Meaux, in France, became herself a nun, and as Sister Helen, beloved by the other nuns, she died.

After Champlain's lamented death a new Governor, Charles de Montmagny, a pious soldier and knight of Malta, was sent out to Canada. On his landing at the foot of Cape Diamond a striking scene took place. Amidst a crowd of black-robed Jesuits and soldiers in brilliant uniforms and the officials and people in their gayest apparel, Montmagny knelt down at the foot of a cross marking Champlain's grave and cried out, "Behold the first cross that I have seen in this country. Let us worship the crucified Saviour in his image." The procession straightway climbed the hill to the church, chanted the Te Deum, and prayed for King Louis. Montmagny was a devout believer in the Jesuits, who ruled with great severity. If a French colonist failed to attend church regularly, he was sent off to prison. They cared nothing for the good things of this world; their only desire was for the salvation of souls. It mattered nothing to them whether the Company of the Hundred Associates made money out of the buying and selling of furs or not. The great ambition of the Jesuits was to make Christians out of the Canadian savages, however remote, and as the Iroquois absolutely refused to be converted, and hated the Jesuits, the priests did not hesitate to join hands with the Hurons and Algonquins to destroy them. So there began to rage a terrible war. The Iroquois, who if not more numerous, were braver and fiercer than the Hurons, swore by the great Manitou never to bury the war-hatchet as long as a single Huron was left alive above the ground. Assault followed assault, the Iroquois braves coming close to the walls of Quebec and burning and torturing their prisoners under the very eyes of the horrified "black robes." On their part the priests, besides being pious, were very brave men and cared nothing for danger. They would push fearlessly past the Iroquois concealed in ambush and carry the gospel amongst the most distant tribes. After a time their letters home describing their adventures made a great stir in France, and a number of wealthy and influential people came forward to help them in their great work. It was at this time that the famous colleges and convents and hospitals of Quebec were founded. The Marquis de Gamache founded a Jesuit college; another priest-nobleman, Noel de Sillery, built a home for Indian converts; the Duchess of Aiguillon, a niece of Cardinal Richelieu, provided the money for the Hotel Dieu, or God's Hospital. Then there was a wealthy young widow, Madame de la Peltrie, who, having no children of her own, decided to devote her life and fortune to establish a seminary for young girls in Canada. In the summer of 1639 she arrived in Quebec in company with Marie Guyard, a silk manufacturer's daughter who had taken vows as a nun and became "Mary of the Incarnation," the Mother Superior of the Ursuline Convent. All of these as soon as they had landed fell down and kissed the earth and evinced great enthusiasm over their future work. When they visited the first Indian settlement, we are told by one of the priests that Madame de la Peltrie and the rest embraced the little Indian girls, "without taking heed whether they were clean or not." Yet at home in Paris these fine ladies would probably not have cared to take the poor dirty little French children to their bosoms.

The Jesuits quickly spread themselves everywhere. No hardship, no danger, no cold was too great for them. Amongst the Huron Indians they soon found their greatest success. There numbered 30,000 Hurons before disaster befell them, considered the most intelligent and progressive of the Canadian Indians. Three fathers, led by the indomitable Jean de Brébeuf, went forth to establish missions amongst them. Brébeuf came of a noble family in Normandy, a tall strong man, who seemed born for a soldier. He could perform wonderful feats of strength and endurance. He penetrated the wilderness in spite of every obstacle, and established a mission at Thonatiria, on Georgian Bay. At first the Jesuits were opposed by the tribe, who foolishly regarded all their sacraments and services as the deeds of sorcerers. Whenever any evil happened to any of them, when the crops were frost-bitten, or even when a child fell ill, the Hurons put it all down to the incantations of the "Black Robes," as they called the missionaries. But gradually the Jesuits lived down all such prejudice. The Hurons saw they were strong, wise men, and at last placed themselves unreservedly in their hands. While the Jesuit fathers made their central station at St Mary on the Wye, a little river emptying into Matchedash Bay, they founded other missions, St. Louis, St. Jean, St. Michael, St. Joseph, in all the country round about. In course of a very few years the missionaries came almost to be the rulers of all the tribes there settled. But the Iroquois hate against the Hurons was fast fanning into flame. Having sworn vengeance upon them because of their alliance with the French, sooner or later they would find them out, and then, alas, the most dreadful, thrilling scenes in the whole history of Canada would happen. While the Hurons and their ministering Jesuits were living in fancied security in their corner of the west, the French in Quebec and Three Rivers were in constant dread of the Iroquois. Day by day the redskins grew bolder. At first, terrified by the French cannon and muskets, they did not venture to approach too near the walls of the French forts. But by degrees that fear wore away, and the sentries, looking out from the bastions, would often see a dozen or two Iroquois braves lurking about the fort in the hopes of catching some straggler unawares and scalping him. One day indeed they were rewarded. Two Frenchmen named Godefroy and François Margerie were captured and dragged away to their lodges. The Iroquois chief, summoning all his forces, prepared a plan. He resolved to offer peace to the French at Three Rivers if they would give up their Indian allies, the Algonquins, against whom and the Hurons the Iroquois were engaged in a war of extermination. As Margerie spoke the Indian tongue, he was told that his life for the present would be spared, that he was to go under a flag of truce back to the fort at Three Rivers and offer these terms to his countrymen. If he did not return, his fellow-captive, Godefroy, would be tortured and slain. The heroic Margerie did not shrink from his task. He journeyed back to the fort and urged the Commandant to reject so dishonourable a proposal. Then, fully counting the cost of his action, he returned to the Iroquois and to his companion Godefroy. Luckily for him, in the meantime, the Governor arrived from Quebec with soldiers to reinforce the garrison at Three Rivers. The Iroquois perceived that it would be hopeless now to storm the fort, and wisely decided to accept ransom for their prisoners. So the brave Margerie and his friend, who had boldly faced death, were now free.

CHAPTER V

THE FOUNDING OF MONTREAL

Of all the great cities of the world you will not find one that has had so romantic a beginning as Montreal. The stories sent home by the Jesuits had stirred all France, and made the more pious and enterprising spirits more than ever resolved to teach the wicked redskins a lesson in Christianity and plant the fear of God in their hearts. The French said they did not believe in treating the savages of the New World in the cruel way the Spaniards had done in Peru and Mexico; they preferred to win them over to civilised ways by kindness and the force of good example.

One night a certain Jerome de la Dauversiére had a dream after he had returned from his office in the little town of La Flèche, in Anjou, where he was receiver of taxes. In this dream an angel came and told him that the surest way to win the redmen of Canada over to Christianity was to set up a great mission on the Island of Mount Royal. This island in the river St. Lawrence, you remember, Jacques Cartier had visited one hundred years before, and had been struck not only by its beauty but by the friendliness of the Indians who lived there. Their town they called Hochelaga. Since Cartier's time Hochelaga had mysteriously vanished (probably owing to one of the frequent redskin feuds), and the French Governor and people of Quebec had made as yet no settlement there. Dauversiére, who was a very holy and zealous man, went to Paris, and to Father Olier, a friendly priest, related his dream. It appeared that the worthy father also had had a vision, in which Mount Royal was pointed out as the future scene of pious labours. Whereupon the two set to work and formed a company of forty persons to build on this island, 3000 miles away, in the heart of New France, a French town, well fortified and able to resist the onslaughts of the infidel savages. The Company of the Hundred Associates agreed to sell them the land, for, of course, the Hundred Associates at this time controlled all the land of New France under a charter from King Louis. All that the promoters of the plan had finally to do was to find a proper person to take charge of the new settlement, which it was decided to call Ville Marie de Montreal, or, as we would call it, Marytown of Mount Royal, in honour of the Holy Virgin. They were fortunate to find just the one they sought in Paul de Chomedy, Sieur de Maisonneuve, a brave and pious soldier, who was forthwith appointed the first Governor of Ville Marie.

With Maisonneuve, when he sailed away from France in the spring of 1641, went Mademoiselle Jeanne Mance. This young woman had dedicated her whole life to nursing the sick and teaching little children, and was to take charge of a hospital in the new colony.

Slow sailing it was in those days, and when Maisonneuve's ship reached Quebec the sweltering heats of August oppressed the city. Governor de Montmagny bade the pioneers welcome, and, after listening to their scheme, told them flatly that he thought it was all a mistake. Instead of venturing their lives so far inland amongst the treacherous Iroquois, much better was it to choose a spot nearer Quebec for their town. But Maisonneuve and his companions, although prevailed upon to spend the winter in Quebec, were resolved to reach Mount Royal, even though, as Maisonneuve said, "every tree on the island were an Iroquois." And so in the spring all set off boldly up the Great River. When they saw the leader's resolution, Governor de Montmagny, Father Vimont, Superior of the Jesuits, and Madame de la Peltrie, head of the Ursuline Convent, consented to accompany them in their ship.

On the 17th May the memorable landing took place. All of the expedition—some fifty in number—fell upon their knees, and from their lips fell a prayer of thankfulness to Almighty God. But they did not deceive themselves as to their danger. They all knew—even the women—that there was to be more work and fighting than praying. As yet no treacherous red-man, tomahawk in hand, lurked behind the tall trees, but the alarm was sure to come, and no time was to be lost. So to the task of chopping and hewing and hammering they flew without delay. The site was quickly enclosed with palisades and several cannon brought from the ship and put in position. As for the hospital which Mademoiselle de Mance had been given the money to build, it could safely be reared outside the walls, being of stone and almost a little fortress of itself. For two centuries and a half this hospital withstood all the attacks of the Iroquois, until a mighty city pressing in upon it forced it to a peaceful surrender to the interests of trade and commerce.

Winter came and went. Spring found Ville Marie quite snug and comfortable, and the inhabitants wondering where the Iroquois were. They had not long to wait. A solitary Algonquin one day fled within the palisades for refuge. He told Maisonneuve that he was being pursued by the Iroquois, coveting his scalp. In a few hours his pursuers had discovered Ville Marie, and, shaking their tomahawks at its inhabitants, vowed vengeance on the bold pale-faces who had ventured to settle in a part of Canada which they had cruelly decreed should for ever remain a desert. Thereafter they patrolled the borders of the town, watching stealthily where they might strike down man, woman, or child. No longer was it possible in safety to sow or reap. Nor were the wooden palisades strong enough for protection. Stout walls and bastions were needed, and accordingly stone was quarried across the river, and willing hands toiled night and day to build what was henceforth little more than a prison. When the colony was two years old, the Iroquois summoned all their braves.

"Let us destroy these insolent Frenchmen," said their chief; "let us carry off their white girls to drudge for us in our lodges."

Maisonneuve covering the Retreat of his Followers, 1644

Maisonneuve, hearing that they had collected a large force, unwisely sallied out to give them battle. It was springtime, but the deep snow had not yet melted.

The little company of French settlers, their hearts beating high with valour and courage, looked about for the foe. Not finding him at first, they were drawn farther and farther into the surrounding forest. Then it was that the redskins, hidden behind trees, darted forth a volley of arrows, and the founders of Ville Marie became an easy target and fell by the dozen. They were unused to this kind of warfare, the only kind the red-men really knew. Maisonneuve, shocked but undaunted, gave the signal for retreat, and the French drew back to the walls of Ville Marie, dragging their dead and wounded with them. Close followed the enemy with ear-splitting yells and flourishing their blood-stained tomahawks. Maisonneuve, pistol in hand, was the last man to enter the gate. Just as he was crossing the threshold an Iroquois chief sprang forward to drag him back, but quick as the savage was, not quick enough was he. The Governor's pistol rang out, and the chief dropped in his tracks. His baffled companions, shrieking in anger and dismay, saw the gates of the little town shut, and for that day the rest of its defenders were safe. To-day, if you should chance to visit the great city of Montreal, you may see the very spot where this encounter took place. It is called the Place d'Armes, and in the middle is a bronze statue of the brave Maisonneuve, on whose pedestal is a representation of his narrow escape from death.

Such terrible experiences were not confined to Montreal alone, or even to Quebec and Three Rivers. About the whole country the Iroquois prowled like wild beasts. Especially did they frequent the northern outlets of the Ottawa River to waylay the friendly Hurons in their passage to the St. Lawrence, bringing furs for barter to the French. Observing this, Governor Montmagny set about building a fort at the mouth of the Richelieu River, and notwithstanding the attempts of 700 Iroquois to destroy it and kill the workmen, it was completed in a short time and christened Fort Richelieu. Forced to retreat, the savages managed to carry off with them a Jesuit priest, Father Isaac Jogues, and two young students named Goupil and Couture, who were coming down the river with a party of fur-hunters. They did not kill their prisoners at once, as they expected, but, after putting them through a course of dreadful tortures, carried them to the home of one of their tribes, the Mohawks. After cutting off Goupil's thumb with a clam-shell, so as to prolong the pain, they scalped him and flung his body down a steep waterfall. Couture, adopted into the tribe, turned Mohawk in order to save his life.

After a time Father Jogues was taken by the Iroquois in one of their trading visits to the Dutch of New Netherlands, now called New York. This is the first time any of the French in Canada had any communication with the European settlers to the south of them, in what are now known as the United States. The Dutch Governor of Albany took pity on the poor Jesuit priest and helped him to escape. Ultimately he was sent back in a ship to France, where he thrilled the King and Court by the sight of his wounds and the story of his wonderful adventures. Never once had he lost courage, but went on baptizing Indian children and giving the sacrament to the dying. Once when no water was forthcoming to baptize a Huron prisoner in the throes of death, Jogues shook off a few scant drops of dew which still clung to an ear of maize that had been thrown to him for food.

After all the intrepid father's starvation and sufferings you would think he had had enough of mission work amongst the red-men and would remain in a peaceful French curacy for the rest of his days. But that is because you do not understand what kind of men these Jesuit priests were. Undaunted by pains or privations, they wished nothing better than to be martyred in the cause of their religion. Isaac Jogues went back again to Canada a year later. In his absence the Mohawks had made peace with the French, and the intrepid priest took up his residence in one of their villages. When it became necessary to visit the Governor of Quebec on business, Jogues left behind him a small box containing a few medicine bottles and other simple things. No sooner was the priest's back turned than the medicine-man or sorcerer of the tribe, who hated the missionaries because they exposed their foolish practices, told the Mohawks that this innocent box contained magic, which would bring all of them ill-luck, disease, and death. Some believed this story, others were incredulous; so that when Father Jogues came back, he found the village divided on the question of killing him or sparing his life. He was invited to a feast, which he dared not refuse. As he entered, a tomahawk clove its way to his brain, and the priest was made a martyr at last. Poor brave Father Jogues was the first to suffer martyrdom in New France. The savages cut off his head and fastened it to a long pole, and the savage children threw pebbles at it in sport.

Alas, the fate of Jogues was destined to be that of the other priests who had established missions in the Huron country.

"Do not imagine," wrote the Father Superior, "that the rage of the Iroquois and the loss of many Christians and converts can bring to nought the mystery of the Cross. We shall die, we shall be captured, burned, and butchered. So be it. Those who die in their beds do not always die the best death. I see none of our company cast down. On the contrary, they ask leave to go up to the Hurons, and some of them protest that the fires of the Iroquois are one of their motives for the journey."

In the summer of 1648 the Hurons wished very much to pay a visit to the French in Eastern Canada. Many canoes had they full of furs which they could exchange for the kettles, hatchets, and knives of the traders. They resolved, therefore, to brave the Iroquois and make the long journey. Five distinguished chiefs accompanied 250 of their best warriors, and by the middle of July, Three Rivers was reached in safety. The Hurons ran their canoes ashore amongst the bulrushes, and began to spread on their war-paint and adorn themselves with feathers and wampum so as to make a distinguished appearance at the fort of the pale-faces. Suddenly an alarm was sounded. The Iroquois were on their track. Snatching their arms, the Hurons ran to meet the foe. This time the Iroquois were outnumbered and were defeated, and the Hurons eventually set out for home, flushed with victory and bearing a number of Iroquois scalps.

At home news of a terrible disaster awaited the victorious Hurons. Taking advantage of their absence, the Iroquois had attacked the Huron town of Teanaustaye, or St. Joseph, where the Jesuit, Father Daniel, was in charge. St. Joseph was one of the chief towns of the Huron nation; it had 2000 inhabitants, and was surrounded by a strong palisade. But on one fatal July day it was all but defenceless: scarce a warrior was to be seen. The arrival of the Iroquois flung the crowd of old men, women, and children into a panic. Daniel, in all his radiant priestly vestments, came to meet the foe at the church door, undismayed by their dreadful war-whoops. There he died. A dozen Iroquois bent their bows and pierced him as he stood, while the chief, armed with a gun he had bought from the Dutch, sent a bullet through the brave priest's heart. The town was set on fire. When the flames reached the church, Daniel's body was thrown into it, and both were consumed together. Nearly one thousand Hurons were killed or taken captive.

Eight months passed, and in the early spring-time the Iroquois came again. This time the Indian converts at St. Mary on the Wye saw heavy smoke curling above the forest three miles away, and cried out, "The Iroquois! the Iroquois! They are burning St. Louis!" And so it was. Had the Hurons acted with better judgment and more valour they might have averted their doom. But ever since the massacre and destruction of St. Joseph they seemed to have lost spirit. The two priests who were stationed here, Brébeuf and Lalement, did their best to arouse them, but they would not take measures to foil an Iroquois assault. Brébeuf and Lalement, implored to flee while there was yet time, both scorned such counsel. Uttering savage yells, the Iroquois swarmed towards the palisades, hacking at them with their hatchets, and they broke through at last, burning and slaying. The two brave priests were seized and stripped and beaten with clubs along the road to St. Ignace, which post the Iroquois had also captured. The fate of St. Mary itself was now trembling in the balance. Here were some 40 Frenchmen, well armed, and besides a large Huron population, 300 more Huron braves were outside the gates, hoping to waylay some of their victorious foes. A battle between the two tribes of red-men ensued, and although this time the Hurons fought with a will, they were obliged at last to give way. Hundreds had been killed or lay weltering in their blood. Only twenty were captured alive by the Iroquois. The enemy's chief was badly wounded, and they themselves had lost a hundred of their best warriors in this fierce battle. You may imagine how the French and Christian Indians shut up in St. Mary waited for the issue of the fight. When they knew that their outer guard was defeated, they gave themselves over to prayer, believing all was lost. They well knew how inflammable were their palisades of wood. When a hundred torches came to be applied only a miracle could save them. At this critical moment panic seized the Iroquois camp. A rumour had spread that a mighty army of Hurons were descending upon them, and they resolved, in spite of their chiefs, to retreat at once. But before fleeing from their imaginary foe, they took nearly all their prisoners and thrust them, bound hand and foot, into the bark dwellings of St. Ignace. They spared neither men nor women, young nor old, not even tiny babes. When they had done this they applied the torch to the town.

Of the two priests, the giant, Jean de Brébeuf, was led apart and fastened to a stake. From thence he called to the others, exhorting them to suffer patiently and God would reward them. They tortured him, but he still stood erect, tall and masterful, and addressed his people. For this the angry Iroquois cut away his lower lip and thrust a red-hot iron down his throat. Round the naked body of Father Lalement they tied strips of bark steeped in pitch and set him in a blaze. As if this were not enough agony, on the heads of both they poured boiling water and cut strips of flesh from Brébeuf's limbs.

"You told us," cried the fiends, laughing, "that the more one suffers on earth the happier he is in heaven. We wish to make you happy. We torment you in this way because we love you; and you ought to thank us for it!"

Still from Brébeuf came no sign of flinching. Baffled in devising further tortures, they cut off his head and tore his body in pieces. The heart of this great man, the founder of the ill-fated Huron mission, was seized by an Iroquois chief and devoured. His friend Lalement, after being tortured all night, was killed by a blow from a hatchet.

Two or three days afterwards, when the fleeing Iroquois were leagues away, the Jesuits at St. Mary came to the smoking ruins of St. Ignace. The scorched and mangled remains of the two martyrs met their horrified gaze. These they carried back to St. Mary and buried, all but Brébeuf's skull, which they preserved as a holy relic. At the Hotel Dieu at Quebec it is shown to the visitor, enclosed in a silver bust of the martyr, which his family sent to the good nuns from France.

Upon the Hurons such a disaster as this told with crushing force. Flight from their country was all they could think of now. Two weeks later they abandoned for ever fifteen towns to roam northward and eastward in the barren, inhospitable wilderness. In various places the fugitives found refuge, some with this tribe, some with that, but as a strong, separate nation they soon ceased to be, and the fort and mission of St. Mary on the Wye was left solitary in the middle of a great waste.

All the love and labour of the Jesuit missionaries for ten years had been in vain. With aching hearts the priests resolved to break up the mission and betake themselves to some less dangerous and more useful station. Several of them followed the wandering Hurons, but a number of priests, with forty soldiers and labourers, established themselves on St. Joseph Island, at the entrance of Matchedash Bay. It is one of three—now known as Faith, Hope, and Charity—islands. Here they toiled, together with a number of Huron converts, in building a stronghold which would defy the dreaded Iroquois. Six or eight thousand souls came to people the island. There not being food for so many, what with hunger and disease, by springtime half had perished. The despairing survivors, resolving to brave the surrounding Iroquois, who roamed on the mainland, and escape, one by one fell into the hands of their lynx-like foes. No refuge was there for the poor persecuted race but in the shadow of the French guns at Quebec.

"Take us to Quebec," cried one of the Huron chiefs to the Jesuit fathers. "Do not wait until war and famine have destroyed us to the last man. We are in your hands. Death has taken more than ten thousand of us. If you wait longer, not one will remain alive."

At last the Jesuits resolved to grant their petition. On the 10th of June 1650 the whole population of St. Joseph (or Charity) Island embarked in canoes, which were packed with all their earthly goods, and paddled sadly towards the east. On the Ottawa River, which was now desolate of native hut or wigwam, they met a large party of French soldiers and Hurons on the way to help the Huron mission.

Too late! The mission, with all its forts and settlements, had been abandoned for ever. The entire party kept on to Montreal, where the Hurons could not be induced to stay because it was too open to Iroquois attacks; and about the end of July the great heights of Quebec came in sight. All disembarked and were hospitably received by the Governor, the priests, the nuns, and the people. Yet the new arrivals could not have come at a worse time, for food was scarce and nearly all were poor.

CHAPTER VI

THE FURY OF THE IROQUOIS

When the poor harassed "Black Robes" and their panic-stricken Indian charges finally rested under the sheltering walls of Quebec, Montmagny was no longer Governor. He had, after twelve years' service, gone back to France, and a new Governor had arrived in his stead. But the Indians still called the new Governor, and all the Governors who came afterwards, by the name of "Onontio." They were told that Montmagny in French signified "Great Mountain," Onontio in the Huron tongue, and supposed it was a title bestowed by the pale-faces on all their rulers in Canada.

Despite the unspeakable horrors, bloodshed, and martyrdom related in the last chapter, nothing of lasting value was accomplished by the hapless mission to the Hurons except a knowledge of the great Lake Superior, which an interpreter, named Jean Nicollet, had discovered a few years before.

Season now followed season, and each saw the French but little better than prisoners in their three towns on the St. Lawrence. If they ventured very far out of these fortified posts, it was only to give the Iroquois a chance to spring upon them and bear back their scalps in triumph to their lodges in the wilderness. The French might have made a treaty of alliance with their English neighbours in New England, who had now set up a number of towns and were flourishing, although they too were at the mercy of the surrounding savages. But the French Governor made it a condition of the treaty that the New Englanders should help Canada to exterminate the terrible Iroquois. This the English colonists were loath to do; they had no wish to bring the Iroquois tomahawks down upon their heads also, as the French had done; and so the plan fell through. After a time one of the Iroquois tribes, having lost a great many of their fighting men in the long war, began to think of making recruits. The idea occurred to them that the unfortunate Hurons and Algonquins, who had joined their fortunes to the French, would be the very men for their purpose, if they could only induce them to desert the alliance. Forthwith they sent courtiers to announce to the Hurons that they no longer bore them any grudge and were willing to adopt them—to receive them into the bosom of their lodges. But it soon appeared that all the Iroquois were not unanimous in their approval of this plan, and as their treachery was well known, the Hurons and Algonquins, now settled on the Isle of Orleans near Quebec, naturally hesitated about accepting the offer. The few foolish ones who trusted in Iroquois good faith were actually tomahawked by their so-called friends on the way to the Iroquois lodges. In attempting to punish a band of Iroquois ambushed near his fort, Du

Plessis Bochat, the Governor of Three Rivers, lost his life; Father Buteaux was killed on his way to his mission, and another priest, Father Poucet, was borne away to a Mohawk village, and after being tortured was sent back to Quebec to offer peace to the French. Peace was indeed welcome, but the French were naturally still suspicious. The truth was that the Iroquois were then too busily engaged in destroying the Eries, a tribe which had burned one of their most illustrious chiefs, to spare time to massacre the pale-faces. As the chief, a Seneca, had stood with unquivering nerve at the stake he had cried out, "Eries, you burn in me an entire nation!" for he knew the Senecas would avenge his death. Much, then, as the Governor, De Lauzon, wanted peace, neither he nor his Indian allies knew how far they could trust the Iroquois. It was at last decided that if the Onondagas, one of the five Iroquois nations, would receive a Jesuit mission, a body of Hurons should be sent under escort to be adopted into their tribe. From the Onondagas there came a message to say they would agree to this, and in June 1656 the expedition set out from Quebec. It consisted of a large body of Hurons, as well as Onondagas, fifty French soldiers, led by the brave captain, Dupuy, and two priests, Dablon and Chaumonot. Scarcely was the party well under way, when a band of Mohawks fell upon them, and before they pretended to discover that they were attacking members of their own confederacy, they had killed and wounded a number of Onondagas. Profuse excuses and apologies followed, the Mohawks explaining that they took them, the Onondagas, for Hurons. The expedition was suffered to proceed. The truth is, the Mohawks were jealous of the Onondagas in obtaining an alliance with the French and Hurons. To show their power and their contempt of the pale-faces, they continued their journey eastward to the Isle of Orleans, and under the very guns of the fort of Quebec surprised the defenceless Hurons who dwelt there, and fiercely murdered or captured all they came upon, even the women and children. In broad daylight they paddled their fleet of bark canoes in front of Quebec, laughing and yelling defiance to the French, and making their unhappy captives join in dancing and songs of triumph. The Governor this time was a weak man, and all he could do was to wring his hands and regret bitterly that he had ever sent any mission to the Onondagas. He began to fear for their safety.

Not wholly unfounded were the Governor's alarms. At first all went smoothly enough with the little band of Frenchmen in the heart of the Onondaga country. This particular tribe of the Iroquois appeared delighted at the coming of the French. But quickly signs of danger began to multiply. The pale-face soldiers grew aware that a plot was on foot to murder them in the little fort they had built, close to where the present prosperous city of Syracuse now stands. Dupuy, being an able and courageous man, resolved by some means or another to foil the savages and escape back to Canada. This is the stratagem he hit upon; it was the custom of these Indians to hold mystic feasts, at which it was a point of honour to eat everything that was set before them by their hosts. If a man failed to eat the whole of a dish—even to the fifth helping—it was taken by the host as a personal insult. Dupuy planned such a feast, and arranged to stuff them so plentifully that not a single brave would be capable of rising from the banquet. The plan worked perfectly, the Indians not observing that the French concealed most of their food instead of eating it, so that by midnight the gorged and drunken Onondagas were sunk in a gluttonous sleep. Dupuy had taken good care beforehand to build secretly within his fort a number of large, light, flat-bottomed skiffs, and now when dawn came the Frenchmen stole away, carrying these with them to the Oswego River, reaching Quebec at last, in spite of ice and rapids, with the loss of only three men, who were drowned. The Indians pursued, but their birch-bark canoes were useless on the icy stream, and they had to give up the chase.

The escape from the Onondagas was a very clever and daring deed, and shows the material the colonists of New France were made of in those days. A deed still more daring and important was to follow. The Iroquois threw off the mask and determined to deal the French in Canada a deadly blow. A mighty force of the Five Nations was organised, to meet at the junction of the Ottawa and St. Lawrence rivers, and swoop down first upon Montreal and then upon the other settlements. It so happened that there lived in Ville Marie at this time a young nobleman, Daulac des Ormeaux, who chose to be known to the other colonists as Adam Dollard. Having left France in order to escape the consequences of some rash act, he burned for some chance to retrieve the honour of his name. The valiant youth now saw with joy the long-looked-for opportunity arrive at his door, and he obeyed the summons. From the Governor did Dollard obtain leave to lead a party of volunteers against the savage foe. Gathering sixteen gallant fellows about him, all swore a solemn oath to give or take no quarter, but by sheer force of their arms break the force of the blow which was about to descend on their beloved town. A mad enterprise truly did it seem, but for sheer valour nothing finer has been known since fearless Leonidas and his handful of Greeks held the pass at Thermopylae. The seventeen heroes, together kneeling, took the Sacrament at the hands of the pale priest, and set forth for the Long Sault (or Rapids) of the Ottawa. There in the dense woods they found a disused old Indian stockade by which the invading host had to pass. Entrenching themselves as well as they could, they waited. A few friendly Hurons and Algonquins joined them, wondering at the hardihood of the pale-face warriors, and shamed into lending them a helping hand. The storm broke. A horde of 700 screaming savages, picked men of the Iroquois, flung themselves upon them. Easy work it seemed to crush out this feeble band. To their astonishment, Dollard and his men beat them back. Again and again they came on, and again and again were they repulsed. By this time, appalled at the fearful odds against them, the friendly Indians had fled from the side of the besieged, all but one Huron chief, Annahotaha, and four Algonquins. These stood firm. Every loophole in the stockade darted its tongue of fire; so faultless was the aim that nearly every time a musket rang out an Iroquois fell dead. Fortunately Dollard had brought plenty of ammunition. Some musketoons of large calibre, from whose throats scraps of lead and iron belched forth, slew and wounded several of the enemy at a single discharge. Thus three days wore away and still the terrible struggle came to no end. In the intervals, by day and night, Dollard and his men offered up prayers to Heaven on their knees in the melting snow. Their food was now gone, and, worse still, they had no water. No hope now remained save to keep the Iroquois a few hours longer at bay; they were certain only of a martyr's reward. On the part of the besiegers so many men had they lost that they sickened of the fight, and some amongst them even counselled going home. But other chiefs shrank from such a disgrace.

"Shall we," they cried, "confess ourselves beaten by so paltry an enemy? Our squaws would laugh in our faces! Let us now rather band ourselves together and storm the fort of the white men, at whatever cost."

A general assault was made. So high by this time was piled the bodies of the Iroquois, that their fellows could now leap over the stockade. Dollard fell, and one after another of the exhausted defenders was slain, although each fought like a madman, a sword or hatchet in one hand and a knife in the other. Amongst the heap of corpses one Frenchman still breathed, and he was dragged out and tortured. This was the end; thus perished Dollard and his valiant sixteen, whose names are imperishably written in the annals of Montreal. Nor did they offer their lives to the Iroquois hatchets in vain. The Iroquois had been taught a lesson, and to their lodges the tribe slunk back like whipped curs. "If," said they, "seventeen Frenchmen, four Algonquins, and one Huron can, behind a picket fence, hold seven hundred of our best warriors at bay, what defence would their hundreds do behind yonder ramparts of stone?" And so the colony of New France was saved.

The cowardly native allies of the French in this fight were not to escape the penalty of their treacherous desertion. The Iroquois turned upon them, burning some on the spot, and making captives of others. Five only succeeded in escaping to carry the tale of the defence, the butchery, and the martyrdom to Ville Marie.

It seemed, however, as if Canada had only been saved in order to perish from other causes. The colony was impoverished and torn, besides, with civil and religious dissensions. The Society of Notre Dame of Montreal, those rich and influential persons in France who had founded the city, now wearied of their enterprise. It was turned over to the great Seminary of St. Sulpicius, and a number of Sulpician fathers were sent out to take charge and to found a seminary in Montreal. Amongst these was the Abbe de Queylus, who hoped the King would eventually make him a bishop. But the Jesuits were too powerful not to prevent any priest but a Jesuit from receiving such an appointment, and at last succeeded in getting François de Laval, Bishop of Petræa, appointed to control the Church in Canada. A striking figure was Laval, playing a great part in the early history of Canada; but in spite of his virtue, he was narrow-minded and domineering, perpetually quarrelling with the various Governors of the colony during the next thirty-five years.

So desperate did the people of New France become at the dangers which surrounded them, at the quarrels between the Bishop and the Governor, at the excesses of the fur-traders, who insisted on intoxicating the Indians and themselves with brandy, that it hardly needed the terrible earthquake which took place in 1663 to make them lose heart altogether. The total population then was some two thousand souls, and the Company of the Hundred Associates had been found powerless to settle, develop, and defend the country properly. Thinking only of the profits of the fur trade, it had shamefully neglected its promises, and when any of its officials made money in Canada, they at once went home to spend it. All this was pointed out by the Marquis d'Avaugour when the Governorship at last fell from his hands; and remembering that others, including Laval, had made the same charge, Colbert, the new Minister of young King Louis the Fourteenth, decided to plead the cause of Canada to his master. It was on his advice that King Louis resolved to take the government directly into his own hands. By royal edict was revoked the charter of the Hundred Associates, and three men appointed as a Sovereign Council in Canada to carry out royal authority. These three officials were the Governor, the Bishop, and the Intendant, the latter having charge of the commerce and finances of the colony. To the post of Governor the Sieur de Courcelle was appointed, and Jean Baptiste Talon became Intendant. The office of Bishop, of course, continued to be filled by Laval.

Dollard strikes his Last Blow, 1658

And now the drooping fortunes of New France began to revive. Soldiers and settlers began to pour into the country. Besides De Courcelle, the King sent also his Viceroy for the whole of his Trans-atlantic domains, the veteran Marquis de Tracy, to report to him personally upon the state of Canada. When De Tracy set sail a throng of eager young nobles accompanied him. Their imagination had been stirred by the tales they had heard of the country by the St. Lawrence River. They thirsted for adventure and renown. There came also the famous disbanded regiment, called the Carignan-Callières, after the names of its commanders, the first regiment of regular troops ever sent to Canada by the King. It had lately been serving in the wars of France against the Turks, and had provoked the admiration of the Turkish Sultan.

On the last day of June 1665 a brilliant scene was witnessed in Quebec. On that glowing summer's day the gallant Marquis and the troops landed at the flowery base of towering Cape Diamond. What a different scene was now presented from that which had taken place but a few seasons before, when the impudent Iroquois had shaken their hatchets from their canoes at the trembling and helpless Governor! The population had doubled as if by magic; thousands were on the ramparts shouting a welcome to the broad white standard blazoned with the arms of France, which floated proudly from fleet and fortress. The river-banks echoed with the hoarse note of cannon. The bells of the church and seminaries pealed in a frenzy of joy. Tracy, a giant six feet and a half high, and his officers stepped ashore, all gorgeously attired in crimson and white and gold. In the vanguard of the procession which climbed that day the heights of Quebec were twenty-four guards in the King's livery, followed by four pages and six valets. On arrival at the square, Laval, in his resplendent pontificals, received them, and noted with pleasure that the old marquis, although suffering from fever caught in the tropics, knelt on the bare pavement. A new order of things everywhere was begun. With the 2000 settlers came young women for wives, as well as horses, oxen, and sheep in abundance. It became Tracy's duty to look to the colony's protection in order that it might increase and multiply, and the only way to accomplish this was by curbing the power of the Iroquois. No time was lost in taking measures to this end. The forts at Quebec, Three Rivers, and Montreal were strengthened, three new forts, St. Theresa, Sorel, and Chambly, were built on the Richelieu River. Reports of the arrival of the troops, and of all their preparations, naturally spread far and wide amongst the Indians, and very soon four of the Five Nations thought it prudent to sue for peace. The fierce Mohawks alone remained defiant; they were not to be cowed by all this martial pomp, and at last Courcelle, the Governor, with Tracy, the Viceroy's, permission, resolved to chastise them as soundly as they deserved. He would take them when they least expected it: surprise them in their lodges in the depths of winter, when his soldiers could travel over the frozen rivers as though on a paved highway. Many who had had experience of winter journeyings in Canada sought to dissuade him from the attempt, but the new Governor was anxious to distinguish himself, and win the approval of the Viceroy and his King. Early in January he and his 500 men began to march. Before they had reached Three Rivers many had their ears, noses, and fingers frozen, while some of the newly-arrived troops were so disabled by the cold, that they had to be left behind.

But the old Indian fighters and native Canadians, of whom there were nearly a hundred, pressed forward bravely in the van, in spite of the heavy loads which all were obliged to carry. For six weeks they travelled to reach the Iroquois lodges, but they lost their way, and came at last to the Dutch settlement of Schenectady. Here they learnt that the Mohawks had gone far afield on a war-like expedition, and that the country they were now in belonged to the Duke of York, afterwards James II. New Netherlands having thus passed into English hands, Courcelle and his troops were asked to quit the territory at once. There was nothing, therefore, to do but to steal away to Canada, whence they had come. It was not an easy feat, for a body of Mohawks hung at their heels tomahawking stragglers. The cold was intense, and, to make matters worse, the provisions gave out. Sixty men perished on the march. Nevertheless, unlucky as Courcelle had been, his expedition had served to convince the Mohawks that they and their families were no longer safe in their lodges. There was no telling what these Frenchmen would do next, so they sent a deputation to offer peace. The Viceroy, in his turn, sent a priest as his ambassador to visit their deputation, but he had scarcely left when tidings came that a party of seven French officers out hunting near Lake Champlain had been set upon and killed by the Mohawks. A cousin of Tracy's had been captured, and a nephew had been slain.

"Now, by the Virgin!" cried the sick old soldier, bringing down his giant palm on the table, "they have gone far enough. Recall the holy father. We must teach these savages a lesson." But the cup of his anger was not yet full. A couple of boastful Mohawk deputies arrived in Quebec and came to his house. When the indignant Tracy happened to mention the murder of his nephew, one of them actually had the effrontery to laugh and exclaim, as he stretched out his arm, "Yes, this is the hand that split the head of that young man!"

The Viceroy, veteran soldier as he was, and used to deeds of violence, shuddered with horror.

"Very well," he said, "never shall it slay any one else. Take that base wretch out," he added to one of the guard, "and hang him in the presence of his fellows!"

It was September. Tracy himself and Courcelle, commanding 1300 men, put the heights of Quebec behind them. Traversing mountains, swamps, rivers, lakes, and forests, they held steadily on their way to the country of the Mohawks. When the gout seized the commander they bore him on a litter, a mighty load. All day long were the drums beating and the trumpets blowing; when provisions had grown low, luckily they came upon a huge grove yielding chestnuts, on which they largely fed. The Mohawks heard of this martial procession and were terrified. They had no wish now to face the French, whose numbers rumour magnified, and whose drums they took for devils. At the last moment they retreated from their towns, one after another. Tracy pursued them, capturing each place as he arrived at it. At the fourth town he thought he had captured them all, but a squaw told him there was still another, and stronger than any they had yet seen. To this town he sent an officer, who prepared for an assault, but, to the surprise of the French, they found within only an old man, a couple of aged squaws, and a little child. These told the French that the Mohawks had just evacuated, crying, "Let us save ourselves, brothers! The whole world is coming against us!" All loaded with corn and provisions as it was, to the town the French that night applied the torch. A mighty bonfire lit up the forest. In despair at losing all their possessions, the two squaws flung themselves headlong into the flames. All the other places were destroyed, and then, chanting the Te Deum and reciting mass, the victors set out on the return march. They had burned the food of the Mohawks, who they knew must now feel the dread pangs of hunger. Terrible was the blow, and the Mohawks suffered much that winter. Their pride was humbled. By these means was a treaty of peace between the French and all the Iroquois declared, and for twenty years Canada enjoyed the sweets of peace.

Old Marquis de Tracy had done his work well, and could now go back to France with his resplendent bodyguard, his four pages, and his six valets, and leave Courcelle and Talon to rule Canada alone.

After this, when they went amongst the Iroquois, cross and breviary in hand, Jesuit missionaries met with no danger or refusal. They made many converts. Not content with their labours amongst the tribes close at hand, they pierced the distant forests north of Lake Superior, established permanent missions at Michilimackinac and Sault Ste. Marie, which joins the Lakes Huron and Michigan. On the banks of the St. Lawrence a new era began. For when the Carignan-Callières regiment was disbanded, the soldiers turned their swords into ploughshares, and the wise and prudent Intendant, Talon, had the satisfaction of seeing farms arise in the wilderness and yield abundant harvests. Talon's hand was seen everywhere; he spared no pains to make Canada prosperous and self-supporting. He set about establishing the fisheries in the St. Lawrence river and gulf, and encouraged the seal-hunts, by which much oil was obtained and exported to France. He ordered the people to grow hemp, and taught the women to spin wool. He also devoted much attention to the timber trade, and to him is owing the first tannery seen in Canada. By the year 1688 as many as 1100 vessels had in a single season anchored in the Quebec roadstead, laden with every kind of merchandise. According to a letter written by one of the chief nuns, "M. Talon studied with the affection of a father how to succour the poor and cause the colony to grow; entered into the minutest particulars; visited the houses of the inhabitants and caused them to visit him; learned what crop each was raising; taught those who had wheat to sell it at a profit; helped those who had none, and encouraged everybody."

But in nothing were Talon's efforts so extraordinary to us as in his providing wives for the colonists of New France. In his first few years of office 1200 girls were shipped out from France. These French maidens were chosen from the country rather than from the city, strong and accustomed to work. But there was also a consignment of "select young ladies" as wives for the officers. When they arrived in Quebec or Montreal, the girls, tall and short, blonde or brunette, plump and lean, were gathered in a large building, and the young Canadian came and chose a wife to his liking. A priest was in readiness, and they were married on the spot, in batches of thirty at a time. Next day, we are told, the Governor caused the couple to be presented with an ox, a cow, a pair of swine, a pair of fowls, two barrels of salted meat, and eleven crowns in money. Besides this bounty, twenty livres were given to each youth who married before he was twenty years old, and to each girl who married before sixteen. All bachelors were heavily taxed. To be unmarried was regarded by the Intendant and the King as a crime. In short, as has been said, the new settler was found by the King, sent over by the King, and supplied by the King with a wife, a farm, and even a house.

Now amongst free-born Britons all this royal interference would have been resented. Britons like to manage their own private affairs. They would call Louis the Fourteenth's system "paternalism," and in truth the system was a failure, because it discouraged the principle of independence. No spirit of self-reliance was stimulated amongst the people. They looked to the Government for everything, not to themselves. The result was that many of the strongest and most self-reliant amongst the young men preferred to live a life of freedom and adventure in the wilderness, hunting, fishing, and trading, rather than suffer the constraints imposed upon them by the well-meaning Talon. Thus came about the creation of a famous class called the *coureurs de bois,* or bushrangers, who at last spread themselves all over Canada, from the Atlantic to the Pacific, owning no laws but their own, living like Indians, taking unto themselves Indian wives, and rearing half-breed children. Talon and all the Governors, Intendants, and Bishops were very angry with these men, who thus set the wishes of the good King at defiance, and made many laws against them. But in vain! The bushrangers, valorous, picturesque, and their companions, the *voyageurs,* continued to flourish almost until our own day.

CHAPTER VII

STRANGE DOINGS AT PORT ROYAL

We left the loyal, undaunted Charles de la Tour, whom his Huguenot father, Sir Claude, had tempted in vain to enter the English service, master once more of Port Royal in Acadia, and in high favour with King Louis the Thirteenth. All Acadia as well as Canada was given back to the French by the treaty of St. Germain-en-Laye, and King Louis and his Court were now inclined to abandon their policy of indifference and begin the work of colonising anew. In the spring of 1632 a nephew of Richelieu's, Captain de Razilly, arrived in Acadia with a shipload of colonists, including artisans, farmers, several Capuchin friars, and some gentry. Amongst the latter were Nicholas Denys and an extraordinary person, Charles de Menou, Chevalier de Charnisay.

The new Governor-General of Acadia was so struck by the natural beauties of La Heve that he fixed his residence there, in preference to Port Royal, which the Scotch had taken care to dismantle before sailing away. Naturally young De la Tour was very jealous at Razilly's coming. He thought the King ought to have appointed him Governor, instead of giving him the mere lordship over a limited territory. With Razilly's death in the following year De la Tour thought his chance had come. But again his hopes were frustrated. It appeared that Razilly had ceded all his rights to Charnisay, his Deputy-Governor, whose first act was to remove from La Heve and take up residence at Port Royal, where he built a new fort.

From this time forward Charnisay and De la Tour were sworn enemies. De la Tour believed in his heart that it was Charnisay's aim to dispossess him of those rights which he had acquired in Acadia by so much energy and sacrifice. It is certain that Charnisay had much more influence at home in France than had his rival. The King tried to settle the dispute by fixing the limits of Charnisay's government at the New England frontiers on the one hand, and at a line north from the Bay of Fundy on the other. Westward of this line was to be De la Tour's province. But in vain. Both rivals appealed to their monarch, and Charnisay's friends having poisoned the King's mind by alleging that De la Tour was a Huguenot in disguise, orders were sent to his foe to arrest him and send him a prisoner to France. By this time De la Tour was dwelling with his young wife and children, his soldiers and Indian followers, in a strong fort he had built at the mouth of the St. John's River, to which he had given his own name. When, to his amazement, he heard that his foe had succeeded in depriving him of his rank as King's Lieutenant, of his charter, and of his share in the fur trade; that Charnisay had, moreover, orders to take him a prisoner to France, his indignation was overwhelming. He took instant measures. Having strengthened Fort la Tour, he defied his enemy to do his worst.

Charnisay was a crafty man and moved slowly. Not until the spring of 1643 was he ready to wreak vengeance on the "traitor," as he called De la Tour. The snows had scarce melted, the trees were putting forth their first pale verdure, when De la Tour perceived several armed ships creeping stealthily into the harbour. Aboard these ships were 500 men whom Richelieu had sent to Charnisay to overpower the loyal subject who had, in a time of stress and temptation, held all Acadia for the French King. Duly the attacking force landed, and Charnisay, his eye kindling with hate and expected triumph, himself led the assault. But he deceived himself: the fort proved too strong and the besieged too valiant. After an hour of hot fighting, Charnisay was fain to acknowledge himself baffled. Yet although he could not storm the fort, he had another resource. He could, he thought, starve it into capitulation. Thus was begun a close siege by sea and land. But in spite of Charnisay's care, a loophole in the line of ships was left, and through this loophole one day De la Tour's keen vision saw, far on the horizon, the long-expected ship, with provisions, merchandise, and gunpowder for Fort de la Tour. To reach that ship was now the hope of De la Tour and his wife, no whit less valiant than himself. In it both would sail to Boston, and there seek to obtain reinforcements from the sturdy New Englanders. In his hazardous extremity De la Tour remembered the lesson his father, now dead, had tried to teach him, and what he had tried to forget all these years, that he was a baronet of England, doubly so, once in his own right and once by right of inheritance. By virtue of the rank the English King had given him, King Charles's transatlantic subjects would not refuse him succour. The next night, therefore, De la Tour and his lady slipped unperceived into a waiting boat and rowed with muffled oars through the blockade. The captain of the *St. Clement* was delighted to see De la Tour. Placing himself under his orders, they sailed for Boston, where, although they dared not give him direct assistance, the Puritan elders of the new town had no objection to striking a bargain, and at a good price permitted their visitor to hire four stout ships and seventy men. Sailing back with his force, De la Tour was able now to make his enemy flee before him. The siege of his own fort being raised, he followed the foiled Charnisay to Port Royal, captured a shipload of rich furs, and would have taken Charnisay himself and his settlement, had it not been for the scruples of his New England allies, who succeeded in patching up a peace. But none knew better than De la Tour that there could be no lasting truce between him and Charnisay.

While his wife went to France to obtain help, the brave Charles set about strengthening Fort la Tour. Once across the Atlantic, Madame de la Tour had a narrow escape from falling into the hands of their enemy, Charnisay, who had also gone to France on the same mission. But she eluded her enemies as well as the King's officers sent to arrest her, and reached England in safety. After many months, she took passage home in a small vessel. She had many adventures. Once she hid in the hold of the vessel while her enemies searched for her. The ship suffered delay after delay ere, to her joy, Fort la Tour at length was reached. Her husband received her with raptures, and at once set out to bribe the Boston folk once more to lend him a helping hand to avert the danger which again threatened him. Now was Charnisay's opportunity. Hardly was his rival gone than he mustered all his ships and men and fell upon the fort. What an easy prey it seemed! Charnisay forgot that a woman sometimes can play a man's part. The fort received him with so hot a fire—so hot that thirty-three of his men were slain—that Charnisay, with loud curses, withdrew to his ships. Long he lay in wait for De la Tour, who dared not now return, and after a second onslaught on the fort, Charnisay began in earnest to despair of success. At this critical junction a scoundrelly traitor, bought by Charnisay's gold, appeared in the fort. In vain the heroic woman spurred on her valiant band to repel the invaders. The latter had been told that her food and powder were nearly spent, and finally, at a signal, the traitor threw open the outer gates of the fort, and the host of the enemy rushed in. Yet even then for three days Madame de la Tour kept them at bay, and Charnisay at last, weary of the bloodshed, was fain to offer her fair terms if she would surrender and depart. She hesitated a moment, but, to spare the lives of her brave garrison, she caused the gates of the inner fort to be opened, and so yielded.

Then it was that Charnisay covered his name to the end of all time with the blackest infamy. His eyes dwelt on the smallness of the garrison, and, ashamed of the terms he had offered, he cried out, "I have been deceived! I have been deceived! Take these wretches out and hang them all one by one!" He ordered a halter to be placed about the neck of the splendid heroine, their intrepid mistress, Marie de la Tour. He forced her to witness the cold-blooded murder of her men, so that she swooned with horror. To Port Royal Charnisay then bore her away, where she fell ill, and in three short weeks was dead.

Alas, poor Marie de la Tour! Her husband was now an exile from Acadia. By the capture of the fort he had lost not only his wife, but all his merchandise, jewels, plate, and furniture worth ten thousand pounds. His debts to the Bostonians being heavy, he became bankrupt. So while Charnisay flourished and grew rich at Port Royal, reigning supreme throughout Acadia, Charles de la Tour was a wanderer on the face of the earth. As a *coureur de bois* he hunted and bartered for furs in the far north. Years passed, when, through a faithful follower, tidings reached him which filled his breast anew with hope. His enemy was dead, drowned in an Acadian river in the very flush and midsummer of his success, which, however, by the wildest extravagance, he had grossly abused. No sooner did De la Tour learn of this event than he took ship immediately for France and poured out the story of his wrongs at the foot of the throne. The King acknowledged the injustice with which his faithful subject had been treated, and, to make amends, created him sole Governor of Acadia, with a monopoly of the fur trade. Once again back in the colony he loved, his fortunes grew bright. His coffers soon filled with gold. But the sight of the widow and children of his life-long enemy troubled him. He knew that they regarded him as profiting by their misfortunes. To make what reparation he could, he presented himself before Madame Charnisay. She did not spurn his attentions, and so he courted, then wedded her, and took her children under his protection.

And now, you will think, this surely is the end of the drama. Nay, there is more to come. Charnisay in his day had had many dealings with a certain merchant of Rochelle named Le Borgne. This fellow now came forward with a trumped-up tale for De la Tour's undoing. He swore that Charnisay had died owing him a quarter of a million livres, and this story he duly unfolded before Cardinal Mazarin, the great Richelieu's successor. Mazarin, an intriguing bigot, suspected De la Tour's loyalty and religion, and ended by giving Le Borgne power to seize the dead Charnisay's estate. On the strength of this authority a force was got together, and Le Borgne sailed away to oust De la Tour and make himself, if possible, master of Acadia. He fell first upon Nicholas Denys, who commanded a fort under De la Tour, captured him, took Port Royal, and made all in readiness to storm Fort la Tour. Matters were in this posture when, like a bombshell, burst a surprise for all parties.

At this time, far away across the Atlantic in England, the Civil War had come to an end. King Charles was beheaded, and Oliver Cromwell ruled in his stead as Lord Protector of the Commonwealth. When war broke out with Holland, Cromwell despatched a fleet to capture the Dutch colonies in America; but not long after the ships arrived at Boston, where they were to be joined by 500 of the English colonists, the latter were chagrined to hear that the war was over. The New Englanders had, however, in the meantime been petitioning Cromwell to make himself master of Nova Scotia, which they said was English by right and a source of danger to themselves. A glorious opportunity was now at hand of carrying out their schemes. The expedition intended for the Dutch was turned against the French in Acadia, and both De la Tour and Le Borgne were compelled to surrender. Nova Scotia once more flew the English flag, and at Port Royal an English Governor was installed, who made the settlers understand that no harm or oppression should befall them.

When these things happened, in the year 1654, De la Tour was long past his prime. After waiting a year he began to see how hopeless it was to expect that France would do anything to save Acadia. He crossed the ocean, this time to England. As Sir Charles de la Tour he obtained audience of the Lord Protector and stated his case fully and frankly. "I am the man for that country, my Lord. For more than sixty years I have laboured there, and settlers and Indians know me. With me it may prosper; without me it is nothing." Cromwell was a keen judge of character. He liked De la Tour's address, and decreed that he should come into his own again. An English Company was formed, consisting of De la Tour, Thomas Temple, one of Cromwell's colonels, and a Puritan minister named William Crowne, to take over the whole of Acadia, both the peninsula of Nova Scotia and the mainland. The partners were given besides the usual trading monopoly. Great projects were planned, and so firm was Temple's belief in Acadia's future that he spent his whole fortune in developing the estate. Long before his death, in 1666, Charles de la Tour sold out his interests to his partners. He divined further trouble, for the Restoration of Charles the Second put a new aspect on the situation. His seventy years of strenuous life made him long for peace and quiet. But the worst he did not live to see. A year after De la Tour died, King Charles put his royal hand to the disgraceful Treaty of Breda, by which all Acadia, Nova Scotia, New Brunswick, and Prince Edward Island, was given back to France, and Temple became a ruined man.

For forty-three years did Nova Scotia remain in the possession of the French. At length in 1713, by the Treaty of Utrecht, it passed to Great Britain, and in British possession it remains to this day. The New Englanders never ceased to regard French Acadia with jealousy. There were constant quarrels about the boundary-line between it and New England, and many deadly raids on both sides. Among the chief characters of Acadia at this time was the Baron St. Castin. He was a French noble who flung off the mantle of civilisation when he arrived in Canada with the Carignan-Callières regiment, and, marrying a squaw, took up his residence with the Indians. St. Castin dwelt in a strong fort on the Penobscot River and made himself lord and master over hundreds of Abenakis Indians. He was greatly dreaded by the English of Maine and Massachusetts.

During this long period, while Frontenac was ruling far away in Quebec, the population of Acadia slowly increased. Settlement was made at Chignecto and in the district called the Basin of Minas. It was the descendants of these settlers whose opposition to British rule caused them in the next century to be banished from the country.

In the meantime you must bear in mind that by water more than a thousand miles separated Port Royal from Quebec. Communication was slow and difficult. There was no high-road, and consequently the colonists on the St. Lawrence showed for a long time hardly more interest in Acadia's fortunes than if it were one of France's far-distant West Indian possessions. Louisburg, that mighty fortress which was to awaken their interest and to centre in itself so much of the power and glory of New France, was not yet built. It was not yet even a dream.

CHAPTER VIII

THE COMING OF FRONTENAC

While the wise and prudent Intendant, Talon, was playing his part of official father to the people, Governor Courcelle was busy with his own duties at Quebec. He found that the Iroquois, although they had buried the war-hatchet, had begun to injure Canada's interests in another way by inducing the Northern and Western Indians to trade with the English colonies. Courcelle made up his mind that the proper policy for the French was to secure a stronger hold on the more distant tribes. A fort and military station was built at a spot on the north shore of Lake Ontario where Kingston now stands. Expeditions were despatched to open up communication with the great and unknown territory west and south of the great lakes. Such was the beginning of a great era of discovery, associated in Canadian history with the name of Frontenac, Courcelle's successor, whose name in Canadian history stands second only to Champlain. It was during Courcelle's governorship, in 1669, that Charles the Second of England granted a charter to the Hudson's Bay Company, who thereby acquired the right to trade for furs in the mighty region bordering upon Hudson's Bay. But although England thus planted her foot in the far regions of the north, it was to a couple of intrepid French Canadian bushrangers that the idea of the Company was due. The names of these bushrangers were Pierre Esprit Radisson and Chouart de Groseilliers, both emigrants from France. At an early age they had been thrilled by the tales of life and adventure in the distant wilderness across the sea. They were hardy and enterprising, well fitted for the arduous life-work which was before them. From a western tribe of Indians called the Assiniboines, Radisson and Groseilliers first heard of the character and extent of the great inland sea to the north, which had long before been named by the English marine explorers Hudson's Bay. Not only did they glean a description of the inland sea, but they also succeeded, while on their wanderings, in obtaining information how they might reach it, not as the English might do by sea, but overland.

In August 1660 the two adventurers found their way back to Montreal after over a year's absence. They were accompanied by 300 Indians and 60 canoes, laden with furs, out of which they made a handsome profit. But they had to reckon with the jealous fur-trading proprietors of Quebec, who sought to restrict them from adventuring into any new fields, and so many obstacles did the pair meet with, that in order to carry out their scheme and establish trading posts on Hudson's Bay they gave up their overland scheme and decided to throw in their lot with the English. They crossed over the ocean and had an interview with King Charles's cousin, the gallant Prince Rupert, and the result was all their hearts could wish for. Money for the enterprise was found, and an English association founded under charter from the King, which took the title of the Merchants and Adventurers of England trading into Hudson's Bay, but better known to us as the Hudson's Bay Company.

On a June morning 1668 the *Nonsuch*, a ketch of only fifty tons' burden, left the Thames for Hudson's Bay. At the end of September it passed safely through Hudson's Straits, and all hands were ordered ashore in Rupert's River to begin the construction of a fort and dwellings, called after King Charles. It was made of logs, in the fashion of those made by the Jesuits and traders in Canada. As some protection from sudden attack it was enclosed by a stockade.

This, at Rupert's River, was the first of the forts and stations of the Hudson's Bay Company. After a time other forts and "factories," as they were called, began to dot the shores of the bay.

Radisson and Groseilliers did not continue very constant in their allegiance; sometimes they were English, sometimes they were French. They were rough-and-ready adventurers both; and it all depended whose purse was largest to command their services. Radisson, however, ended his days in the receipt of a pension from the Hudson's Bay Company.

Naturally, the French were not at all pleased at this enterprise which the English had set on foot, and soon began to take measures to get the fur trade of the most distant parts into their own hands.

Governor Courcelle despatched an explorer, a brave fellow named Nicholas Perrot, to summon deputies from the far western tribes to a conference, and take them all under the protection of King Louis. It was while on this expedition that Perrot heard from the Indians of a mighty river flowing southwards, which they spoke of as the Mississippi, or Father of Waters. The rumour caused great interest in Canada. It was not long, as we shall see, before another expedition started from Quebec to ascertain what truth lay in the story. But that was in Frontenac's time.

Louis de Buade, Count of Frontenac, was a grandson of one of the knightly paladins who had fought with Henry the Fourth in the wars of the League. He was a very shrewd, courageous, and ambitious man. He entered upon the government of Canada, as he entered upon everything he undertook in his life, with great enthusiasm. In almost his first letter home he wrote: "I have never seen anything so fair or so grand as the site of Quebec. That city could not have been better placed had it been purposely founded as the expected capital of a great Empire." Soon after lie arrived, Talon retired from his post of Intendant, fearing a conflict with the indomitable spirit of the new Governor. For Frontenac, with all his excellent qualities, could endure no opposition. He chafed at any criticism of his authority. And opposition and criticism were to be his lot for years. He soon became engaged in bitter disputes with the officials of the colony, with Bishop Laval, who was as stern and unbending as himself, with the new Intendant, Duchesneau, and with the Governor of Montreal. Frontenac disliked the Jesuits; he was constantly seeking to curb their influence. This unhappy three-cornered conflict lasted all through

Frontenac's first governorship of ten years. He became more and more despotic, banishing members of the Council who offended him, and finally sending Governor Perrot of Montreal, as well as a hostile priest named Fenelon, back to France, where the former was imprisoned in the Bastille.

He had many enemies, but Frontenac had also many friends. These idolised him, and to one, the brilliant and adventurous La Salle, he stood firm as a rock. We have seen how Frontenac's predecessor, Courcelle, had planned a fort on Lake Ontario. This plan Frontenac warmly approved, and believing the post ought to be a strong one, he sent 400 men to construct the works and to serve as garrison. He also established another fort at Niagara. The project of discovering the vast stream which the Indians called the Mississippi also greatly interested the Governor, and a strong and able priest, Father Marquette, and a fur-trading explorer named Jolliet left the St. Lawrence in its quest. Frontenac, La Salle, and the others still cherished in their hearts a vision of a short route to China. At that time no one knew how far away the Pacific Ocean lay—no one dreamt that thousands of miles of mountain range and prairie separated Quebec and New York from its shores. Marquette and Jolliet, with a few followers, pushed on to the north-west of Lake Michigan. After much paddling and many portages their canoes brought them at last into the swelling flood of the greatest river in the world. What emotions they felt! In wonder and triumph they descended the Mississippi, and during the month which followed, passed the mouths of three other great rivers, the Illinois, the Missouri, and the Ohio. They had many talks with friendly Indians on the banks; they saw much beautiful scenery and many strange sights. At last they drew near to the mouth of the river of Arkansas, where savages who had never so much as looked on the face of a white man were not so friendly. Jolliet and his companion deemed that they had gone far enough. By this time they had made up their minds that the great river emptied not into the Pacific ocean but into the Gulf of Mexico. Reluctantly they turned back, and not till the following summer did the two explorers reach Canada again. All through this memorable journey Jolliet had noted down in a book a description of all that had attracted his attention, besides sketching carefully a map of the course. This book he guarded jealously, intending it for the eyes of the Governor, of King Louis, and the people of France. Alas, just as he had run Lachine rapids and was in sight of home, his canoe capsized and the precious volume floated away on the rushing waters! It was a cruel disappointment for Jolliet. Frontenac received him graciously, heard his story, and reported what he had heard to his royal master. As for Jolliet's companion, Father Marquette was wholly worn out by his exertions. Less than two years later he lay down and died by a little river pouring into Lake Michigan, baffled in his dream of converting whole tribes of Indians in what was then the Far West. Neither he nor the Canadian-born Jolliet have been forgotten in this region. To many towns and counties have their names been given, and their statues in bronze and marble are to be seen in several places in America to-day.

Jolliet and Marquette had begun the work; it now remained for another strong, ardent, adventurous spirit to continue it. Such a one was close at hand in the person of Réné Robert Cavelier, Sieur de la Salle. As a young man he had come to Canada from his native city of Rouen, filled with the most romantic ideas of winning fame and wealth in the wilderness. To learn the Indian language and ways he had left the towns and led the roving life of a bushranger, making long, lonely canoe journeys and dwelling in the Indian wigwams. He, too, had heard of the Father of Waters, the vast Mississippi, and tried to reach it, but, as we have seen, Jolliet was there before him. But La Salle did not accept Jolliet's conclusions. He refused to believe that the Mississippi emptied into the Gulf of Mexico—he thought it led to the Pacific. He was full of faith in the existence of a short route to China. When any one met him on his return from an expedition, however short, they would jokingly ask him, "Venez vous de la Chine?" ("Do you come from China?") La Salle had bought an estate not far from Montreal, and this estate came at last to be called in derision La Chine, and Lachine it is called to this hour. But La Salle was not the kind of man to be discouraged. He was determined to settle the matter one way or another, and into his plans Frontenac entered heartily. But for some years other work claimed La Salle's attention—work of a pioneering sort. He believed that before the French could lay strong hands on the west, where the English had already begun to penetrate, forts and stations ought to be built and a firm alliance made with the Indians. With Frontenac's approval, he assumed control of Fort Cataracoui, on Lake Ontario. Once in his hands, La Salle tore it down, built a stronger one of stone, and rechristened it in honour of his patron, Fort Frontenac. Moving westward, he began to clear land and to build small ships to carry the cargoes of furs he had bargained for. The first he built on Lake Erie in the year 1679 he called the *Griffin*, in which he sailed to the Green Bay Mission on Lake Michigan. There the *Griffin* was packed with costly furs and bade God-speed on her return voyage eastward. Weeks passed, then months and years, but the *Griffin* never came back. Her timbers and the bodies of her crew have long rotted somewhere at the bottom of one of the Great Lakes. The loss was a sad blow to La Salle; it was one of the first of that series of great misfortunes which followed him through his career until he was cruelly done to death by foul traitors in the remote forest.

But by this time La Salle was not alone in his wanderings. In Henry de Tonti he had a fiery and trusty lieutenant, and a devoted follower in a Recollet friar, Father Hennepin. Before coming to Canada, Tonti had lost a hand in battle, its place being supplied by one of steel, covered by a glove. The Indians stood amazed at the blows Tonti could deal with his mysterious gloved hand, blows which would have shattered their own members to fragments. Tonti often had reason to bless his hand of steel. Three years after the ill-fated *Griffin* went down, La Salle saw his way clear to carry out his great purpose. He embarked on the waters of the Mississippi on a voyage to its source. The explorer, with Tonti and his party, met with a friendly reception from most of the Indians on their journey. Some were disposed to be hostile, and when this happened to be the case, strong, quick paddling soon put the French out of their reach. Finally, on the 19th of March, as the sun shone hot and trees and flowers were in bloom, their canoes entered the mouth of the Father of Waters, which is divided into three channels. La Salle, in his canoe, entered one, Tonti the second, and Captain d'Autray the third. All disembarked, and on some high, dry ground La Salle caused a column to be raised, and upon it this inscription was placed:

LOUIS THE GREAT,
King of France
and of Navarre,
reigns.
The ninth of April 1682.

La Salle took possession of the country for the King, and bestowed upon it the name, in his honour, of Louisiana. It took the explorers a full year to get back to Quebec, for the current was strong and the difficulties many. There he received a warm reception. But nothing could console him. Much to his sorrow and dismay, he found a new Governor installed. The enemies of Frontenac, headed by Laval, had triumphed, and the greatest and strongest man in Canada had been recalled by the King. Never could this measure have happened at a worse time. For, while La Salle had been absent, after years of peace, the restless Iroquois had dug up the war-hatchet. Upon a pretext of having received offence from the Illinois tribe, which was under French protection, they threatened to deluge the land in blood. To this policy they had been urged by the English Governor of New York, Colonel Dongan, who saw with alarm the growing enterprise, both in fur trade and exploration of the French. While he continued in Canada the doughty Frontenac was more than a match for the Iroquois chiefs. He sent for them instantly to Fort Frontenac, saying that if they had been wronged by the Illinois he would see that they had proper satisfaction. The Iroquois, having the English Governor at their back, at first returned a defiant answer. "If you want to see us, friend Onontio," they said, "you must come to our lodges." With flashing eyes and with knitted brows, Frontenac sent back the messenger to the Iroquois commanding them to keep their hands off his Indians or take all consequences. He had, he said, asked them to come and meet him at Fort Frontenac. Now he added, if the Iroquois wished to see him, they would have to come to Montreal. His sternness and the fear of his displeasure overcame the braves of the Five Nations. Changing their tone, they sent an embassy to Montreal, promising the peace which they hated. Scarcely had they done so than Frontenac the Lion was replaced by La Barre, the Lamb.

Like every one else, La Salle, on learning the evil news, saw the folly and danger of the change. To France straightway he sailed, where the King heaped him with honours, and, seizing the opportunity, he unfolded a project for establishing a French colony in Louisiana. Ships were freely given him and many soldiers and supplies to reach the Gulf of Mexico by sea. But La Salle, though he never would admit the fact, was no sailor. His navigation was fatally at fault; he wholly missed his intended destination, the mouth of the Mississippi, sailing hundreds of miles beyond. He landed, and through the forests and swamps, and stricken with fever, he led his colonists. After much miserable wandering, in which most of the little army perished, his followers mutinied. La Salle was murdered and his corpse flung to the jackals and vultures.

Far more successful were the adventures of the Chevalier de Troyes. The Chevalier de Troyes was a Canadian nobleman who had long fought for his king, and had seen service on many of the bloody battlefields in Europe. Now, when age began to creep upon him, and scars lined his cheek and brow, he had retired to his estate on the banks of the silvery St. Lawrence, to spend the rest of his days in peace and the companionship of his books. In his retirement the news of the increasing power and wealth of the Hudson's Bay Company reached him; it told him that unless this power was checked the prosperity of the French fur-hunters and fur-traders would be utterly crushed. An idea flashed across the brain of the Chevalier de Troyes, who believed he now saw an opportunity of winning enduring distinction, to rival, and may be surpass, the exploits of Champlain, La Salle, and the other hero-pioneers of New France.

In the depths of winter he summoned all his dependants and all whom his eloquence could attract, locked up his library, and set out for Quebec on snow-shoes. From the Governor he procured, on Christmas Eve 1685, official permission to steal upon the English and drive them, at the point of the sword, from the shores of Hudson's Bay. He was empowered to "search for, seize, and occupy the most advantageous posts, to seize the robbers, bushrangers, and others whom we know to have taken and arrested several of our French engaged in the Indian trade, whom we order him to arrest, especially Radisson and his adherents, wherever they may be found, and bring them to be punished as deserters, according to the rigour of the ordinances." The rigour of the ordinances was but another word for death.

Fourscore Canadians were selected to make up the expedition against the Hudson's Bay Company's posts by the Chevalier de Troyes. For his lieutenants the leader chose the three sons of a nobleman of New France named Charles le Moine. One, the eldest, a young man of only twenty-five, was to bear an enduring distinction in the annals of France as one of her most able and intrepid naval commanders. This was the Sieur d'Iberville. His brothers, taking their names, as he had done, from places in their native land, were called the Sieurs de Sainte-Hélène and de Marincourt. Thirty soldiers were directly attached to the Chevalier's command, veterans who had, almost to a man, seen service in one or other of the great European wars. That they might not be without the ministrations of religion, Father Sylvie, a Jesuit priest, accompanied the expedition.

"The rivers," writes a chronicler of the Troyes expedition, "were frozen and the earth covered with snow when that small party of vigorous men left Montreal in order to ascend the Ottawa River as far as the height of land, and thence to go down to James's Bay." At the beginning of April they arrived at the Long Sault, where they prepared some canoes in order to ascend the Ottawa River. From Lake Temiscamingue they passed many portages until they reached Lake Abbitibi, at the entrance or most southern extremity of which they built a small fort of stockades. After a short halt they continued their course onward to James's Bay.

First doomed to conquest by Troyes and his companions was Moose Factory, a stockade fort with four bastions. In the centre stood a house 40 feet square and as many high, terminating in a platform. This fort was escaladed by the French late at night, and of the palisades short work was made by the hatchets of the bushrangers.

Not a man amongst the garrison appears to have attempted a decent defence save the chief gunner, whose skull was split into fragments by Iberville, and who thus perished bravely at his post of duty. A cry for quarter went up, and the English were made prisoners on the spot. They were sixteen in number, and as the attack was made at night, they were in a state of almost complete undress. Troyes found in the fort twelve cannon, chiefly six and eight pounders, three thousand pounds of powder, and ten pounds of lead.

It is worth telling that this conquest was made with an amount of pomp and ceremony calculated to strike the deepest awe into the hearts of the fifteen unhappy traders, who knew nothing of fighting, nor had bargained for anything so perilous. For so small a victory it was both preceded and followed by almost as much circumstance as would have sufficed for the Grand Monarque himself in one of his theatrical sieges. The Chevalier announced in a loud voice that he took possession of the fort and island "in the name of his Most Christian Majesty the Most High, Most Mighty, Most Redoubtable Monarch Louis XIV. of the Most Christian names, King of France and Navarre." According to romantic custom, a sod of earth was thrice raised in the air, whilst a cry of "Vive le Roi" rang out over those waters wherein, deep down, lay the bodies of Henry Hudson and his brave followers.

Flushed with his triumph, the Chevalier de Troyes next bethought him of an attack on either Fort Rupert or Fort Albany. He did not long hesitate. News came that a boat containing provisions had left Moose Factory on the previous day bound for Rupert's River. Iberville was therefore sent with nine men and two bark canoes to attack a sloop belonging to the Company, then lying at anchor at the mouth of the latter river. Fourteen souls were aboard, including the Governor. To accomplish this feat it was necessary to travel forty leagues along the sea-coast. The road was extremely difficult, and in places almost impassable. A small boat was built to carry a couple of small camion. When he had arranged all his plans, Troyes left for Fort Rupert.

Ste. Hélène was sent on in advance to reconnoitre the English fort. He returned with the information that it was a square structure, flanked by four bastions, but that all was in a state of confusion owing to repairs and additions then being made. The cannon had not yet been placed, being temporarily accommodated outside on the slope of a redoubt.

Ere the attack, which could only have one issue, was made by the land forces, Iberville had boarded the Company's sloop, surprised captain and crew, and made all, including Governor Bridgar, prisoners. Four of the English were killed.

On the heels of this exploit, Iberville came ashore, rejoined his superior, and overpowered the almost defenceless garrison of Fort Rupert.

The French forces now united, and Ste. Hélène having been as successful as his brother in securing the second of the Company's ships, all embarked and sailed for the remaining post of the Company in that part of the Bay.

Neither Troyes nor Iberville knew its precise situation; but a little reconnoitring soon discovered it. Fort Albany was built in a sheltered inlet forty yards from the borders of the Bay. Two miles to the north-east was an estrapade, on the summit of which was placed a seat for a sentinel to sight the ships expected from England, and to signal them if all was well. But on this morning, unhappily, no sentinel was there to greet with a waving flag the Company's captured ship, on the deck of which young Iberville held vigilant and expectant watch.

Two Indians, however, brought Governor Sargeant tidings of the approach of the enemy, and his previous successes at Moose and Rupert rivers. The Governor immediately resolved upon making a bold stand; all was instantly got in readiness to sustain a siege, and the men were encouraged to behave with fortitude. Two hours later the booming of cannon was heard, and soon afterwards a couple of skirmishers were sighted at a distance. Despite the Governor's example, the servants at the fort were thrown into the greatest confusion. Two of their number were deputed by the rest to inform the Governor that they were by no means disposed to sacrifice their lives without provision being made for themselves and families in case of a serious issue. They were prevailed upon by the Governor to return to their posts, and a bounty was promised them. Bombardment by the French soon afterwards began, and lasted for two days, occasionally replied to by the English. But it was not until the evening of the second day that the first fatality occurred, when one of the servants was killed, and this brought about a mutiny. Elias Turner, the chief gunner, declared to his comrades that it was impossible for the Governor to hold the place, and that, for his part, he was ready to throw himself on the clemency of the French. Sargeant, overhearing this declaration, drew his pistol and threatened to blow out the gunner's brains if he did not return to his post, and the man slunk back to his duty. The French now profited by the darkness to bring their cannon through the wood closer to the fort; and by daybreak a series of heavy balls struck the bastions, causing a breach. Bridgar and Captain Outlaw, then at Fort Albany, were convinced that the enemy was undermining the powder magazine, in which case they would certainly all be blown to pieces.

From the ship the French had thrown up a battery, which was separated from the moat surrounding the fort by less than a musket-shot. None ventured to show himself above ground at a moment of such peril. A shell exploded at the head of the stairway and wounded the cook. The cries of the French could now be distinctly heard outside the fort—"Vive le Roi, Vive le Roi." In their fright and despair the English echoed the cry "Vive le Roi," thinking thereby to propitiate their aggressors. But the latter mistook the cry for one of defiance, as a token of loyalty to an altogether different monarch, and the bullets whistled faster and thicker. Sargeant desired to lower the flag floating above his own dwelling, but there was none to undertake so hazardous a task. Finally, Dixon, the under-factor, offered to show himself and placate the French. He first thrust a white cloth from a window and waved a lighted torch before it. He then called in a loud voice, and the firing instantly ceased. The under-factor came forth, fully dressed, bearing two huge flagons of port wine. Walking beyond the parapets, he encountered both Troyes and Iberville, and by the light of a full moon the little party of French officers and the solitary Englishman sat down on the mounted cannon, or on the ground beside it, broached the two flagons and drank the health of the two kings, their masters.

"And now, gentlemen," said Dixon, "what is it you want?"

"Possession of your fort in the name of his Most Christian Majesty, King Louis the Fourteenth."

Dixon, explaining that he was not master there, offered to conduct this message to his chief, and in a very short time the French commanders were seated comfortably within the house of the Governor. The demand was here repeated, it being added that great offence had been given by the action of the English in taking captive three French traders, the previous autumn, and keeping them prisoners on ground owned and ruled by the King of France. For this compensation was demanded, and Sargeant was desired at once to surrender the fort. The Governor was surprised at such extreme measures, for which he was totally unprepared, but was willing to surrender upon terms of capitulation. On the following morning these were arranged.

It was agreed that Sargeant should continue to keep all his personal effects; and further, that his deputy, Dixon, three domestics, and his servant should accompany him out of the fort. It was also agreed that Troyes should send the clerks and servants of the Company to a neighbouring island, there to await the arrival of the Company's ships from England. In case of their non-arrival within a reasonable time, Troyes promised to assist them to such vessel as he could procure for the purpose. The Frenchmen also gave Sargeant the provisions necessary to keep him and his companions from starvation. All quitted the fort without arms, save Sargeant and his son, whose swords and pistols hung at their sides. The Governor and his suite were provided with passage to Hays Island, where he afterwards made his escape to Port Nelson. The others were distributed between Forts Moose and Albany, and were treated by their captors with considerable severity and hardship.

Having attended to the disposition of his prisoners and their property, Troyes, accompanied by Iberville, departed on 10th August for Montreal. The gallant Chevalier and his associates would have been glad to have pursued their successes by crossing the Bay and capturing York Factory. But although two ships belonging to the Company had fallen to their lot, yet they could find none competent to command them. The distance between Albany and Port Nelson was by water 250 leagues, and the road overland was as yet unknown to the French. But it was not their purpose that it should long remain so. In a letter to his official superior at Quebec, Troyes, who wanted to plant the fleur-de-lys over the whole bay, boasted that the next year would not pass without his becoming acquainted with it.

Wherefore Troyes suffered himself to be prevailed upon by Iberville and be content with the victories already won. They carried with them in their journey more than 50,000 beaver skins as a trophy of their arms. Many of the Hudson's Bay Company's servants were employed in bearing the spoils. During the dreary march several of these unhappy captives were killed through the connivance of the French with the Indians; and the survivors reached Quebec in a dreadfully emaciated and halt condition.

You may believe that the victories of the Chevalier were blazoned to the skies. He was hailed in Montreal, Three Rivers, and Quebec as equal to any of the heroes of olden times, and his return was celebrated with great pomp. As to his future, the career of the Chevalier de Troyes ended abruptly and tragically in 1687, when he and all his men, to the number of ninety, were massacred by the Indians at

Niagara.

Governor la Barre, as you have heard, was an altogether different sort of man from Count Frontenac. The Iroquois tribes, especially the Senecas, who had now become the strongest nation, noticed the difference at once when they resumed negotiations. Instead of the dignity of command, La Barre wheedled their deputies, sending them away from Montreal loaded with presents. Soon afterwards, when he despatched a trading expedition to the Illinois region, the Senecas stopped it in its course, overhauled the canoes, and confiscated all the valuable goods with which La Barre (with an eye to great private profits) had packed them. Such a high-handed proceeding touched the Governor in a very sore place—his pocket. He became very wroth with the rascally Senecas, and swore to punish them for their knavery and presumption. A force of 900 men being raised, La Barre himself led them to the land of the Senecas on the south side of Lake Ontario. But so badly laid and badly carried out were his plans that, having got as far as the spot, since called the Bay of Famine, Governor la Barre called a halt and there encamped. Each day saw some of the soldiers stricken down by death and disease. The prospect was so gloomy that finally La Barre thought it best to come to terms with the enemy, and he therefore patched up an inglorious peace.

The name of the Seneca deputy at the peace conference was La Grande Gueule, or Big Jaw, so called from his gift of sustained eloquence. Big Jaw openly boasted that the Iroquois had not the slightest intention of sparing the Illinois tribe, whether the French liked it or not. Frontenac would have smitten the fellow down where he stood, but La Barre was obliged to pocket this affront, and the next day the remnant of his troops, full of anger and indignation, marched away.

Such a peace could not, of course, long endure. The Iroquois torch had been kindled, an evil wind was blowing, and it would take more than La Barre's feeble efforts to extinguish it. Tardy in war and too eager for peace had the Governor shown himself, and when he returned to Quebec found, to his mortification, that the King, his master, had superseded him. His instant return to France was ordered, the Marquis de Denonville being appointed in his stead. Little pains did His Majesty take to conceal his dissatisfaction with the treaty, or his anger at the abandonment of the Illinois.

The new Governor very quickly found that the English colonists were intriguing with the Iroquois, upholding and encouraging them in acts of hostility against the French. War, and war in earnest, had to come, and when 800 fresh soldiers arrived from France, Denonville began to prepare for it. In this he had the loyal support of the brave and wise man who also came out as the new Governor of Montreal, De Callières. Unluckily, Denonville began with an act of treachery. It was a strange deed for a soldier and a Christian. A number of Iroquois chiefs were enticed to Fort Frontenac, where they were seized, and, after being flung into prison, were sent to France to work all the rest of their days in the galleys. What a fate for such haughty braves, who never worked, but left all labour to their poor squaws! What wonder the revenge of the Iroquois was terrible!

Creeping along the St. Lawrence with his army, Denonville crossed Lake Ontario, built a new fort, and leaving 400 men to guard it, marched towards the Seneca lodges. In the middle of July 1687 a hot battle took place with 800 Senecas, in which, after losing six men killed and twenty wounded, the French drove the foe into the forest. Four hundred thousand bushels of Indian corn (maize) and several herds of swine were found and destroyed. In the meantime, however, while the Senecas were being punished, the danger to Montreal and the other towns was imminent, owing to their being without strong military protection. To defend Chambly 120 bushrangers were armed, and on the island of Montreal, Callières built twenty small forts for the inhabitants to take refuge in, should the Iroquois descend upon them in force. For by this time, as you can imagine, the whole of the Five Nations were blazing with rage, as if they had been so many bloodthirsty wolves. Even in their rage they were cunning. They had no intention of attacking Canada in force; that was not their method of warfare. Crossing the border silently in batches, each singled out his prey, some sleeping village, or mayhap an unsuspecting farm. Next day a few mangled corpses here, a heap of smoking ruins there, told the terrible tale of the Iroquois raid.

After a time the wiser heads amongst the Five Nations began to consider whether a conquest over the French would not make the Colonial English (whom they called *Ang'ais* or Yankees) too powerful. Suddenly they openly professed a desire for peace. A deputation was sent to Canada to say that, strong as the Iroquois knew themselves to be, they did not mean to press for all the advantages they had the right and power to demand. "We know," they said, "how weak you are. We can at any time burn the houses of your people, pillage your stores, waste your crops, and raze your forts." To this boasting Denonville replied that Colonel Dongan of New York claimed the Iroquois as English subjects. "If you are English subjects, then you must be at peace with us, for France and England are not now at war." "Onontio," exclaimed the chief of the Envoys, "the Five Nations are independent! We can be friends to one or both, or enemies to one or both. Never have we been conquered by either of you."

In the end a truce was proclaimed, but truce or no truce, a great many skirmishes and massacres still went on, on both sides. All they could do to prevent a peace being signed, the Hurons of Michilimackinac, allies of the French, did. To them peace meant utter ruin; their numbers were too few, and they well knew Denonville could not protect them from the fury of the Iroquois. Amongst the Hurons was a tall chief famous for his prowess in war and his gift of eloquence. He was, according to those who knew him, the bravest and most intelligent chief on the whole Continent. Kondiaronk, or "The Rat," was mortally offended that the French should have made even a truce without so much as consulting the wishes of their native allies. To take his revenge on Denonville, he resolved to make peace impossible. When the Iroquois envoys were on their way to Montreal to sign the treaty, "The Rat" lay in ambush with a band of his trusty Hurons. He surprised and made them all his prisoners, slaying one. When they angrily explained that they were peaceful envoys, the crafty Kondiaronk professed to be greatly surprised, because, said he, "the French Governor himself sent me here on purpose to waylay you. But if, as I believe, what you say is true, behold, I set you at liberty!

May the gods curse Onontio for having committed such an act of treachery!" Thus saying, he loaded the deputies with gifts and bade all but one go free. After which Kondiaronk, glorying in his perfidy, hastened to Michilimackinac, shaking his fist in triumph and crying, "I have killed the peace!" He spoke then the truth. The Iroquois prisoner he took with him, under the pretence of adopting him in place of one of his Hurons slain by the deputies on being attacked, was handed over to the French Commander of Michilimackinac as a spy. In vain the victim protested that he was an envoy of peace between the Five Nations and the French. In vain did he try to explain the circumstances of his capture. Kondiaronk laughed in his face, telling the French Commander he must have taken leave of his wits, and the unhappy wretch was led to the stake. An Iroquois captive was released by Kondiaronk and bidden to return to his tribe with this message, that while the French were making a show of wishing peace, they were secretly slaying and capturing the men of the Five Nations.

Months passed while the Iroquois brooded on vengeance. Denonville's protestations were received in contemptuous silence. There was now nothing to prevent formal war, for France and England had recommenced hostilities. King James the Second had fled from his throne and palace to France. William of Orange, the mortal enemy of King Louis, reigned in his stead. A new English Governor, Andros, was sent out to New York to foment the deadly feud between the Iroquois and the Canadians.

In the month of August 1689 burst at last the storm of the Iroquois' hatred and revenge. One night, during a heavy shower of hail, 1500 dusky warriors crossed Lake St. Louis, landing silently and stealthily on the beautiful island of Montreal, the "Garden of Canada." By daybreak they had grouped themselves in platoons, one platoon around every large dwelling for several leagues along the road at Lachine almost to the gates of Montreal. The inhabitants of Lachine were wrapped in sweet slumber, soon and ruthlessly to be exchanged for that other slumber which knows no mortal awakening.

Let us conjure up the terrible picture. At each door, in war-paint and feathers, stands a group of savages with upraised hatchets and huge mallets. The signal is given; it is the dread Indian war-whoop; the next moment doors and windows are driven inwards. Sleeping men, women, and children are dragged from their beds. In vain they struggle in the hands of their butchers, in vain they appeal to those who know no pity. They might as well appeal to wild beasts. A few houses resist their attacks; when these are fired 200 unhappy beings, the hope and pride of the colony, are burnt alive. Agonising shrieks rend the air. The knife, the torch, and the tomahawk spare none, not even the little children. Those who do not now die under their tortures are led away to nameless cruelties, which will furnish rare sport to the lodges of the Five Nations.

Such was the awful massacre of Lachine; such the vengeance of the Iroquois. So swift and sudden had been the blow that the citizens of Montreal were paralysed. All that dreadful day the savages moved on, and for many days afterwards, and none came to arrest their course. Governor Denonville, to whose policy the calamity was due, seems entirely to have lost his nerve. A few miles from Lachine a body of 200 troops, led by a brave officer named Subercase, asked to be led against the murderers of their countrymen. But Denonville, in a panic, ordered Subercase to take refuge in Fort Roland. All were forbidden to stir. Another body of men, commanded by one Larobeyre, attempting to reach Fort Roland, were set upon and cut to pieces. More than half the prisoners were burnt by their conquerors. Larobeyre, wounded and unable to flee, was led captive to the Iroquois wigwams and roasted alive at a slow fire. The bloodthirsty tribes remained by the St. Lawrence as long as they pleased; their ravages of the countryside continued for many weeks. Not until October did the last of them disappear. A small party sent by Denonville to make sure that they had really gone, came upon a canoe bearing twenty-two departing Iroquois paddling across the Lake of the Two Mountains. The chance was not one to be foregone. Too long held in check, the Canadians drew near the savages, who fired upon them without damage. Then with a fierce joy the white men singled out each his man, raised their muskets, and when the explosion came eighteen Iroquois toppled over into the lake. But considering the hundreds of Canadians who had been massacred, this was a paltry retribution indeed.

What wonder now that the men and women of Canada longed for the strong right arm and sagacious brain of Frontenac! Is it any marvel that they rejoiced to hear that, menaced with the loss of his North-American dominions, King Louis had entrusted the gallant, fiery old soldier once more with the government of New France. Frontenac's return was hailed by all, nobles, soldiers, merchants, artisans, farmers, even by the Jesuits, who five years before had striven to send him away. He was escorted to the fort with a multitude of torch-bearers. Well he knew what a great task awaited him. He had now to battle not only with the Iroquois, but with the Anglo-American colonies, the Yankees, as they were called by the Indians, just as his master, King Louis, had to combat five powers at once—England, Germany, Holland, Spain, and Savoy.

Was Frontenac equal to the task? Was the strain now to be placed on his shoulders too great for the powers of a hero seventy-two years of age? That question let the next chapter answer.

CHAPTER IX

"QUEBEC FOR KING LOUIS"

When Count Frontenac arrived at Quebec the massacre at Lachine had just thrilled all Canada with horror. It was time to be up and doing if the French Canadians were not to be utterly exterminated, if New France was to be saved for King Louis, then at the height of his power and renown. Callières, the Governor of Montreal, saw in the presence not of the Iroquois but of the English in New York the root of all Canada's troubles. He urged his sovereign to strike, and King Louis had resolved to deal them a blow once and for all, from which they would never recover. He would banish them from New York and plant a colony of Frenchmen instead. The plan was entrusted to Frontenac to execute. Unfortunately for the success of this scheme, sufficient ships and troops and money were not forthcoming at the right moment from France. There followed vexatious delays, and when the French fleet at length crossed the ocean and anchored at Chedabucto, in Acadia, the season was too far advanced to begin operations. Meanwhile Frontenac was not the man to let time dwell on his hands. Against the English colonies three war-parties were organised whose deeds of blood were long remembered in American homesteads and in Indian wigwams. Frontenac saw that French prestige had sunk so low amongst the northern and western tribes that all were ready to make peace with the dreaded Iroquois on any terms. At the very name of Frenchmen the meanest brave amongst the Five Nations laughed and spat contemptuously on the ground.

"Now, by St. Louis," cried Frontenac, "they shall see how weak we are!"

His fiery soul could not wait upon the seasons. The three expeditions he sent forth marched amidst the ice and snow of mid-winter, for it was by such a stroke of daring that Canada could be saved. The first started from Montreal, led by Mantet and Ste. Hélène, one of the three sons of the brave Canadian named Le Moine, and after incredible hardships reached the village of Schenectady, on the Hudson. They burst upon the sleeping, unsuspecting villagers in the middle of the night, killing many and taking numerous prisoners. When the fighting was over they burned nearly the whole settlement to the ground. The Indians of the party were indignant at not being able to torture the prisoners unhindered, for the French-Canadian leaders were not cruel by nature. They showed gratitude to an English colonist named Glen, who, on a previous occasion, had treated certain French prisoners with kindness. Glen barricaded his house, resolved to sell his life dearly, but the Canadian captain called out to him to have no fear. "We are your debtors, not your enemies. Moreover, if you have any kinsmen amongst the captives we have taken, point them out, and they shall go free." The Quebec Indians looked on sulkily while the Englishman took advantage of this handsome offer and named several of the prisoners. "This Yankee pale-face has a terribly large family," their chief was heard to grumble.

The second war-party from Three Rivers, led by the redoubtable François Hertel, wiped out the village of Salmon Falls, butchering most of the inhabitants; while the third, under the command of Portneuf, attacked and captured the fort and settlement at Casco Bay. To the disgrace of Portneuf, he broke faith with the heroic garrison when they surrendered, and abandoned his prisoners to his Indian allies, who scalped and burnt them all.

By feats such as these the tide was turned. At last the French had exhibited proofs of their prowess, and the Iroquois were not slow in acknowledging that they had made a mistake when they branded them with the name of cowards. Frontenac could strike still as heavy a blow as in the past. The wavering North-West tribes made haste to assure him of their support, and the haughty Iroquois, in spite of the arguments of the English, sent deputies to Quebec to congratulate Ontio on his return to the land. The furs which had been collecting for three years in the distant ports, with none daring enough to venture upon their transport, now began to pour into Montreal in hundreds of canoes. Trade began to revive, and the drooping spirits of the colonists were exchanged for gladness and hope.

Could the redoubtable Frontenac have thought that the English colonists would bear this terrible treatment tamely? No! every mind and bosom there was excited by the desire for revenge. Moreover, they knew that now France's chief strength lay in Frontenac himself. With England flying at the throat of Old France, the King, to whom Frontenac applied, told him bluntly that he had need for all his soldiers in Europe. "Your demands," wrote King Louis, "come at a wrong time. A defensive policy is the proper one for you to pursue." True, William the Third of England also could give little help to the New Englanders. They, too, must fight their own battles. To their own arms was it left to inflict chastisement on the Canadians in the north. Accordingly, all the colonies met in consultation, and by great efforts a fleet of seven vessels and several hundred men was raised in Boston. Sir William Phips led them forth, and Port Royal, in Acadia, was taken without much trouble. Sufficient booty was captured to cover the cost of this expedition, and the New Englanders returned flushed with triumph and eager for a more daring blow. Meanwhile a land force of 1300 men, under Colonel Winthrop, had failed, through sickness and mismanagement, to reach Montreal by way of Lake Champlain. A portion of this little army had followed Captain John Schuyler onwards, and, crossing the Canadian border, killed a few Frenchmen near Montreal. When it had done that, it beat a hasty retreat.

Such raids as these—for raids is all they were—afforded little satisfaction to the English colonists, burning with a desire to sweep the lilies of France from the New World. Silently and speedily a plot was matured, and by the next summer it was ripe. Frontenac, thinking all was secure for the present, had left Quebec to entertain a band of Iroquois at Montreal to a great feast and war-dance. One morning a messenger arrived post-haste to tell him that the enemy in their ships were sailing up the St. Lawrence. Not a moment was to be lost. Summoning the Governor of Montreal and De Ramsay of Three Rivers to follow him with every man who could shoulder a musket, the lion-hearted Frontenac pressed forward with all his speed. Ere he could reach Quebec the enemy's fleet had anchored off the Isle of Orleans. Quebec was almost in a panic, but Frontenac's arrival instantly assuaged their fears. He filled all with his enthusiasm. They resolved to die rather than yield. Great trunks of trees and casks filled with stones were hastily heaped up where the walls were weakest. On the enemy were trained the rows of cannon, and 2700 men firmly awaited the onslaught. Was the danger then so great? Who was the man—who were the men—who thus hoped to storm the strongest citadel in New France?

A humble blacksmith's son was William Phips, born at Fort Pemaquid, in Maine. In his boyhood he herded a drove of cattle. But he was a clever boy, and having learned ship-carpentry, he built a little vessel of his own, and as a trader went to sea. Phips was a born sailor. In one of his many long voyages he heard stories of a Spanish galleon filled with gold and silver sunk off the Island of Cuba. Phips learnt all the particulars, satisfied himself of his ability, and then determined to raise that ship and make himself master of her wealth. At first people laughed at him, but he persevered, and at last the King had given him the command of a warship. As he had promised, so Phips carried out his plan, bringing to England a fortune of £300,000. With the praise of King Charles the Second ringing in his ears, as Sir William Phips he returned to New England, prepared for any deed of note and valour which fate might offer.

To Phips, then, his New England fellow-countrymen had entrusted their fleet, thirty-two vessels, large and small, with 2000 men. Phips sailed forth in a confident spirit, but when he first cast his eyes on the great rock of Quebec and the white fleur-de-lys floating above in the autumn air, he may have felt some misgivings. These he sternly repressed: it were best to put the boldest front on the matter. Choosing a young major, he sent him with a peremptory summons to Count Frontenac to surrender the city. Immediately on landing from the boat with his flag of truce, Phips's emissary was blindfolded and led by a roundabout path to the Castle of St. Louis, where Frontenac and most of the chief men of the colony were assembled. His demands Phips had written out on a sheet of paper. He was anxious, he told Frontenac, to avoid shedding blood, and that if the Count would surrender the fort, the city, the stores, and their persons without delay, they may expect mercy from him as a Christian. Otherwise it would go hard with the French. Capitulation was demanded within one hour.

The bandage was taken from the messenger's eyes and the paper read and translated to the company. Then the New England major took a large silver watch from his pocket and laid it on the table, saying haughtily, "Gentlemen, you will perceive it is now ten o'clock. My general expects an answer by eleven."

Whereat the French officers assembled, flushed with anger, only Frontenac's face remaining impassive. "You need not wait so long," he said. He told the envoy that the French rejected the demand.

"Will your Excellency put that in writing?" asked the envoy.

Frontenac's eyes darted fire.

"My Guns will give my Answer," Frontenac, 1690

"It is by the cannon's mouth and by musket-shot that I will send my answer. I am not in the habit of being addressed in the style he has chosen to adopt. Let your master do his best; I will do mine."

Once more blindfolded, the messenger was escorted to his boat. A little later the batteries of Quebec's lower town opened fire on the fleet. Some of the very first shots brought down the flag of Phips's own vessel, seeing which from the shore, several bold Canadians immediately swam out, and, regardless of the musket fire from the fleet, fished the dripping prize out of the water. Afterwards this flag was hung as a trophy to the ceiling of Quebec Cathedral, and there it remained until the siege and capture of the city by General Wolfe, when it and the building that sheltered it were consumed by fire.

For two whole days Phips remained in a state of indecision. The enemy was of sterner stuff than he had supposed, and an effective plan must be concerted. On the 18th of October 1690 Major Walley, the second in command, with 1300 men and some small field cannon, landed at Beauport. They had resolved to cross the St. Charles River there and attack Quebec in the rear. At the same time the guns of the ships opened fire. So vigorously replied the ramparts that Phips was obliged to draw off for a while, not renewing his bombardment until the next morning. By this time the New England commander saw that unless the troops on shore could manage to force their way into the city and capture it by assault, his chances of success were gone.

Valiantly, doggedly did Walley and his men try to cross the St. Charles River. The banks were covered with deep mud; each time they tried to cross, the Indians and bushrangers sent by Frontenac beat them off. After three days of cold and hunger they were fain to give up the attempt. When they retreated to the ships, five of their cannon were left sticking in the Beauport mud. Yet even had they succeeded, what a task was left them to do! There was Frontenac watching them sharply, ready, if need be, to go to the rescue of the outposts of carabiniers with 2000 men. In these circumstances Sir William Phips's siege of Quebec turned out an utter failure. Frontenac was more than a match for him: Quebec was not Port Royal.

On the following day the townsfolk and soldiers on the heights saw the discomfited fleet of the foe passing out of sight homeward down the St. Lawrence. They had lost only some sixty killed and wounded,—Ste. Hélène had fallen,—while before Phips got back to Boston, what with those slain by bullets and the hundreds drowned on the several ships lost in the November storms, his loss was heavy indeed. While Quebec sang a Te Deum and dedicated a chapel to "Our Lady of Victories," Boston was plunged in gloom. Phips's ignoble failure had involved the whole colony in debt and mortification. King Louis the Fourteenth, hearing the good news, ordered a medal to be struck bearing the inscription: "Francia in Nova Orbe Victrix; Kebeca Liberata A.D. MDCXC."

If Frontenac hoped that the Iroquois would cease after this to give him trouble, he was destined to disappointment. All his endeavours to conciliate them failed; their chiefs were still convinced that they had more to hope for as allies of the

English, and took measures accordingly. English and French colonists now hated one another with a hate that was never to slumber for the next seventy years, until Wolfe was to plant the blood-red flag of England on the frowning heights of Quebec.

During the winter of 1691 and 1692 there were numerous terrible border raids, in one of which the Abenakis devastated more than fifty leagues of English territory and utterly destroyed Yorktown. Both French and English used the Indians as so many packs of human bloodhounds to track their foes to death. Both sides resorted to the practice of paying a price for the bodies, alive or dead, of the hostile savages. A French regular soldier received ten louis for the scalp of an Iroquois; a volunteer received twenty. If he had to hunt the red-man like any other wild animal, he could claim fifty louis for his scalp. This practice was not confined to the Canadians. Corresponding premiums were paid by the English.

Living captives were often handed over to their Indian allies to appease their delight in human suffering and bloodshed. Once one of Frontenac's officers, ravaging the country of the Oneidas, found a solitary old man in a certain village. He was nearly a hundred years of age, but do not imagine his years awakened any compassion in his captors, who at once handed him over to their savage allies. The old brave awaited his fate as calmly as any of those Roman senators whose city was taken by the Gauls. Father Charlevoix tells us the story. He says it was a strange sight to behold more than four hundred savage tormentors forming a circle round a decrepit object from whom they could not wring a single cry, and who, as long as the breath remained in his body, taunted them with being the slaves of weak and foolish Frenchmen. Only once did he complain, and that was when one of his butchers, on purpose to finish the scene, stabbed him repeatedly in the breast.

"Ah," he murmured hoarsely, "why did you not wait until you had done your worst, so that you might behold how a man ought to die!"

At another time Frontenac captured two Mohawk warriors whom he condemned to die by torture. One of them immediately despatched himself with a knife, which a pitying priest threw him in prison. But his fellow-captive, disdaining such an escape, walked boldly to the stake singing his death chant. In his song he boasted that not all the power of man could extort a groan or a murmur from his lips, and that it was enough happiness for him in the hour of trial to remember that he had made many a Frenchman feel the same pangs he was about to feel. When bound to the stake, he looked round on his executioners, their instruments of torture, and the multitude of French spectators with a smile of composure. For some hours he endured a series of barbarities that make our blood even now, as we read of it, chill in our veins, and at last a Frenchwoman implored the Governor to order him to be dealt a mortal blow and so put him out of his agony.

Thanks to the incessant raids of the Iroquois into Canada, the farmers dared not till the fields and sow the seed. Those who might have protected them were everywhere up in arms, coping with their implacable savage foes, who seemed to rise out of the ground on every hand. In vain was one band beaten and cut to pieces; another sprang up to take its place.

Heroic Defence by Madeleine de Verchères and her Brothers, 1692

Many were the heroic deeds performed by both Canadian men and women, but none is more thrilling than that which is told of a beautiful young girl of fourteen, Madeleine de la Verchères. She was the daughter of Seigneur of Verchères, and lived in the fortified seignory ten miles from Montreal, on the south side of the great river St. Lawrence. One morning her father was absent at Quebec, and all the farm-folk were working in the fields. To guard the fort, her father had left two soldiers, an old man eighty years old, her two little brothers, and herself. Suddenly the terrible war-whoop of the Iroquois pierced the air, and scarce time had the soldiers to barricade the doors and windows before a mighty host appeared before the fort. So fierce was their fire, that the soldiers deemed it useless to continue to struggle. But not so Madeleine. Seizing a musket, she ordered the falterers to their posts. Day and night for a whole week did this heroic girl hold the band of Iroquois at bay. She taught her little brothers to load and fire so rapidly, that the Indians fancied a garrison of twelve men at least held the fort. At last a reinforcement arrived, and the Iroquois beat a retreat. The gates of the fort were flung open, and the pale, weary girl of fourteen, captain of the garrison of Verchères, flung herself into her father's arms.

And now let us return for a moment to the shores of Hudson's Bay. It was not likely that the forts which the Chevalier de Troyes had wrested from the English would continue to remain in French possession without an effort being made to regain them. One Captain Moon, returning from Port Nelson, endeavoured, with twenty-four men, to surprise the French at Fort Anne, which was the new name bestowed upon the captured Fort Albany. Moon built a station eight miles away, but Iberville, who had been again sent to the Bay, instantly got wind of it, and, marching thither, drove the English out. When two Hudson's Bay Company's vessels arrived in these waters, winter overtook them, and they became locked in the ice. The crews landed, and had nearly built a fort when Iberville fell upon them and made them all prisoners.

But there was one stronghold in the northern bay which continued to defy the French. This single fort was considered of so much importance, that the gain or loss of everything in Hudson's Bay depended upon it. To capture it, however, required a stronger force than Iberville could at present command, whereupon he sailed away to France to ask assistance from the King. He revealed to His Majesty his plans for the capture of Fort Nelson, and was at length promised two ships in the following spring. The royal promise was duly kept. After a hot bombardment of three weeks, the English Governor was obliged to surrender and the French standard hoisted over the captured stronghold. Only for a year, however, did the stronghold remain in the enemy's possession, when it was recaptured by the Company, and threescore Frenchmen sent prisoners to England. When Iberville heard of this fresh turn which events had taken, he ground his teeth with rage. "Am I," he cried, "to go on capturing this fort from the English, only to have it repeatedly slip through our hands?" He then and there vowed to have nothing further to do with Hudson's Bay, he who had fought so many battles and won there so many victories.

As for the French prisoners, no sooner were they released than they crossed the Channel and sought audience of their King. Gazing upon this emaciated band of fur-hunters and bushrangers, Louis the Fourteenth would have been craven indeed if he had not attempted to retrieve their misfortunes. Four ships of war were promised them. "And," said the King, "Iberville shall lead you." But Iberville was then at Placentia, in Newfoundland, bent on finding other fields for his energy and martial prowess. No other man was so well equipped at all points, in knowledge of the great bay and of the conditions of fighting there, as this hero, so the four captains found him out at Placentia, and, embarking in the *Pelican*, he took command.

Iberville's flag-ship mounted fifty guns. The others of the fleet were the *Palmier*, the *Weesph*, and the *Violent*. The attack on Fort Nelson this time was to be no child's play. Almost at the very moment when the wind was filling the sails of the French ships in the Channel, there sailed from Plymouth a fleet belonging to the Hudson's Bay Company, the *Hampshire*, the *Hudson's Bay*, the *Dering*, and *Owner's Love*. The two first-named vessels were no strangers to the Bay, and had participated in the conquest of the previous year. Although each was ignorant of the other's movements, it was a race across the Atlantic, and the English fleet entered the Straits only forty hours before the ships of the French, and, like them, was much impeded by the ice, which was unusually troublesome. Passage was made by the enemy in the English wake. One French ship, commanded by Duqué, pushed past the currents, taking a northerly course, which brought her commander into full view of two of the Company's ships. Shots were exchanged; but owing to the difficulties engendered by the ice, it was impossible to manoeuvre with such certainty as to cut off the Frenchman's escape. While this skirmish was in progress, Iberville in the *Pelican* succeeded in getting past the English unknown to them, and reached the mouth of the Nelson River in sight of the fort. His presence, as may be imagined, greatly surprised and disturbed the Governor and the Company's servants; for they had believed their own ships would have arrived in season to prevent the enemy from entering the Straits. Several rounds of shot were fired as a signal, in the hope that a response would be made by the Company's ships, which they hourly expected in that quarter.

On his part the French commander was equally disturbed by the non-arrival of his three consorts, which the exigencies of the voyage had obliged him to forsake. Two days were passed in a state of suspense. At daybreak on the 5th of September three ships[2] were distinctly visible; both parties joyfully believed they were their own. So certain was Iberville, that he immediately raised anchor and started to join the newcomers. He was soon undeceived, but the knowledge of his mistake in no way daunted him.

The Company's commanders were not prepared either for the daring or the fury of the Frenchman's onslaught. It is true the *Pelican* was much superior to any of their own craft singly, being manned by nearly 250 men, and boasting 44 pieces of cannon. The Company's ships lined up, the *Hampshire* in front, the *Dering* next, with the *Hudson's Bay* bringing up the rear.

The combatants being in close proximity, the battle began at half-past nine in the morning. The French commander came straight for the *Hampshire*, whose captain, believing it was his enemy's design to board, instantly let fall his mainsail

[2] The fourth, the fire-ship *Owner's Love*, was never more heard of. It is supposed that, separated from the others, she ran into the ice and was sunk, with all on board.

and set his fore-top-sail. Contact having been by these means narrowly evaded, the scene of battle suddenly shifted to the *Pelican* and the *Dering*, whose main-sail was smitten by the terrific volley. At the same time the *Hudson's Bay*, veering, received a damaging broadside. The Company's men could distinctly hear the orders shouted by Iberville to discharge a musket fire into the *Dering's* forecastle, but in this move he was anticipated by the English sailors, who poured a storm of bullets in upon the Frenchman, accompanied by a broadside of grape, which wrought havoc with her sails. While the cries of the wounded on the *Pelican* could be distinctly heard, all three of the Company's ships opened fire, with the design of disabling her rigging. But the captain of the *Hudson's Bay*, seeing that he could not engage the *Pelican* owing to Iberville's tactics, determined to run in front of her and give her the benefit of a constant hull fire, besides taking the wind from her sails. Iberville observed the movement; the two English vessels were near; he veered round, and by a superb piece of seamanship came so near to the *Hampshire* that the crew of the latter saw that boarding was intended. Every man flew out on the main deck with his pistol and cutlass, and a terrific broadside of grape on the part of the Englishman alone saved him.

Hotter and fiercer raged the battle. The *Hampshire's* salvation had been only temporary; at the end of three hours and a half she began to sink, with all sails set. When this occurred, Iberville had ninety men wounded, forty being struck by a single broadside. Notwithstanding this, he decided at once to push matters with the *Hampshire's* companions, although the *Pelican* was in a badly damaged state, especially the forecastle, which was a mass of splinters.

The enemy made at once for the *Dering*, which besides being the smallest ship, had suffered severely. She crowded on all sail and managed to avoid an encounter, and Iberville, being in no condition to prosecute the chase, returned to the *Hudson's Bay*, which soon surrendered. Iberville was not destined, however, to reap much advantage from his prize, the *Hampshire*. The English flag-ship was unable to render any assistance to the *Hudson's Bay*, and soon went down, with nearly all on board.

To render the situation more distressing, no sooner had some ninety prisoners been made than a storm arose, so that it became out of the question to approach the shore with design of landing. They were without a long-boat, and each attempt to launch canoes in the boiling surf was attended with failure.

Night fell; the wind instead of calming grew fiercer. The sea became truly terrible, seeking, seemingly, with all its power to drive the *Pelican* and the *Hudson's Bay* upon the coast. The rudders of each ship broke; the tide rose, and there seemed no hope for the crews, whose destiny was so cruel. Their only hope, in the midst of the bitter blast and clouds of snow which environed them, lay in the strength of their cables. Soon after nine o'clock the *Hudson's Bay* and its anchor parted with a shock.

"Instantly," said one of the survivors, "a piercing cry went up from our fore-castle. The wounded and dead lay heaped up with so little separation one from the other that silence and moans alone distinguished them. All were icy cold and covered with blood. They had told us the anchor would hold, and we dreaded being washed up on the shore stiff the next morning."

A huge wave broke over the main deck and the ship lurched desperately. Two hours later the cable parted, and the ship was hurled rudderless to and fro in the trough of the sea.

By the French account, matters were in no more enviable state aboard the *Pelican*; Iberville, however, amidst scenes rivalling those just described, did his best to animate his officers and men with a spirit equalling his own.

"It is better," he cried, "to die, if we must, outside the bastions of Fort Bourbon than to perish here like pent sheep on board."

When morning broke, it was seen by the French that their ship was not yet submerged, and it was resolved to disembark by such means as lay in their power. The Company's servants were more fortunate. The *Hudson's Bay* had drifted eight miles to the south of the fort, and was wrecked on a bank of icy marshland, which at least constrained them to wade no deeper than their knees. The French, however, were forced to make their way through the icy water submerged to their necks, from the results of which terrible exposure no fewer than eighteen marines and seamen lost their lives. Once on shore they could not, like the English, look forward to a place of refuge and appease their hunger with provisions and drink. They were obliged, in their shivering, half-frozen state, to subsist upon moss and seaweed, but for which indifferent nourishment they must inevitably have perished.

The Company's garrison witnessed the calamities which were overtaking the French, but not knowing how great their number, and assured of their hostility, did not attempt any acts of mercy. They perceived the enemy camped in a wood, less than two leagues distant, where, building several fires, they sought to restore their spirits by means of warmth and hot draughts of boiled herbs.

While the fort was being continually recruited by survivors of the two wrecked ships, the other three French vessels had arrived on the scene. The fourth, the *Violent*, lay at the bottom of the Bay, having been sunk by the ice. The *Palmier* had suffered the loss of her helm, but was fortunate in not being also a victim of the storm. The French forces being now united, little time was lost by Iberville in making active preparations for the attack upon the fort.

On the 11th the enemy attained a small wood, almost under the guns of the fort, and having entrenched themselves, lit numerous fires and made considerable noise in order to lend the impression to the English that an entrenchment was being thrown up. This ruse was successful, for the Governor gave orders to fire in that direction; and Iberville, seizing this opportunity, effected a landing of all his men and armaments from the ships.

The fort would now soon be hemmed in on all sides, and it were indeed strange if a chance shot or firebrand did not ignite the timbers and the powder magazine were not exploded. Governor Bailey was holding a council of his advisers when one of the French prisoners in the fort gave notice of the approach of a messenger bearing a flag of truce. He was recognised as Martigny. The Governor permitted his advance and sent a factor to meet him and insist upon his eyes being bandaged before he would be permitted to enter. Martigny was conducted to where the council was sitting, and there delivered Iberville's message demanding surrender. He was instantly interrupted by Captain Smithsend, who, with a great show of passion, asked the emissary if it were not true that Iberville had been killed in the action. In spite of Martigny's denials, Smithsend loudly persisted in believing Iberville's death, and held that the French were in sore straits and only made the present attack because no other alternative was offered to desperate men to obtain food and shelter. Bailey allowed himself to be influenced by Smithsend, and declined to yield to any of Martigny's demands. The latter returned, and the French instantly set up a battery near the fort and continued, amidst a hail of bullets, the work of landing their damaged stores and armaments. Stragglers from the wreck of the *Hudson's Bay* continued all day to find their way to the fort, but several reached it only to be shot down in mistake by the cannon and muskets of their own men. On the 12th, after a hot skirmish, fatal to both sides, the Governor was again requested, this time by Sérigny, to yield up the fort to superior numbers.

"If you refuse, we will set fire to the place and accord you no quarter," he wrote to Bailey.

"Set fire and be d— —d to you!" responded Bailey.

He then went to work, with Smithsend, whose treatment as a prisoner in the hands of the French some years before was still vividly before him, to animate the garrison.

"Go for them, you dogs!" cried Bailey. "Give it to them hot and heavy; I promise you forty pounds apiece for your widows!"

Fighting in these days was attended by fearful mortality, and the scarcity of pensions to the hero's family, perhaps, made the offer seem handsome. At any rate it seemed a sufficient bribe to the Company's men, who fought like demons.

A continual fire of guns and mortar, as well as of muskets, was kept up. The Canadians sallied out upon a number of skirmishes, filling the air with a frightful din, borrowing from the Iroquois their piercing war-cries. In one of these sallies St. Martin, one of their bravest men, perished.

Under protection of a flag of truce, Sérigny came again to demand a surrender. It was the last time, he said, the request would be preferred. A general assault had been resolved upon by the enemy, who were at their last resort, living like beasts in the wood, feeding on moss, and to whom no extremity could be odious were it but an exchange for their present condition. They were resolved upon carrying the fort, even at the point of the bayonet and over heaps of their slain.

Bailey decided to yield. He sent Morrison to carry the terms of capitulation, in which he demanded all the peltries in the fort belonging to the Hudson's Bay Company. This demand being rejected by the enemy, Bailey later in the evening sent Henry Kelsey with a proposition to retain a portion of their armament; this also was refused. There was now nothing for it but to surrender, Iberville having granted an evacuation with bag and baggage.

At one o'clock on the following day, therefore, the evacuation took place. Bailey, at the head of his garrison, and a number of the crew of the wrecked *Hudson's Bay* and six survivors of the *Hampshire*, marched forth from Fort York with drums beating, flag flying, and with arms and baggage. They hardly knew whither they were to go, or what fate awaited them. A vast, and inhospitable region surrounded them, and a winter long to be remembered for its severity had begun. But to the French it seemed as if their spirits were undaunted, and they set forth bravely.

The enemy watched the retreat of the defeated garrison not without admiration, and for the moment speculation was rife as to their fate. But it was only for a moment. Too rejoiced to contemplate anything but the termination of their own sufferings, the Canadians hastened to enter the fort, headed by Boisbriant, late an ensign in the service of the Compagnie du Nord. Fort Nelson was once more in the hands of the French.

On the St. Lawrence the Count of Frontenac, old as he was, sickening of the perpetual raids, led a great war force into the very midst of the Iroquois. Rebuilding Fort Frontenac, which had been destroyed, he launched his men straight against the Onondaga lodges, wiping out all their stores of food and their maize harvests. He laid low also the land of the Oneidas, and the warriors of both tribes fled before him. If they could raid and butcher, by St. Louis, so could he! The Iroquois looked to the English for help against the French. Whatever they might have done, their hand was stopped. News arrived in 1697 of the signing of the peace at Ryswick between the warring kingdoms of England and France. Tired of the conflict grew the haughty Five Nations, and deputies were sent to Quebec to bring it to an end. They offered, as before, to cease fighting the French Canadians, but not their Indian allies in the west. This would not satisfy Frontenac: he would make no peace which could not be lasting. The Governor of New York interfered.

"The Iroquois," he told Frontenac, "are under the King of England's protection. They cannot make either war or peace on their own account. I have told them to be at peace with you. Henceforward you must not treat them as enemies."

"I will make my peace with the Five Nations," Frontenac thundered forth to the Indian deputy, "but it shall be on my own terms. If we continue to fight and you aid them, by St. Louis! the blood will be on your own hands."

A few weeks later, when the reward of his firmness was in sight, the lion-hearted Frontenac, now in his seventy-eighth year, sickened and died, amidst the sorrow of his people. It was a great loss to Canada, and fortunate was it that his successor was as brave and wise as Governor de Callières.

CHAPTER X

KING LOUIS BUILDS A MIGHTY FORT

Afar off, in the little Dutch town of Ryswick, the two kings, William and Louis, had signed the treaty of peace. It was agreed that all the places captured by either French or English soldiers during the war should be given back again. What did this mean to Canada and America? Only this: that all these eight years of bloodshed had been in vain. Neither French nor English were a whit the richer or more powerful than before. You must always remember that what both sides were really fighting for was the mastery of the North-American continent. Vast as it was, there was not room enough for both. One side or other must possess it. Should it be French or English? No lasting peace could there be as long as the question remained unsettled.

A great advantage was gained for Canada when the Iroquois at length gave way. Their chiefs, journeying to Montreal in 1701, smoked the calumet with Governor de Callières and handed him the belt of wampum—which signified that there should be no more fighting between Onontio and the Five Nations. Never again did the Iroquois make serious trouble for the people of Canada, and the fetters which had so long bound the fur trade were for ever removed.

But the very next year after this had happened the Peace of Ryswick came to an end. It had lasted only five years, and it was the reckless ambition of Louis the Fourteenth that killed it. He, too, like Kondiaronk, "The Rat," could exclaim to his courtiers, "I have killed the peace!" The new war is known in Europe as the War of the Spanish Succession, because Louis wanted to put his Bourbon nephew on the vacant throne of Spain. In America it is always called "Queen Anne's War." William the Third had died that year, and Queen Anne had succeeded him on the English throne.

The English colonists were still as much in earnest as ever about the importance of overcoming by any means in their power the "French danger," as they called it. They did not hesitate to employ the tribes of Indians, however remote, in the work of harrying the French settlements, both east and west. Port Royal was again attacked, only this time the attack was ignominiously repulsed. Meanwhile the French were not idle. De Calliéres had strongly advised the establishment of several posts on the lake for the reception of furs and merchandise. In June 1701 La Motte Cadillac, with a Jesuit priest and 100 men, was despatched to build a fort at Detroit. Governor de Calliéres hesitated to attack Albany until he could feel confident that the long-dreaded Iroquois Indians would not return to the old allies, the

English. He was still making up his mind when illness seized him, and in 1703 he died. His successor was the Marquis de Vaudreuil.

But if the authorities at Quebec doubted the wisdom of provoking Indian hostility in their quarrel with the New Yorkers, Vaudreuil and his friends felt sure of Abenakis friendship. This famous tribe had long hated the New Englanders with a deadly hate. They had committed terrible outrages for many years upon the unfortunate Yankee settlers. De Vaudreuil feared that if the Abenakis were to be at peace too long, they might forget their hatred and even become on friendly terms with the Americans. So Canadian priests and soldiers were sent amongst them to stir up their zeal. They did not want any pitched battles or long sieges. Their policy was to persecute and slay the outlying farmers and woodmen, to make settlement outside of the large towns impossible.

One of the most terrible of these raids occurred at Deerfield in Massachusetts. This place was on the river Connecticut. A party under De Rouville crept up Lake Champlain in mid-winter, and, following the river on the ice, reached Deerfield in the dark. What had happened at Schenectady and Salmon Falls happened here. The surprised people could make no defence, the town was burnt, fifty people slaughtered, almost without resistance, and a hundred more carried away prisoners. A man never laid his head on the pillow at night without the fear that a red assassin might scalp it ere morning dawned. A little later the Abenakis were induced to attack the town of Haverhill in broad daylight. Fierce fighting ensued, because this time there were fifty soldiers present to aid the inhabitants in their resistance; but all was in vain. The massacre at Haverhill is still spoken of with horror in New England. You can imagine the storm of indignation which swept through the English colonies when they heard of these dreadful raids, how strong was their anger against the Abenakis! Bands of stout colonists were sent against them, eager for vengeance and showing no mercy, and as a result the chiefs of the Abenakis at length decided that it would be safer for them to cross the border and set up their wigwams in Canada. From Canada they could raid New England as usual. But, to their surprise, they were by no means heartily welcomed by the French. Canadians well knew by this time the treacherous nature of the Indian. Guns and food were given them, and a smiling face hid the Governor's real embarrassment. Fortunate for him if that were to be his only embarrassment!

Although repeatedly foiled, the people of both New and Old England again plotted on a large scale the destruction of French power in Canada, Acadia, and Newfoundland. One day a ship reached Quebec with tidings that an English army was on its way to join with two other forces in an attack upon Quebec. The report was true, but certain accidents occurred which prevented carrying out the plan for that season. In the following year (1709), however, they fell upon Port Royal. The English intention was to sail on to Quebec, but the danger of being caught in the ice prevented them, and Nicholson appearing before the Acadian capital, called upon the brave Subercase to surrender. Port Royal had not expected an attack; both powder and provisions were low, but Subercase was not a man to yield without firing a shot. So gallant a resistance did he offer, although his garrison was in a half-starved state, that when at last he could fight no more, Nicholson granted him the honours of war. With the fleur-de-lys flying in the icy breeze, with the roll of drums and the sound of the trumpet, the last of the shattered band of Frenchmen sailed out of Port Royal, which was to be Port Royal no more. In honour of Queen Anne, Nicholson rechristened the place Annapolis Royal, and thereafter it was held by the Queen's successors on the English throne.

Acadia now being English and garrisoned by the colonists, it remained to deal a deadly blow at Quebec. Up to this time the chief difficulty had been to procure sufficient soldiers from England, for during all the years since the outbreak of Queen Anne's war England had been drained of her first-class fighting men. The great Marlborough had wanted them for Oudenarde, Ramillies, and those other great battles which you read of in the history of that time in Europe. But now, flushed and confident with his many victories, Marlborough could afford to spare a few regiments for the conquest of Quebec. No child's play it was to be this time, no half-hearted attempt. Nicholson himself was there at the English Court to press the scheme upon Queen Anne and her ministers. A large and splendid fleet of fifteen warships, besides forty-six transports and store ships, was got ready, and with the fleet seven of Marlborough's best regiments were ordered to set sail for Canada.

But it is not always big armaments, many men, many ships, many guns, that win the famous battles of history. Sometimes, as we have seen, so far from winning the battle, they do not even strike a blow. This expedition was England's shame. This, which might have conquered Quebec for the English flag, melted away in sorrow, disease, and disgrace, all because of the utter incompetency of its leaders. The Admiral, Sir Hovenden Walker, was both foolish and perverse. As for the commander of the land forces, Sir John Hill, he was chosen not because of his war-like talents, but because he was a brother of Mrs. Masham, the Queen's great personal friend.

You may be interested in learning something of his personal history as afterwards written by the Duchess of Marlborough. "Abigail Hill's brother, whom the bottle man afterwards called 'honest Jack Hill,' was a tall boy whom I clothed (for he was all in rags) and put to school in St. Albans. I afterwards got my Lord Marlborough to make him groom of the bedchamber to the Duke of Gloucester, and though my Lord always said that Jack Hill was good for nothing, yet to oblige me he made him his aide-de-camp and afterwards gave him a regiment."

Under such a commander the fleet and army, crossing the Atlantic, arrived at Boston. Here they were joined by two Massachusetts regiments under the command of Samuel Vetch, a New Englander, who had been made Governor of Annapolis. The plan decided upon was that Canada should be attacked, simultaneously with Quebec and Montreal, by 12,000 men. Surely, with such a force, it seemed impossible to fail! But failure had marked the enterprise for its own. A dense fog hung over the gulf and river of St. Lawrence. In vain Admiral Walker was warned that to steer to the north was to advance to certain destruction. Walker simply laughed at the advice. But his laughter had scarcely died away ere the shrieks of drowning men rang in his ears. Eight ships, packed close with brave soldiers eager for the fray, were shattered to pieces in the black fog. A terrible night ensued, a night which has no parallel in the annals of the British Navy. When day dawned, some Indian and French fur-traders found 1000 bodies strewn on the beach. There were some women amongst them, hapless soldiers' wives, who from early times have accompanied British expeditions, and have been present in defeat and victory.

After this terrible disaster the question arose whether the attack on Quebec should be abandoned or not. There was still a great land force left, enough to plant the British flag on the heights of Quebec if valour and endurance could do it. The officers and soldiers looked with one accord to General Hill, their commander, who had it in his power yet to atone for the disaster which had overtaken his comrade, Admiral Walker. When Hill spoke, it was not to say, "Gentlemen, we will retrieve our misfortunes," but, "Gentlemen, we will turn back." Vetch implored him to reconsider, but orders were given to turn about the prows of the remaining ships.

After fatal delays the ill-starred fleet reached Portsmouth again about the middle of October. But even when safe in dock, misfortune went with it to the last. The Admiral's flag-ship *Edgar* by some accident blew up, killing 400 seamen, and 30 of the townsfolk of Portsmouth who had gone on board to learn from the sailors the melancholy tale of the expedition. Well might the English people have been angry, and their anger descended swiftly and heavily upon the foolish and stubborn admiral's head. He was driven from England, to die at last, broken in heart, rank, and fortune, on a West Indian island.

But what further rejoicings in Canada! What gratitude, what repeated Te Deums for the narrow escape the colony had had from almost certain destruction! General Hill had caused to be printed beforehand, and took with him, a bundle of proclamations, calling upon the French Canadians to acknowledge the rule of Queen Anne. A bundle of these documents had been washed ashore, and were now distributed amongst the people amidst derisive laughter. So grateful did the Quebec folk feel to Heaven for having preserved them from such peril, that they built a memorial in Our Lady of Victories, as the church in the lower town of Quebec was called. De Vaudreuil appealed to the people to help him in making yet stronger the fortifications of Quebec, and he did not appeal in vain. Fifty thousand écus poured into the Treasury for this purpose.

While Quebec and Canada were thus saved, by the Treaty of Utrecht in 1713 Great Britain obtained cession of Acadia, Newfoundland, and the countries bordering Hudson Bay. Forced to give up so much, yet the French retained Cape Breton, with the right to fortify it. King Louis made great efforts to get Nova Scotia back into his power, but in vain. Foiled in this, he well knew the value of Cape Breton, and here it was resolved to erect a great fortress to dominate the whole seaboard of Nova Scotia and New England. In a very few years Cape Breton became the centre of intriguing governors and priests, always in touch with the French population in Acadia to teach them to be discontented and dangerous to the English rulers. Vaudreuil did not cease to govern Canada till his death in 1725. He always clung to the hope of regaining Acadia; he always prevented the Abenakis from making peace with the colonists of New England, and encouraged them to attack the outlying settlements. Vaudreuil still dreamed, as Frontenac had done before him, of France ruling the whole of the great north and west of the continent, and it was hard to see how that prize could be wrested from her. As the eighteenth century wore on, the chain of great inland lakes were as French as those two great rivers, the St. Lawrence and the Mississippi. Little by little French priests and fur-traders pushed their way through the wilderness, making peace with new tribes and founding forts at the heads or junctions of important rivers. Before Vaudreuil died, he saw all New France prospering and in peace.

Profit was even wrested from calamity. Once a great ship, *La Seine*, bearing clothes and merchandise to Quebec and Montreal, had been captured and carried a prize to England. The loss had caused much distress in Canada, because up to this date the people had not grown flax and hemp, and had spun no wool, and their clothing, therefore, came across to them from France. In this emergency the Canadians, particularly the women, were obliged to show their ingenuity, and soon they began to weave coverings, blankets, and even small carpets. They found the fibre of a nettle would make good cloth, and the bark of the white wood cotton-tree was pressed into service. Slowly but surely the industry grew, until there were twenty-five different branches of trade producing druggets, cloths, and linens. The nuns commenced to make bunting for their own dress, black serge for the priests, and blue serge for their pupils.

At first there were no horses in Quebec or Montreal. But at the beginning of the eighteenth century hundreds of these animals were being bred, and to possess and train them became a passion amongst the young men. The result was that many who had before been very skilful in the use of snowshoes soon grew lazy and drove about in sleighs. This came to the notice of the Governor, who told them that Canada could not afford to have her young men unaccustomed to snow-shoes. It was by means of snow-shoes that they were able, even when a blizzard was blowing, to move silently and swiftly in time of war. He issued a decree which forbade any habitant to own more than two mares and one colt. After a certain day any colonist possessing more would be visited by an official ordered to kill the extra horses, and the order was carried out.

The population of Canada had now grown to 50,000 souls. As to life in the colony, we get an excellent picture from the writings of Father Charlevoix, who visited Canada in 1720, and spent some time in making personal observations. He tells us that the country about Montreal was wholly unsettled by Europeans excepting several fortified posts and block-houses, such as Frontenac, Niagara, Detroit, Michilimackinac, and other trading stations in the west. "In Quebec," he wrote, "one finds nothing but what is select and calculated to form an agreeable society. A Governor-General, with his staff, a high-born officer and his troops, an Intendant with a superior council and inferior court, a Commissary of Marines and other officers, and a Superintendent of Waters and Forests, whose jurisdiction is certainly the largest in the world; merchants in easy circumstances, or at least living as if they were, a Bishop, a seminary, and three convents.

"Other circles elsewhere are as brilliant as those surrounding the Governor and Intendant. On the whole, it seems to me there are for all classes the means of passing the time agreeably. Every one contributes to his utmost, people amuse themselves with games and excursions, using caleches in summer, sledges and skates in winter. There is a great deal of hunting, for many gentle folks have no other resources for living in comfort. The news from Europe comes all at once, and occupies a great part of the year, furnishing subjects of conversation of the past and future."

"The Canadians," continues this eye-witness, "breathe from their birth the air of liberty, which renders them very agreeable in social intercourse. Nowhere else is our language spoken with greater purity. One observes here no defective accent. There are here no rich people; every one is hospitable, and no one amuses himself with making money. If a person cannot afford to entertain friends at table, he at least endeavours to dress well."

From the foregoing you may be able to form a fair picture of Canada under the Old Régime.

Two hundred years ago, when Newfoundland was ceded to the English, all the French officials and fishermen removed to the eastern coast of Cape Breton. Cape Breton, despite its name, is an island, and was known to the French as Isle Royale. The place whither the French retired was a safe and spacious inlet, up to that time known as English Harbour, and it was English Harbour that the French king chose as the site of the greatest and most celebrated fortress in the New World. To it was duly given the name of Louisburg. Vauban, a celebrated engineer of his day, was called upon to design it. "Spare neither money nor labour," said the King; "we shall make it another Dunkerque." This Dunkerque, you may remember, was a fortified seaport on the north-east coast of France, upon which millions of money had been spent, and it was generally believed that no enemy could take it. To build its equal, hundreds of engineers, stonecutters, masons, bricklayers, and workmen sailed across the Atlantic. When finished, Louisburg fortress occupied an area of 100 acres, the harbour being defended by batteries on an island at the entrance. Within the fort and town dwelt never less than 2000 people. With such a stronghold so near at hand, it was not strange that the French in Acadia should dwell firmly in the belief that the flag of the lilies would once more wave over them. If few English colonists came to Nova Scotia, none at all migrated to that portion of it which was still called Acadia.

While these things were happening in the far east, in the west notable pioneers were forging a path to French dominion. The far north-west was opened up by Sieur Verendrye with his three valiant sons, a Jesuit priest, and a handful of bushrangers. Verendrye struck out westward through Michilimackinac. He had heard of the great Lake Winnipeg from the Indians and resolved to reach it. Coming upon the Lake of the Woods, there he built a strong fur-trading post, Fort St. Charles, where his party were met by the Sioux, a fierce western tribe. In the battle one of Verendrye's sons was slain. After the explorer had finally reached Lake Winnipeg, he crossed its waters and paddled with his party up the Red River. One morning they came to where the river Assiniboine joins the Red River, and there Verendrye halted and built Fort Rouge. Hard by a settlement grew up, which settlement has in our day expanded at length into the great and flourishing city of

Winnipeg.

Nothing could daunt Verendrye and his sons, neither heat nor cold, hunger nor thirst. They pressed on through the forest and over the prairie, exploring and building trading posts. The news of their travels and successes with the Indians reached Quebec and Montreal, and a horde of hardy bush-rangers were soon following their example. The forts in the far wilderness grew closely packed with costly furs. Heavily-laden canoes by the hundred found their way by river and lake and toilsome portage to the great stone warehouses of Montreal, some of which are yet upstanding in the city.

It was after the leader Verendrye's death that one of his sons, on New Year's Day 1743, first amongst French Canadians, beheld the lofty snow-clad pinnacles of the Rocky Mountains. Truly, in spite of many discouragements, the fleur-de-lys was being borne westward valiantly.

CHAPTER XI

HOW LOUISBURG SURRENDERED AND WAS GIVEN BACK

Twenty-seven years of peace! It was a long respite, but long as it was, French and English were ready to fly at each other's throats with renewed vigour when war broke out again. Quickly did the flames of the conflict spread to the New World.

Looking out from the ramparts of his strong fortress of Louisburg, it seemed to the Governor that the moment was a most favourable one to recapture Nova Scotia for France. The iron was struck while it was hot. One thousand men, led by Duvivier, were despatched to Annapolis, which, under the name of Port Royal, has been the scene of so many vicissitudes.

On the way thither the French easily took Canso, at the entrance of the strait of that name, and sent its garrison prisoners to Louisburg. Flushed with this victory, Duvivier marched by land to Annapolis, held for the English by Paul Mascarene. But if the French thought they would frighten Mascarene into surrendering, they were mistaken. Of Huguenot extraction, Mascarene was yet a brave and sturdy Englishman. "We are expecting," wrote Duvivier, "the arrival of three ships of war, carrying respectively seventy, sixty, and forty guns, and a regiment of soldiers. Not that we need these, for I have already sufficient forces to storm your fort." "Really," ran Mascarene's reply, "it will be time to consider the question of surrender when your French fleet is in the harbour." Then it was Duvivier sent his brother proposing a truce and asking for the conditional capitulation of the garrison. The brave Mascarene called his officers together and found that they were not disinclined to accept the French terms.

"We have no chance," they said; "we are abandoned and our men losing heart; let us capitulate while we can." They spoke so strongly, that Mascarene allowed three of them to confer with the French commander and obtain his proffered terms in writing. But no sooner had he cast his eye over the paper than Mascarene steadfastly refused to sign. In vain his officers implored him to put his name to the deed of surrender. He rebuked them and set about with tact and energy to raise the spirits of his men and reanimate them with courage. The French renewed their attack on the fort. Day after day and night after night they tried to wear out the garrison, but Mascarene had now, by his patience and good spirits, brought all to his way of thinking. Try as they would, the French could make no impression on the sturdy ramparts of Annapolis.

Duvivier sickened of the siege, and during October returned to Louisburg. No sooner had he gone than the French Acadians were filled with fear. They had supposed that all Acadia would have been won for King Louis, and, realising their mistake, they hastened to send deputies to Mascarene declaring that they had refused to take any part in the expedition. At the same time they wrote to the defeated French commander to say, "We live under a mild and tranquil government, and we have good reason to be faithful to it. We hope, therefore, that you will not separate us from it, and that you will grant us the favour not to plunge us into utter misery."

Soon I will have to tell you how these same Acadians, because of their continued treachery to the English Government, had to be transported from this land of their birth or adoption. A great deal has been written about the poor Acadians to excite our sympathy for them at the fate which shortly awaited them. You will see that they brought it upon themselves, or rather that their leaders and ill-advisers brought it upon them. Perfectly happy and contented were they under English rule, but base priests and agitators amongst them tried hard to instil into their minds the idea of a grievance and stirred up treachery and disaffection in their hearts. Bitterest and most unscrupulous of these agitators was a priest named Le Loutre. Although an able man, he was a terrible coward, and shrank from no crime, no falsehood, to gain his ends. Of Le Loutre and the results of his policy we will speak hereafter.

The English prisoners taken at Canso spent many weeks shut up in Louisburg. They did not wholly idle away their time, but, examining all they saw with such care and to such purpose, they were able on regaining their freedom to describe with accuracy the plan and condition of this great fortress. Once a French officer had said that Louisburg was so strong that it might be held against any assault by an army of women. Yet these English prisoners thought they saw how Louisburg might be taken, and their hopes were eagerly seized upon and shared by the Governor of Massachusetts.

Governor William Shirley was a lawyer by profession, full of energy and enterprise, and once he had set his mind to do a thing, difficulties seemed to fade away. He now set his mind to the capture of Louisburg. He believed that unless the English had control of the whole coast from Cape Sable to the mouth of the St. Lawrence, the safety, nay, the very existence of New England was in constant jeopardy. Shirley listened eagerly to what the returned prisoners had to tell him. They had observed the discontent and the bad discipline of the Louisburg garrison, which consisted of 1300 men. Their plan of the fort showed him that it was built on a point of land jutting out into the Atlantic, while all behind it on the land side was treacherous marsh. From 30 to 36 feet high were the walls on the other side of a ditch 80 feet wide. One hundred and sixty-four guns were mounted on the walls, besides many mortars and cohorns. On a little island opposite Louisburg there was a battery mounted with thirty-two heavy cannon. The ramparts were, however, seen to be defective in more than one place, and, besides this, if the French ships which came over sea with provisions and reinforcements could be intercepted, Shirley felt there was a fair chance of success. He wrote instantly to

London asking King George to help him with ships, but without waiting for a reply a little fleet was raised and a land force of 4000 men hastily got together. It was not a very imposing army in appearance, as you may imagine. It was chiefly composed of artisans, farmers, fishermen, and labourers, commanded by a merchant named William Pepperell. Although without any military experience, Pepperell had courage and good judgment, and was anxious to distinguish himself. On the 24th March 1745 the ships left Boston, and reached Canso ten days later. Here they remained three weeks, waiting for the ice to melt in the bays and harbours. It was at Canso that Pepperell and his brave New Englanders were joined by the English commodore, Warren, whom King George had sent to help him in the capture of Louisburg. Instantly Pepperell and his army set off, while Warren cruised about with a fleet of ten ships to prevent any news or assistance from reaching the fortress.

The Governor of Louisburg was M. Duchambon. On the fateful night a ball was given in the town, which the Governor, his officers, and soldiers attended. Before the people had got to sleep it was almost dawn, and their slumbers were quickly disturbed. A captain, attired in his night-clothes, came rushing into the Governor's chamber to report that a strange fleet had been sighted by the sentries entering Gabarus Bay, five miles distant. "French ships?" cried Duchambon. "No, sir," answered the officer, "I fear the English are upon us." Next moment the cannons were booming loudly from the walls and a peal of bells rang through the town. Pepperell made a pretence of landing his troops at a certain point, so as to deceive the French. A skirmish took place, in which the French were beaten back and some of them taken prisoners. Before nightfall 2000 of the New Englanders had planted foot on the shore, and the next day they were joined by the rest of their comrades. The siege of Louisburg was begun. A hard and dangerous task was the landing of the artillery and stores, owing to the rolling surf. There being no wharf, the men had to wade through the sea to bring the guns, ammunition, and provisions on shore. This alone took an entire fortnight. Batteries were thrown up, in spite of sallies made from the town by French and Indians to prevent them. An outside battery was captured, mounted with twenty-eight heavy guns, which now belched forth shot and shell amongst the besieged. Warehouses and other places took fire, and great columns of smoke hid the fort from view for days at a time. The walls were at last seen to crumble, and when the guns of the Americans began to close up on the fortress, Duchambon was summoned to surrender. He replied that he would surrender when forced to by the cannon of the foe. The New Englanders at last silenced the island battery, so that the English fleet could enter the harbour and turn upon him its 500 guns. The expected supply ship from France, the *Vigilant*, had been captured, and Duchambon's supply of gunpowder was exhausted. He gave himself up to despair, and now it was that the flag of truce was sent to the British camp asking for terms of capitulation.

The terms offered by Pepperell were accepted. For forty-nine days Duchambon had defended Louisburg bravely. He had done his best, and when the time came to surrender he was permitted to march out his soldiers with colours flying and drums beating. While he abandoned the fortress by one gate, Pepperell at the head of the victorious besiegers entered by another. The day wound up with a great banquet; all was rejoicing at so glorious a victory. But terrible was the defeat and humiliation for more than 4000 of the French in Louisburg. They were embarked on ships and sent back to France.

Meanwhile the French flag was not lowered from the parapets, so as to lure in any French ships approaching those waters. The ruse was successful. Two East Indiamen and one South Sea vessel fell into the trap, and these prizes were afterwards found to be worth six hundred thousand pounds. In prize money the share of an ordinary seaman is said to have been eight hundred guineas.

No wonder the bells in Boston and Salem rang out with jubilation when the tidings of the capture of Louisburg arrived. Nor were King George II. and his ministers less pleased. From palace and tower cannons fixed their salute of rejoicing; many bonfires were lit in London, and whole streets were illuminated. Pepperell was created a baron and a colonel in the Army. Shirley was also rewarded. Warren was promoted to be an admiral. There is, however, a melancholy side to this picture. The troops left in possession of Louisburg were too elated by success to behave themselves properly. Many men can stand defeat who cannot endure success. The stores of liquor in the fort were stolen, and in spite of all the efforts of the English commandant 1000 men were found every day intoxicated. A terrible illness raged throughout the garrison, and when spring came it was found that out of 3000 men 1200 had died.

At first the people in France and in Canada could not believe the news that Louisburg had fallen. They had looked upon it as the key to French power in North-America. When at length there could be no doubt that the news was true, one thought, one ambition filled the minds of all—the fortress must at all hazards be retaken. It was resolved at Versailles that an expedition should be sent out to Cape Breton for that purpose. One of the finest fleets that ever left the shores of France sailed away from Rochelle the following year, commanded by the Duke d'Anville, which consisted of thirty-nine ships of war and many of the best soldiers in France. D'Anville had orders to recapture Louisburg and Nova Scotia, to ravage Boston, and turn all New England into a scene of desolation. But man proposes, God disposes. Not only were two of D'Anville's ships captured by English cruisers, but he encountered such a succession of storms and one mighty tempest, that the whole squadron was dispersed. When, at Chebucto, D'Anville arrived with the remnants of his fleet, his mortification was so great as to bring on an apoplectic stroke, from which he died.

On an island in what is to-day known as Halifax Harbour, his body was buried. On the afternoon of the very day on which the French commander died, his Vice-Admiral, Destournelles, arrived with three more ships, on board one of which was Canada's new Governor, General Jonquière. When Destournelles took command the outlook was most desperate. More than 2000 men were stricken with fever, and eventually died. Destournelles, seeing no hope for success, proposed that the expedition should be abandoned and the vessels return to France. Jonquière and most of the officers resisted this plan. If they could not take Louisburg, at least they could attack Annapolis and seize Nova Scotia. Annapolis was weak and had a small garrison, and once it were captured, Acadia was regained for France. Moreover, was not the priest, Le Loutre, at hand to give the signal to the Acadians to rise against their English masters? On seeing that they were all against him, Admiral Destournelles retired. He thought it reflected on his character and honour, and next morning they found him stabbed through the breast. He had lost his reason and flung himself upon his sword.

It was now Jonquière's turn to lead the forlorn expedition. But ere he could get to Annapolis another great storm arose, scattering his fleet, and nothing remained at last but to return dispirited to France. At least 2500 brave Frenchmen had been lost in this ill-fated expedition. Still undaunted by these terrible reverses, next year the Marquis de la Jonquière made another attempt with another fleet. But the English admirals, Anson and Warren, were on the watch; a battle was fought off Cape Finisterre, in the Bay of Biscay, and a signal defeat inflicted on the French. This time Jonquière himself was captured and carried to London. It seemed as if he were fated never to reach his Governor's château at Quebec.

Balked in her endeavours to obtain Louisburg again at the point of the sword, France had now recourse to the arts of diplomacy.

In 1748 was signed the Treaty of Aix-la-Chapelle. The French, you may remember, had met with many successes in Europe and in India. They had, for one thing, captured the province of Madras, and so had something to offer England in exchange for what they considered to be a greater prize than all they had won. A bargain was therefore struck between the diplomatists of France and England, the former to yield back Madras if the English would give up Louisburg. King George did not consult the New Englanders who had striven so hard and so valiantly to win him the prize. He consented to the exchange, and Louisburg was handed back to France.

Of course when the bargain was known in Massachusetts and New York there was great indignation. But the wiser heads amongst the colonists saw that the welfare of a whole empire is greater than the welfare of any part, and so bided their time, knowing full well that another and final blow would some day be struck. Meanwhile, all the money that the colonists had spent on their expedition was given back to them by Britain.

Although eight years of peace followed the Treaty of Aix-la-Chapelle, it was a peace only in name. In Canada and America there were two nations who could never be free from war until one had conquered the other. One of the great causes of offence and perpetual squabbling was that as yet neither knew the precise boundaries of French and British territory. It seems strange that where so much land existed and so few people, that there should be any fighting over boundaries; but if you study the wars of history you will see there is nothing that nations are so ready to quarrel over as this question of boundaries. Besides, there was a vast region constantly being explored, and even surveyed, upon which dwelt tribes of Indians whose allegiance was claimed by one of the two parties to the dispute. So while the Marquis de la Jonquière languished in an English prison, the acting Governor-General of Canada, Galissonière, was kept extremely busy. It was his idea, and he was never tired of expressing it, that although Acadia had been surrendered to England, Acadia meant only the peninsula of Nova Scotia. As for the great region of the west now known as New Brunswick and Eastern Maine, that he claimed to belong to France. He sent out several hundred French agents to conciliate the Indian tribes, to warn off English traders, and to mark out the boundary line between New England and Canada. The Governor ordered forts to be built at Gaspereau and Beauséjour, and another on the St. John River. In the west many other forts were built, including Fort Ticonderoga, at the head of Lake George. He asked King Louis to send him 10,000 colonists to settle along the line of the Alleghany Mountains, and so form a barrier against the English on the east. But, however anxious he was to keep New France, by this time King Louis thought he had lost sufficient of his subjects in the late wars, and refused the request.

The English traders and frontiersmen were meanwhile pressing westward. If France's title to all the country on the other side of the Alleghanies was to be something better than waste-paper, something more must be done to assert it. Galissonière therefore resolved to take swift and effective action.

And so the curious episode called "The Planting of the Leaden Plates" began.

CHAPTER XII

THE ACADIANS ARE BANISHED FROM ACADIA

The French had really no grounds for their claims to sovereignty over the valley of the Ohio except in the explorations of La Salle in the previous century. All the country south of Lake Erie was almost unknown to the French Canadians. The regions in the vicinity of the Ohio River were generally regarded as belonging to the English colonies of Pennsylvania, Virginia, and New York.

If you will look at the old maps of America, you will see that the map-makers never gave any boundary-line on the west of the thirteen colonies. There was no boundary-line. At this time, as was said in the last chapter, English traders had crossed the Alleghany Mountains on their fur-trading expeditions, and the Indians, in turn, had visited the people living in the three provinces I have named. But Galissonière had a special reason for wanting the whole Ohio valley in French possession. Canada and Acadia were not the only French colonies on the North American continent. Far to the south there was Louisiana, which since La Salle's time had grown and flourished exceedingly. A Canadian, De Bienville, one of the sons of Charles le Moine, had even been sent to govern it. So, you see, it was of the utmost importance to the French way of thinking that Canada and Louisiana should be joined together by a stretch of territory flying the French flag. It would be fatal for Louisiana to be cut off from Canada by English colonies, or even forts and trading posts. For this reason Galissonière now set about proclaiming French sovereignty over the entire Ohio valley, as this region was called.

In the French service there was a captain named Céléron, a Chevalier of the Order of St. Louis. This officer the Government despatched in the summer of 1749 with a small force of some 200 French soldiers, Canadian bushrangers, and Indians. With him Céléron carried a large stock of leaden plates with engraved inscriptions. These plates were eleven inches long and seven and a half inches wide, and Céléron was ordered to bury them at the foot of certain trees marking the boundary-line which Galissonière had drawn up on his map. Besides these leaden plates Céléron carried an immense stock of tin shields bearing the arms of the King of France. Every time he buried a leaden plate at the foot of a tree, he nailed up one of the shields on the trunk.

Now it so happened that one of these plates was dug up by an Indian soon after the French party had marched on. It was sent by a Cayugan chief to a famous English trader and colonist named William Johnson. The chief asked Johnson to tell him what the French meant by planting such a plate in their territory. He thought it might be some sorcery on the part of the northern pale-faces. Johnson had no love for the French. He knew exactly what they were aiming at, and he spoke very plainly to the chief of the Cayugas. "Brethren," said he, "this is an affair of the greatest importance to you. Nothing less than all your lands and your best hunting-places are concerned. You are to be shut off entirely from us and the rest of your brethren, the Pennsylvanians and the Virginians, who can always supply you with goods at a much lower rate than the French ever did or ever could do. Under our protection you are, and ever will be, safer and better treated than under the French, who are your implacable enemies. The writing on this piece of lead is sufficient of itself to convince you of their villainous designs." The Governor of New York afterwards sent the plate to England, where it attracted great attention, for it showed quite clearly what the designs of the French were.

By this time English statesmen began to consider whether the step they had taken in giving back Cape Breton to France so hastily was not a mistake. But something to offset it might still be done. Although Louisburg was no longer theirs, yet they had the power to retrieve much of the prestige and many of the advantages they had lost. Governor Shirley dinned constantly into their ears the value of settling an English population in Nova Scotia to counter-balance the French Acadians who were planted there. So at last King George was induced to issue a proclamation offering to all officers and private men retired from the Army or Navy, and to many others, a free passage to Nova Scotia, besides supporting them for a year after landing and giving them arms, ammunition, and a grant of land to build a dwelling. Parliament having voted £40,000, in the summer of 1749 more than 2500 settlers, with their families, arrived at Chebucto, now rechristened in honour of the Earl of Halifax.

The commander of the expedition and the chief of the new colony was Colonel Edward Cornwallis, a man both able and lovable. Owing to his care, a beautiful city gradually arose on the shore of the splendid harbour, afterwards to be crowned by the famous citadel of Halifax.

Soon after Cornwallis's arrival he issued a proclamation in French and English to the Acadians calling upon them to assist the new settlers. He did not fail to remind them that while they had so long enjoyed possession of their lands and the free exercise of their religion, they had been secretly aiding King George's enemies. But His Majesty would forgive and forget all this if they were at once to take the oath of allegiance and act in future as British subjects.

Some 13,000 Frenchmen were at this time settled in the ten villages of Acadia. To the northward the French had built a fort of five bastions which they called Beauséjour, and another one much similar at Baie Verte. Their idea was to keep up communication with Louisburg until they could strike a blow against the English and get back Acadia again into their own hands.

It was at Fort Beauséjour that the priestly traitor Le Loutre continued to create dissatisfaction and sow the seeds of revolt amongst the thrifty, ignorant Acadians, who otherwise would have been happy and contented. Their minds filled with Le Loutre's threats and promises, they refused to take the oath of allegiance, and even to supply the English settlers with labour, timber, or provisions, though good prices for these were offered. Cornwallis warned them. "You will allow yourselves," he said, "to be led away by people who find it to their interest to lead you astray. It is only out of pity for your situation and your inexperience in the ways of government that we condescend to reason with you. Otherwise the question would not be reasoning, but commanding and being obeyed."

He was very patient with them. He told them that they had been for more than thirty-four years the subjects of the King of Great Britain. "Show now that you are grateful for his favours and ready to serve your King when your services are required. Manage to let me have here in ten days fifty of your people to assist the poor to build their houses to shelter them from the bad weather. They shall be paid in ready money and fed on the King's provisions."

Shortly thereafter Le Loutre descended from craft to the crime of bloodshed. He aroused the native Indians of the province, known as the Micmacs, against the English newcomers. He sent them out stealthily to slay and to destroy. Twenty Englishmen were surprised and captured at Canso while gathering hay. Eight Indians, pretending to barter furs, went on board two English ships and tried to surprise them. Several of the sailors were killed. A saw-mill had been built near Halifax. Six unsuspecting men went out unarmed to hew some timber. Four were killed and scalped, one was captured, and one escaped. So frequent became the Indian attacks that the men of Halifax formed themselves into a militia, and a sentry paced the streets every night. Cornwallis offered £100 for the head of Le Loutre. Ten guineas were offered for an Indian, living or dead, or for his scalp.

It now became necessary also to build a fort to counterbalance the Fort Beauséjour of the French. The latter was erected on the western bank of a little stream called the Missiquash which the French claimed as the boundary between Canada and Acadia. Opposite, at Chignecto, Colonel Lawrence was sent with 400 men to build the English fort. Le Loutre and his Acadians did their best to prevent the English landing and building the fort which became known as Fort Lawrence. The commander of this post was named Captain Howe, a man of charming manners who spoke French fluently. Howe reasoned with the stubborn Acadians, many of whom saw the good sense of his remarks, and in a short time the captain became extremely popular. All this Le Loutre saw with misgivings. He felt that Howe was obtaining an influence amongst the Acadians, and so marked him down for destruction. One bright autumn day a Frenchman in the dress of an officer advanced to the opposite side of the stream waving a white handkerchief. Howe, ever polite, advanced to meet him. As he did so, some Indians who were in ambuscade pointed their guns at him and shot him dead. La Corne, the French commandant, was filled with shame and horror at this treacherous murder. He would like to have got rid of Le Loutre, but the priest was too strong for him. His influence at Quebec was great, as it was amongst the Acadian people, who dreaded his fierce anger.

Notwithstanding all this, there were a number of Acadians who at last consented to take the oath of allegiance to King George. When the French Governor at Quebec heard of their doing so, he issued a proclamation that all the Acadians must swear loyalty to France and be enrolled in the Canadian militia, or suffer the penalty of fire and sword. By way of rejoinder, the English Governor of Nova Scotia proclaimed that if any Acadian, taking the oath of allegiance to King George, should afterwards be found fighting amongst the French soldiers, he would be shot. Thus were the poor Acadians between two fires. A considerable number of them removed their settlements to the Canadian side of the boundary. Some travelled even as far as Quebec. But the majority who remained continued to cause great anxiety to the English authorities in Nova Scotia.

In 1754 the French planned an invasion of Nova Scotia, and Halifax was filled with alarm. For they knew that in the absence of the English fleet, Cape Breton could send a force in a few hours to overrun the country. As for provisions, were not the Acadians there to furnish them to the French invaders? In forty-eight hours 15,000 armed Acadians could be summoned to Fort Beauséjour. The outlying English forts would be destroyed and Halifax starved into surrender. When this had been captured, New England would be the next victim. So reasoned Lawrence and Governor Shirley of Massachusetts. Taking counsel together, they resolved to strike a blow instantly before troops from France or Quebec could arrive. They would seize Fort Beauséjour and drive the French out of the isthmus. Two thousand men were raised and the command given to an English officer, Colonel Monckton. On the 1st June 1755 the English war-party arrived in Chignecto Bay.

No longer was the gallant La Corne commandant at Fort Beauséjour; another, dishonest and incompetent, ruled the French stronghold. His name was Vergor. Vergor thought little of patriotism, but only of his purse and how much money he could make by defrauding his King. When he saw the English ships approach, Vergor issued a proclamation to the Acadians round about to hasten to his defence. Fifteen hundred responded, and three hundred of these he took into the fort. The others he ordered to retire into the woods and stealthily harass the enemy.

While the New Englanders prepared to launch their force, the French spent the time trying to strengthen their bastions. The strong, simple Acadians, accustomed to hard labour, were set to work. Over them stood Le Loutre in his shirtsleeves with a pipe in his mouth, encouraging them to toil. But in spite of his zeal and his promises, so huddled and exposed was their condition inside the fort, that many Acadians deserted.

Duly the bombardment began. When it was at its height, and Vergor was hourly expecting help from Louisburg, a letter arrived to say that assistance could not come from that quarter. An English squadron was cruising in front of Louisburg harbour, and so prevented the French frigates from putting out to sea.

When this disquieting news leaked out at Beauséjour, more Acadians became disheartened, and in spite of the threats launched against them, deserted by dozens. The bombardment continued. Next morning at breakfast a shell from an English mortar crashed through the ceiling of a casemate, killing three French officers and an English captain who had been taken prisoner. Vergor saw that he had begun to strengthen his fort too late. There was now no hope—the guns of the English were too near. He despatched a flag of truce and surrendered Fort Beauséjour.

Having got Fort Beauséjour, henceforward to be known as Fort Cumberland, into his hands, the victorious Monckton sent summonses to the other French stronghold at Baie Verte to surrender. Seeing the situation hopeless, the French commandant complied, and the campaign was over. Immediate danger to English settlers in Nova Scotia was happily removed for ever.

And now we come to a tragedy—the most pathetic passage in Canada's history. It is known as the expulsion of the Acadians. You have seen the dilemma in which the English found themselves. They could not trust the Acadians, nor could they spare an army large enough to render treachery harmless. On the other hand, they could not treat all those thousands of people as rebels, for the great majority of them had not fought against them at Beauséjour and elsewhere, but had remained quiet in their villages. The long patience of the English was now almost worn out. Yet once again Governor Lawrence urged them to take the oath. Once again they stubbornly refused.

What else could be done? Nothing. So the decree of exile went forth. Ignorant of the trades and callings by which they could earn a livelihood in those countries, the Acadians could not be sent to France or England. Colonists they were, and the sons of colonists, suited only for a colonial life. On banishment they would be distributed in batches amongst the English colonies along the Atlantic coast.

It was a terrible thing to do, and many hearts, even among the rude soldiers, beat warmly for the fate of the unhappy Acadians. Those who had taken the oath were safe in their homesteads. A number escaped into the woods. As for the rest, the military officers were given their instructions. At Beauséjour 400 men were seized. Without warning the people, Colonel Winslow marched rapidly to Grand-pré. He summoned the men of the village to meet him in the chapel, and there he read them the decree of banishment. In vain they tried to escape; the doors were shut and guarded by English soldiers. The people of village after village were seized, until 6000 souls had been gathered together. Many of the Acadians never believed that the threat would be carried out. For a long time they had to wait for transports to bear them away. Many had to be placed on the ships by force. Old and young, men, women, and children, were marched to the beach. Sometimes members of the same family became separated from each other, never to meet again. But the soldiers did their best to perform their painful duty as humanely as they could. No unnecessary harshness was permitted.

From Minas, Chignecto, and Annapolis ship after ship carried away their weeping burdens to Massachusetts, Connecticut, Pennsylvania, New York, Virginia, North and South Carolina, and Georgia. One of the vessels, hailing from Annapolis, was captured by its cargo of exiles, who overpowered the crew and made themselves masters of the ship. This they sailed up the river St. John, where they ran it ashore and escaped to Quebec. A few decided to struggle southwards, however, until they reached Louisiana, where some of their descendants are to this day. Others, after months and even years, returned again to Acadia, where, when Quebec and the French flag had fallen, they were no longer a danger to the Government. Such of the Acadians who reached Quebec were treated very coldly and almost died of famine. It is said that they were reduced to four ounces of bread per day, and sought in the gutters of Quebec to appease their hunger. Many were forced to eat boiled leather during the greater part of the winter. As if this were not enough, smallpox broke out amongst them, and many entire families were destroyed. Such, alas! was the fate of men "whose attachment to their mother-country was only equalled by her indifference."

The expulsion of the Acadians may seem to us a cruel act, but it was forced upon the English by the hardest necessity—the necessity of self-protection.

CHAPTER XIII

TERRIBLE FIGHTS OVER THE BORDER

The Marquis de Jonquière was released at last from his English prison and sailed away to succeed Galissonière as Governor of Canada.

Jonquière's term of office is looked back upon with shame by the people of Canada, but is it strange that the servants of King Louis the Fifteenth in any quarter of the world where the French flag yet flew should be animated by low motives and a desire for gain? See what an example their monarch set them! Jonquière was an able man, but he was mercenary, and thought only of lining his own pockets and those of his creatures with the profits of the Canadian fur trade. With him went Francis Bigot to fill the important office of Intendant. Bigot's is one of the most infamous names in French Canadian annals. He was a lawyer, ambitious, intelligent, and fond of luxury and display. Yet with all his intelligence he fell easily a prey to the wiles of a certain Madame Péan, who turned the King's service to her private advantage. Servants, lackeys, upstarts were, by her influence, placed in responsible positions. If they happened to be ignorant and dishonest, it was no bar to their promotion. Taxes were multiplied and the poor people of Canada were made to suffer. Bigot and his official band of robbers held office to the last moment of French dominion in Canada, but Jonquière died in the midst of his peculations and money-making schemes.

In 1752 his successor, the Marquis Duquesne, appeared on the scene. Before setting out from France, the new Governor had been ordered to arrest the pretensions of the English to the Ohio and western region and drive them from the territory. No English were to be allowed to carry on trade there. Duquesne began by sending out 300 Canadian Militia to build a French fort on Lake Erie, the command of which was afterwards given to Legardeur de St. Pierre. A second fort was built twenty miles away.

In the meantime the English colonists continued to cast their eyes lovingly on this great and fertile region to the west. Almost every month exploring parties went out, and returned full of enthusiastic reports of its commercial advantages. By and by a body was formed called the Ohio Company, including amongst its members many of the leading men of Virginia. To this Company King George granted 500,000 acres, on condition that 100 families should be settled on the territory within seven years and that a fort should be built.

Seeing this, the Pennsylvanians became jealous of Virginia and formed plans to secure the Ohio region for themselves. Each told different and conflicting stories to the Indians. The Virginians tried to stir up suspicion against the Pennsylvanians, and the Pennsylvanians retorted by creating distrust of the Virginians. The result of all this was that the tribes, who up to now had been faithful to England, began to look suspiciously upon the actions and the policy of both these colonies. All this, of course, was playing into the hands of the French. An English fort or two was built, but in spite of the efforts of the Governors of New York, Pennsylvania, and Virginia, very little was done for several years to assert English sovereignty. The qualities the Indians admire are vigour and courage. When the tribes saw the bold and daring efforts of Canada to Frenchify the western country, they were naturally led to range themselves on the Canadian side.

All that happened during the next few years, of the battles and skirmishes, the forts that were taken, and the massacres that were carried out, does not properly belong to Canadian history. It must, however, be mentioned that it was at this time, when Governor Duquesne in his citadel at Quebec was rejoicing at the prospect of bringing the western region under French rule, that we first hear of a young Virginian whose name was destined to be world famous. The name of this youth was George Washington. He was only twenty-one years of age when Governor Dinwiddie of Virginia sent him to expostulate with a party of French Canadians who had just captured an English trading fort. Getting no satisfaction from the Commandant there, young Washington went on to Fort Le Breuf, where, as we have seen, Legardeur de St. Pierre was in charge. St. Pierre received Washington courteously, but could not give him any satisfaction. The French were there, and there they meant to stay, in spite of all the English protests. It was now plain that there was serious trouble looming ahead. All these proceedings being reported to England, at last, after many delays, King George's ministers decided to send a large force to America to drive the French back across the Canadian border. The command of this force was given to General Braddock, a stern and peppery old soldier, wholly ignorant of Indian warfare. Before Braddock could cross the Atlantic with his regiments, English and French were at each other's throats in earnest. The French had built Fort Duquesne, and Colonel Washington, with a force of regulars and backwoodsmen, was sent to capture it. A bloody battle was fought, in which Washington was defeated; and now the Indians were more than ever on the French side. But the schemes and labour of the last three years had undermined Governor Duquesne's health, and a new Viceroy appeared in Quebec. This was the Marquis de Vaudreuil, a native of Canada, whose father had formerly also been Governor.

Vaudreuil entered with spirit upon the duties of his office. He needed all his faculties, for stirring times were in prospect. General Braddock and his Englishmen were in the north awaiting soldiers who were crossing the Atlantic. The French were also resolved to maintain what their Canadian advance guard had won. Field-Marshal Baron Dieskau was appointed to command six regiments of French soldiers who left their native shores in a squadron of fourteen battleships, four frigates, and many transports.

You must remember that during all this time there had been no war. If you had asked any of the French courtiers or ambassadors they would have told you that perfect peace existed between the two nations. But that was only a diplomatic fiction. At all events, whatever was happening in Europe between Old France and Old England, on the other side of the great ocean New France and New England were engaged in a life-and-death conflict. It was not strange that the hand of both mother-countries was extended to help them. Only if England could have looked into the future five-and-twenty years and seen her ungrateful American children tearing down her noble old flag with taunts and insults, perhaps she might not have given her help or spilt her blood so freely to protect America from the French. After all, it may be as well that nations do not know all the evils that are to happen. Their course is to do their duty manfully and honestly for the present; posterity can take care of itself. Moreover, the separation of America from England was no real evil, because that separation was to build the foundation of Canada's greatness in the British Empire and loyalty to the British crown and flag.

On the arrival of General Braddock the various colonial Governors held a consultation. They decided that the three forts, Duquesne, Niagara, and Crown Point, at the head of Lake Champlain, should be captured. We have already seen that another French fort, Beauséjour, was doomed to destruction. It was while Beauséjour was being surrounded by Monckton and his New Englanders that the other expeditions were setting out for their destinations. Braddock decided to take Fort Duquesne himself. Governor Shirley led the expedition against Niagara, and Colonel William Johnson was ordered to take Crown Point. Braddock took 1000 English veterans and 1200 Virginian Militia into the heart of the wilderness. The commander of Fort Duquesne was Contrecoeur. When he was told the size of Braddock's army he saw little hope of standing a siege, but he might intercept the English soldiers in the woods. It was a splendid opportunity for the kind of warfare Indians loved. Two hundred Frenchmen and 500 redskins were sent to lie in ambush on the trail which Braddock would take with drums beating and fifes playing. On a beautiful July day the scarlet-coated regiments of Braddock moved on unconscious to their doom. Every moment they looked to see the great walls of the Fort Duquesne burst upon their gaze. Through the forest they came to the river, the Monongahela, and forded it. Hardly had they crossed, when a strange apparition sprang into the middle of the wide woodland path. He wore war-paint and flaming feathers, but in spite of this dress he was really a French officer. He flung his right arm into the air as a signal, and instantly the forest rang with savage yells. A shower of bullets, fired by unseen hands, fell upon the advancing English. Astonished and taken at such a disadvantage, they yet did not hesitate to return the fire. The intrepid French leader who had given the signal so openly, paid for that act with his life; but it was not easy to fight, however valiantly, against a hidden foe. Braddock and his officers thought it cowardly to fight behind trees; they charged hither and thither in pursuit of the enemy, and were mowed down like grass. The troops became at length huddled together in a panic, shooting, if they shot at all, blindly and without aim. In vain did the General's aide-de-camp, Washington, urge him to scatter his men singly under cover. Braddock, on horseback, galloped fearlessly in every direction ordering the ranks to advance. Not until four horses had been shot dead beneath him did he order a retreat. The command had scarcely passed his lips ere a bullet pierced his body, and he fell, to rise no more. His last words were, "We shall know better how to deal with them another time." The retreat soon became a disgraceful flight. Arms, baggage, and artillery were abandoned. Yelling Indians pursued them, only stopping in order to scalp the helpless wounded. Had it not been for the hope of plunder, very few of the British forces would have escaped death or captivity. Cannons, stores, arms, and papers fell into the hands of the victorious French. Upwards of sixty British officers had been killed, and of all Braddock's army less than half took refuge in the English Fort Cumberland.

Tidings of Braddock's defeat were carried by the swiftest couriers to Canada, and there caused much rejoicing. The Marquis de Vaudreuil sent the good news off at once to his King, but his letter never reached its destination. The ship that bore it, *Le Pierre Alexandre*, was overhauled by an English man-of-war in August, and the captain threw overboard the bag of Canadian letters. Not till nearly two months after the battle had been fought did the news of the victory reach France by way of England. But it was otherwise on the American side of the border. It put an end at once to Shirley's expedition against Niagara. For a time it was thought that the attack on Crown Point would also be given up. It might have been had it been entrusted to another man than Sir William Johnson. Johnson was a settler on the Upper Hudson River. He had married Mollie Brant, sister of the celebrated Chief Brant of the Mohawks, who had acquired great influence with the Iroquois tribes in his locality, and it was on his account that the Mohawks refrained from joining the French. Johnson was not a skilled soldier, but he was wise and daring. Braddock's papers, which had fallen into the hands of Governor Vaudreuil at Quebec, convinced him that Crown Point would be attacked.

Baron Dieskau was sent with 3500 men, half of them Canadian farmers, to go to the defence of Crown Point. Johnson had behind him some 5000 men, raw Militia from Massachusetts and Connecticut. Before attacking Crown Point, Johnson deemed it prudent to build another fort on the Hudson, known as Fort Edward; from this fort he marched to the foot of a large lake, to which he gave the name of his sovereign, and there built Fort George. He was still engaged in building it when the French general marched upon Fort Edward. A scout brought Johnson the news, and immediately he despatched 1000 men to oppose his defence. Dieskau, remembering the success of the manoeuvres against the hapless Braddock, thought to repeat them here. He arranged to keep his own men out of sight amongst the trees and bushes until the enemy should pass by. Had this plan been carried out it is probable that none of the English forces would have escaped alive. But the redskins set up their war-whoops a little too soon, and the English, seeing that they were about to fall into an ambuscade, beat an instant retreat upon Fort Edward. Dieskau now made a hasty resolve to bring the whole strength of his forces to bear upon Fort George. Johnson had made this fort of great strength, protecting it by forming trees into a sort of breastwork, from behind which his cannons and musketry could be used with fatal effect, but Dieskau was not to be turned aside. He ordered his troops to fling themselves on the fort. Legardeur de St. Pierre was killed. Dieskau led forth the French veterans unsupported, leaving the Canadians and Indians scattered behind the trees. These, you will remember, were precisely the tactics which had led to Braddock's defeat. The soldiers advanced gallantly, and, like the English before Fort Duquesne, were mowed down like grass. Dieskau's body was pierced by three bullets. A Canadian who attempted to drag him from under the walls of the fort was shot dead, falling across his General's legs. None now came to his assistance. The French were beaten back and Fort George was saved. The New England troops left their defences. General Dieskau, while leaning against a tree, suffering from the wounds he had received, was fired at and again wounded by a renegade French Canadian, who some years before had deserted. Dieskau reproached him for firing on a wounded man, but the fellow answered that it was better to kill the devil than be killed by him. The French commander was carried to Johnson's own tent and treated kindly. The Iroquois wanted to torture him to death, but Johnson sternly refused. For this victory Johnson was made a Baronet and presented with a purse of £5000. He had begun his career as a private in the army, and had risen to distinction from sheer force of character. As for Dieskau, he never recovered from his wounds, and although he was carried back to France, it was only as a bedridden invalid, to die.

The French still held the positions at Niagara and Crown Point. Three out of the four English expeditions had failed to achieve their purpose, the French remained undisputed masters of the Ohio valley, and their victory over Braddock enabled them to attack the undefended frontiers of Virginia and Pennsylvania. During the winter of 1755-6 French war-parties from Fort Duquesne repeatedly attacked the settlements of the English, behaving very cruelly, and killing or carrying away as prisoners more than 1000 souls. In spite of these temporary successes of the French, Vaudreuil and the Indians were not happy. All this fighting had drawn the farmers away from the soil, and the harvest was very scanty. The necessaries of life became very dear, but, worse than all, dishonesty and corruption were eating out the very heart of Canada. The Intendant Bigot was at the height of his infamy; he descended to every trick of rascality to achieve his ends.

Trade had almost ceased, the supply of beef given out, and the people were reduced to eat horseflesh. As the famine increased the Governor ordered flour to be given to the people; crowds attended at the bakers' shops struggling to be served. At first they were given one pound apiece, afterwards only half a pound. Owing to the scarcity of money, the promises to pay, written on cards, were made to pass as currency. Bigot began to issue what were called ordinances; he issued these notes recklessly. Money was sent from time to time from France, but it was not enough to fill the need. The value of the paper money went down and down, and when England finally acquired Canada it was found that 41,000,000 livres of ordinances were in circulation. Bigot got up a Company to import commodities from France and to buy up all the grain in the country districts. The poor people had to deal with this Company and to pay their charges. The supplies for the King's service had to be bought from the Company in Quebec. The citizens could procure bread only through the Company's stores, which in the two leading cities were known as "La Friponne" or "The Cheat." It was in this way that gigantic frauds were committed which paralysed the colony only to enrich a few individuals. Canada was costing France 15,000,000 francs a year, and France had already spent upon her 80,000,000 francs, but, distressed as she herself was, she did not grudge these sums to her colony.

In the spring of 1756 the people welcomed with joy the arrival of a fresh fleet bearing 1000 soldiers, a supply of food and ammunition, and a large sum of money. Almost as great a boon King Louis bestowed upon Canada when he sent her the new Commander-in-Chief of the Canadian army, the Marquis de Montcalm. This hero was forty-six years old, a splendid soldier, of high character, culture, and determination. Could Canada be saved to the flag of the lilies? If so, surely it was the virtuous Montcalm who could achieve this great task.

CHAPTER XIV

HOW THE GALLANT WOLFE TOOK QUEBEC

If we were to tell the story of Canada faithfully for the next few years, it would be only of further battles, sieges, skirmishes, and massacres between the French and English colonists, aided by savage Indian warriors.

Never before had Canada boasted so many French soldiers as were now arrayed under the command of Montcalm. He fell upon Oswego and destroyed it, taking 1400 prisoners and great booty. Against him was sent the English Earl of Loudoun, no match for the French commander, and afraid to strike an overwhelming blow. Loudoun at last sailed away for Halifax with his army, thinking to make another attack by and by on Louisburg, still in French hands. A terrible mistake this of Loudoun's, and just the opportunity Montcalm looked for. The French had built a strong fortress at Ticonderoga, and now that the danger of Loudoun's army was removed, 6000 of their troops moved swiftly out of the fortress and attacked Fort William Henry.

Undaunted by the great force brought against him, the commander, Colonel Munro, answered Montcalm's summons to surrender by saying that he would defend his post to the death. The French planted their guns and the siege commenced. Day and night the wooden ramparts of Fort William Henry were splintered by Montcalm's cannon balls. Munro, brave Scotsman that he was, hoped vainly that the English garrison at Fort Edward would come to his rescue, but their commander was afraid to send them over. He knew that there were nearly 2000 bloodthirsty redskins roaming at large in the woods. They dreaded the tomahawk and scalping-knife more than the sword and musket. Well did they know what their fate would be if they fell into the hands, wounded or prisoners, of those relentless savages.

So at last one sweltering August day Munro realised that no hope remained. He could hold out no longer. His fort was nearly a mass of ruins, and reluctantly he hoisted the white flag asking Montcalm for terms of capitulation.

The French commander allowed the brave Munro and his soldiers to march out with the honours of war, pledging himself to protect them from his savage followers. Alas! Montcalm had reckoned without his host. He might as well have tried to fetter the summer breeze that blew across Lake George as to balk his redskin allies of their destined prey. They thirsted for the blood of the English. They could not understand the French code of honour. Of terms of capitulation they knew nothing. The soldiers of the garrison, with their wives and children, with a French escort, filed slowly through the woods on their way to a refuge at Fort Edward. Suddenly the Indians, sending up a terrible war-yell, darted upon them. One of the most dreadful massacres in history now took place. The soldiers could do nothing to defend themselves, because they had given up their muskets to the French. They were scalped by dozens and hundreds. Helpless women were brained by hatchets and little children were dashed to death against the trunks of trees.

At the risk of their lives, Montcalm and his officers strove to save the fugitives, but not until nearly 1000 had been slain did they succeed. Montcalm was pale with horror at the awful disgrace which had stained the French name. He had given his word that the garrison should march out unharmed, and now his brave foes were lying in heaps of mangled corpses in the heart of this once peaceful forest.

In fear lest he should punish them in his great anger, the treacherous redskins slunk away with their scalps and plunder. Such was the massacre of Fort William Henry. Afterwards the fort itself was levelled to the ground.

This was not the only disaster the English suffered. Twelve thousand soldiers and eighteen battleships were sent to capture Louisburg, but after cruising about for many weeks and losing several vessels, the weak and cowardly Lord Loudoun did not venture upon an attack, and sailed back to England to meet the contempt of his fellow-countrymen.

You can see what a critical period this was in the history of Canada. To many it seemed a critical period in the life of the English colonists in America. But the French triumph was soon to be cut short. A new and vigorous minister was called by King George to his councils. The energy and fire of the great William Pitt put new life into the hearts of the English people in every part of the Empire. Crushing his right hand down upon the map of the New World, Pitt decreed that French dominion in Canada must be brought to a close. Easy it was to say this. Other English ministers had said it before, but their misfortune was that they did not know how to make the right plans, or to find the right men to carry out their plans. They could not kindle the soldiers into a flame of enthusiasm by their zeal and eloquence. Pitt could do this. He could choose his generals for their worth and fighting qualities, and when he wanted a live ardent soldier, upon whom he could rely, he chose James Wolfe. Who would have dreamt that in the long, gaunt figure, with pale face and straight red hair, that shuffled into the minister's ante-chamber in the spring of 1758, was the future conqueror of Quebec!

General Wolfe was then thirty-two years old. His appearance little revealed his character. A born soldier, he had already distinguished himself on the battle-fields of Europe. In those sleepy days, before Pitt came, his fellow-officers could not understand Wolfe's enthusiasm. One of them told King George that he believed Wolfe was mad. "Then," cried the King, remembering the defeats his army had suffered, "I only hope he will bite some of my generals!"

Court influence succeeded in giving the nominal command to General Amherst, but Wolfe was the real leader. With Amherst and Wolfe sailed a powerful fleet under Admiral Boscawen. By June 1758 the whole of this great force drew up before the fortress of Louisburg, within whose walls was a population of 4000 souls. The garrison consisted of the bravest men the French could furnish, veterans of many battlefields. The Commandant was Drucour. But it was in vain now that the French defended their splendid fortress. After an heroic defence, Drucour was at last obliged to surrender, and all the garrison were sent to England as prisoners of war. Louisburg would give the English trouble and anxiety no more. As if it were but a tiny sandcastle built by children on the seashore, these mighty stone bastions were swept away. After the surrender the English soldiers were ordered to the duty of destroying the stronghold of France in Cape Breton, pulling it to pieces with pickaxe and crowbar, filling the crevices with gunpowder, until at last hardly a vestige remained. If you ask to see Louisburg to-day, you will be shown only a rolling meadow upon which sheep graze peacefully.

Wolfe was now eager to push on to Quebec, but he had to wait nearly a year. In the meantime the French had triumphed on Lake Champlain. General Abercrombie had tried to take Fort Ticonderoga with 15,000 men, but Abercrombie was no such soldier as James Wolfe. He had, however, with him Lord Howe, a brave and able young officer, who was the second in command. Had not a stray bullet struck him down on his way to the battlefield, the story of Ticonderoga might have had a different ending. He was beloved and trusted by his soldiers, and when he died their courage seemed to die away also.

Abercrombie foolishly thought that by his superior numbers he could force Ticonderoga without cannon, but Montcalm knew his strength. He was surprised when he saw the English general hurling his soldiers in four strong columns upon the front of his fort. It was a battle in which superior numbers, bravery, and perseverance were thrown away. Six times did the English doggedly come on, and six times did the cannon of the French sow carnage amongst them. There was a regiment of Highlanders fighting like tigers, some of them hacking the wooden stocks of the outposts with their claymores until a cannon-ball carried away their limbs. When at last, at the close of that long bloody day, Abercrombie drew off his troops, he left 2000 English corpses in the glacis outside the walls of the French fort.

Was it strange that the hearts of the survivors turned against him? that they did not conceal their rejoicing when the King, after this fearful defeat, relieved Abercrombie of his command?

It was not, however, all a tale of repulses and humiliation for the English. Colonel Bradstreet had crossed Lake Ontario and captured Fort Frontenac. General Forbes had made the French abandon Fort Duquesne. On its site a new stronghold arose, to which the name of Fort Pitt was given. Here in our day is the great and flourishing city of Pittsburg. This was not all. In the spring of the fateful year 1759, Fort Niagara fell.

The news of the capture of Louisburg, which caused such rejoicings in America and England, cast a terrible gloom over French Canada. Quebec, that splendid stronghold which had defied the English, was now their last hope. The town and citadel on the summit of Cape Diamond which Champlain had founded and Frontenac guarded so well, seemed to laugh at cannon and bayonet. Stern was the task set before the man who should presume to scale those heights and force the proud city to surrender. Behind its confident aspect Quebec was the scene of despair and corruption. Amongst the officials reckless extravagance reigned. While Canada's fate was trembling in the balance, the Intendant Bigot, who should have been a pattern to the community, spent his nights in riot and gambling. Although the King had forbidden games of hazard, Bigot would often play amongst a party of forty people, losing many thousands of francs in a few hours. The King sent out his gold to help Canada, the people crushed by taxation gave theirs, but all the money found its way into the pocket of Bigot and his accomplices.

Provisions and clothing that should have gone to the hungry, shivering French soldiers were sold at La Friponne to reap a profit. Distant forts held bravely for the French cried aloud for succour, but the scoundrelly Intendant put them off with excuses, and the money intended for them was devoted to gaming and dissipation. In two years alone Bigot's robberies amounted to nearly a million pounds sterling. A time of retribution was at hand. Montcalm wept at the vices and irregularities around him, but, being only military commander, he could do little or nothing. The Governor, De Vaudreuil, answered his warnings haughtily, for he was jealous of Montcalm. So the end approached.

Never had England sent out an army so full of zeal, courage, and discipline as the army which sailed away from her shores under Wolfe to take Quebec. Their commander well knew that he had to attack one of the strongest forts in the world, defended by all the soldiers that Montcalm could muster, fighting in defence of their country, their flag, and their religion. Wolfe had only 9000 men against the 18,000 French Canadians, but he rejoiced in his Englishmen. "If valour could make amends for want of numbers," he wrote to Pitt, "we shall succeed."

On the first day of June 1759, the ships sailed out of the harbour of Halifax for the river St. Lawrence. The harbour rang with the cheers of the soldiers, and the bands struck up the old melody "The Girl I left behind Me." When they reached the mighty river they ran great danger for want of a pilot. A French prisoner on board began wringing his hands, declaring that they would all go to the bottom. An old British captain of a transport laughed in his face: "I will show you," he roared with an oath, "that an Englishman shall go where a Frenchman dare not show his nose." And he steered his ship through in safety. The boast was no empty one. Vaudreuil wrote to France to say "that the enemy have passed sixty ships of war where we dare not risk a vessel of 100 tons by night or day."

In Quebec, Montcalm during the long days of early summer awaited the coming of the English. Not a man was idle. Drilling and building of earthworks filled up nearly every hour of the day. Montcalm's 18,000 men were as strongly entrenched as Nature and the art of war could make them. On the 27th of June the French in Quebec snatched their first glimpse of the masts of the English battleships. A few hours later the English fleet had halted before the Isle of Orleans, and Wolfe and his red-coated infantry landed on its shores. Mounting the point of land to the west, the young general took out a telescope and turned it towards the heights of Quebec, four miles away. As he scanned the mighty rock he felt that it was indeed a hard task which England had sent him to accomplish.

Vaudreuil did not wait for the English commander to make the first move; he attempted to destroy the English fleet with fire-ships. One dark night a number of old vessels, filled with pitch, gunpowder, bombs, and antique cannon, packed to the muzzle, were towed out into the channel and set on fire to float to the English fleet. The whole countryside seemed to burst in lurid flames, and a hail of grape-shot and bullets flew in all directions. But the English soldiers were not frightened; they rowed out in their boats, grappling courageously with the flaming monsters, and towed them to shore. Vaudreuil's explosive experiments proved a total failure. During that very night Wolfe was busy with pen and paper writing his first manifesto to the Canadian people. "We are sent by King George," he said, "to conquer this province, but not to make war upon women and children, the ministers of religion, or industrious people. We lament the sufferings which our invasion may inflict upon you, but if you remain neutral we proffer safety to person and property, with freedom in religion. We are masters of the river; no succour can reach you from France; General Amherst with a large army has sailed to the southern frontier. Your cause is hopeless, your valour useless. Your nation has been guilty of great cruelties to our unprotected settlers, but we seek no revenge, we offer you the sweets of peace with the honours of war. England in her strength will befriend you; France in her weakness leaves you to your fate." But although the English commander spoke so confidently, he had many misgivings in his heart. If Amherst did not get through to Montreal and down the St. Lawrence by the autumn, it meant the winter would be lost, and where was he to find food for his troops? How could he face amidst the snow and ice the 18,000 men of Montcalm, as brave and as hardy as his own?

Victory was only to be won by quick and vigorous action. Seizing the heights of Point Lévis opposite Quebec, Wolfe set up his batteries so as to bombard the city. He planted a large force on the north bank of the river St. Lawrence, near the Falls of Montmorency, leaving some regiments encamped on the Isle of Orleans. Fleet and army now only waited a given signal to attack the city. On board the fleet were some, as yet unknown, officers, who were destined to rise to great fame in the world. A young midshipman there was, named Jervis, who became the great English Admiral Earl St. Vincent. Palliser too, who figures in history as Admiral Sir Hugh Palliser, was on board the frigate *Mercury*. On another vessel was Robison, destined to be a noted Professor of Science in Edinburgh, and the partner of James Watt, inventor of the steam-engine. The humble sailing master of the *Mercury* was none other than James Cook, who became the most famous scientific navigator that ever left the shores of England.

Quickly did the fire of the English ships, joined to that of the batteries, work destruction upon the outer walls of the grim fortress. In the lower town the buildings were soon reduced to ruins, and even in the upper town many dangerous fires broke out. Indeed, before the siege was brought to a close, more than 500 buildings fell a prey to the flames, including public and private structures, the Cathedral and other churches. Yet while the summer wore away, in spite of Wolfe's terrible bombardment, Montcalm played a waiting game. Wolfe was in despair. By the end of July half of Quebec was shattered away by his cannon-balls, and still the French commander could not be drawn out to a battle; so the Englishman decided to attack the enemy at close quarters, just on the other side of the river Montmorency. But a fierce repulse awaited him; 12,000 French soldiers poured a storm of bullets against the brave grenadiers, who tried to get a footing on the river slopes. They were beaten back, 500 of Wolfe's best troops having fallen in the fatal charge. Wolfe fretted with impatience; he knew the time was precious. If he could only draw Montcalm out to battle! But Montcalm was wise; he refused to be drawn.

"You may destroy the town," came the French message under the flag of truce, "but you will never get inside it."

"I will take Quebec," replied Wolfe, "if I stay here until November."

One plan only now remained: it was to creep up in the night and scale the heights. It was a desperate move, but the only one that remained that offered a chance of success. In the midst of his plans the young English commander fell ill. He had always been of a delicate constitution, ever struggling with sickness. Days elapsed, but his heroic spirit conquered, and on the 11th of September the English troops were directed to be ready to land and attack the enemy. While a portion of the troops made a feint to the eastward to disguise Wolfe's intentions from the enemy, Wolfe and his troops drifted up stream with the tide. When the tide began to ebb, boats full of soldiers were cast off, reaching in safety a little cove three miles above Quebec.

In the first boat to land was the young general himself, who, as the oarsmen plied their muffled oars, murmured softly to his officers, the famous lines in Gray's *Elegy*:—

> The boast of heraldry, the pomp of power,
> And all that beauty, all that wealth e'er gave,
> Await alike the inevitable hour—
> The paths of glory lead but to the grave.

"Gentlemen," said Wolfe, "I would rather have written those lines than take Quebec."

As the boat's prow touched the shore, the sentinel's challenge rang out in the darkness, "Qui vive." To hesitate was to be lost. Instantly a Scotch captain, who spoke French perfectly, answered, "La France!"

"A quel régiment?"

"De la Heine," replied the Highlander boldly.

His quickness averted a calamity. The sentry was satisfied; his comrades had been expecting provision boats from Montreal, and he thought they had arrived. Sentry after sentry was passed by Wolfe and his men with the same result.

Up the dread heights the English soldiers clambered. Day was just dawning when they reached the top. They could see a cluster of French tents close at hand, and, dashing forward, they captured their occupants. This was the first outpost. The victors' huzzas rang out, and at this signal all Wolfe's red-coated battalions began climbing the cliffs, and soon joined their companions on the top. Their eyes beheld a great plain stretched out.

Wolfe's Army scaling the Cliff at Quebec. 1759

In the early days of the colony Master Abraham Martin had owned this tract of ground, which he had planted with corn. The people called it the Plains of Abraham, and Wolfe now chose it for his battlefield. On one side of him was the garrison of Quebec, startled by hearing of his mad adventure; on the opposite side was another French army under Bougainville; behind was the edge of the steep cliff and the river.

Montcalm, deceived by the firing of the English fleet, was far away. But at six o'clock he mounted and galloped thither as fast as his horse would carry him. Two miles away he could discern the red ranks of the British soldiers.

"This is a serious business," he said coolly, riding over the bridge of the St. Charles to gather his troops for the fray. Fervently they rallied at his command, never doubting but that they would sweep Wolfe and his men wholly from the heights. The eyes of the Indians, as did their tomahawks, glittered with expectancy; as did too, the eyes and bayonets of the white-coated battalions of Old France and the native Canadians, whose homes were at stake.

Brandishing his sword and again putting spurs to his noble war-horse, Montcalm led his ranks against the English infantry.

Wolfe waited until the French were only forty paces away, and then from kilted Highlander and English red-coat poured one tremendous sheet of flame. The French staggered, but still came on. Another fatal volley met them, inflicting awful slaughter. As they wavered, Wolfe flourished his sword, and amidst the weird uproar of the bagpipes, the shrieks and groans of the wounded, the war-whoops of the Indians, the mad shouting of the English, and fierce slogan of the Highlanders, Wolfe pushed on over dead and dying, behind a moving wall of bayonets. A bullet shattered his wrist, another pierced his body, but he kept on; a third lodged in his breast, and Wolfe fell upon the ground.

Two or three stalwart grenadiers bore their beloved general quickly to the rear. "There is no need for a surgeon," he said; "it is all over with me!"

One of the grenadiers looked up and cried out, "They run! See how they run!"

The dying Wolfe opened his eyes and murmured, "Who run?"

"The enemy, sir; they give way everywhere."

The general roused himself by a superhuman effort.

"Go, one of you, to Colonel Burton," he said in quick terms of command. "Tell him to march Webb's regiment down to Charles River to cut off their retreat from the bridge." Then, turning on his side, he whispered faintly, "Now, God be praised, I die in peace."

In a few moments the gallant Wolfe was no more.

How fared it meanwhile with his brave enemy, Montcalm? As he galloped about on horseback the tide of French fugitives pressed him back towards the gates of Quebec. He was nearing the walls when a shot passed through his body. Mortally wounded though he was, he kept himself seated in the saddle, two soldiers supporting him on either side.

As his life-blood streamed from Montcalm's body down his horse's limbs, the frightened crowd of women within the gates exclaimed in grief and terror, "The Marquis is killed! the Marquis is killed!"

"It is nothing, it is nothing," replied the dying Montcalm: "do not be troubled for me, my good friends."

When, some hours later, his spirit had breathed his last, Montcalm was buried under the floor of the Ursuline Convent. No workman could be found during the panic to make a coffin, and so an old servant gathered a few boards and nailed them together into a rough box. No bell tolled, no cannon fired a salute as Montcalm was laid to eternal rest.

Not thus was the funeral of the victorious Wolfe. His body was embalmed and borne across the sea to England, where the greatest and most powerful gathered to do him honour and reverence at his funeral in Westminster Abbey.

Yet history has struck the balance. To-day in Quebec, marking the scene of the death-struggle on that fateful September day, a single shaft of stone rises to heaven to commemorate at the same time a victory and a defeat. On the one side is graven the single word "MONTCALM" and on the other "WOLFE."

CHAPTER XV

LÉVIS AND THE NOBLES RETIRE TO OLD FRANCE

It was while Montcalm, high-spirited and valorous, yet lay dying, that Vaudreuil, now quartered on the Beauport Road, called a council of war. Tumult, fear, and confusion reigned. Montcalm, seeing the sands of his life fast running out, despatched a brief reply. "You have a threefold choice," he said: "to fight the English again, to retreat to Jacques Cartier, or to surrender the colony."

Over which choice to make, Vaudreuil hesitated. With Bougainville's troops he could muster 3000 men. These added to the Quebec garrison, the Canadian militia and artillery at Beauport, would give him a force far larger than that which had been mustered by the heroic Wolfe on the Plains of Abraham. When he asked the advice of the council of war he found, to his chagrin, that all his officers voted for retreat. "In vain," he reported to the King, "I told these gentlemen that we were superior to the enemy, and should beat them if we mustered. Still I could not at all change their opinion, and my love for the service and for the colony made me subscribe to the voice of the council. In fact, if I had attacked the English against the advice of the principal officers, their ill-will would have exposed me to the risk of losing the battle and the colony also." But the real reason why the officers were against fighting afterwards appeared. It was that they thought their commander, Vaudreuil, unfit to lead them to the fray. So Quebec, which might even now have been prevented from falling into the hands of the English, was left to its fate. Weary and footsore, almost dead for want of sleep, leaving their cannon, tents, and provisions behind them, Vaudreuil and the Beauport army set out for the distant hill of Jacques Cartier, where they were certain of a refuge that very night. Never was such disorder seen before. "It was not a retreat," wrote one of the officers afterwards, "but an abominable flight, with such disorder and confusion that, had the English but known it, 300 men sent after us would have been sufficient to cut all our army to pieces. The soldiers were all mixed, scattered, dispersed, and running as hard as they could, as if the English army were at their heels."

But the English, under General Townsend, were not so foolish as to risk the fruits of their victory by making an attempt to pursue the French across the St. Charles River. The people of Quebec, realising that they were deserted by the army, without provisions or munitions of war, and that the defences were insufficient to repulse a bombardment and assault, wished to surrender at once. Seeing that they refused to fight the enemy, the commandant, Ramésay, could only send out a flag of truce to the hostile camp and begin negotiations for capitulation.

But within the walls of Quebec dwelt a doughty patriot, the town-major, named Joannès. He called upon the soldiers and citizens to fight with their last breath, to die as Montcalm had done rather than let Quebec pass into the hands of the enemy. In his rage at the cowardice about him he beat two of the garrison with the flat of his sword. When the white flag was raised Joannès, the bravest man in the city, instantly hauled it down with his own hands. But alas! it was but fighting a battle against fate. His superior officer, Ramésay, commanded him sternly to repair to the English camp and get the best terms of peace he could. Through the pelting rain the town-major of Quebec, his head thrown back defiantly, his hand on his empty scabbard, sought the quarters of General Townsend. There he spun out the hours in a parley, hoping against hope that the recreant Vaudreuil would return and try to succour the city. Joannès kept up the negotiations as long as he could. Losing patience at last, Townsend sent him back to the French general with the message that if Quebec were not surrendered before eleven o'clock, he would capture it by assault. Ramésay, seeing all was lost, put his name to the articles of capitulation, and Joannès, with a heavy heart, carried the document back to the English commander. Scarcely had he put the walls of the city he loved behind him, when a troop of sixty Canadian horsemen appeared with the news that the Chevalier de Lévis was on the way with troops and provisions to rescue Quebec. The tidings came too late! The French general had surrendered; he would not now break his word. Ramésay dreaded too much the vengeance of the English in case the news borne by the sixty horsemen was not true, but false. How shall we picture the feelings of the town-major Joannès? When he returned he hid himself in a cellar and wept, while the blood-red cross of St. George was flaunted from the summit of the citadel. Thus at length, on the 18th September 1759, the capital town and rock-bound fortress of New France fell into the hands of the English.

General Townsend recognised too well the danger of his position not to grant favourable terms to the enemy, whose troops and sailors were allowed to march out of the garrison with the honours of war and granted passage in English ships to France. The persons and property of the inhabitants were promised protection, and their religion was not to be interfered with.

But now the question was with the English, should they keep Quebec or destroy it, as they had destroyed Louisburg? For a moment the city's fate trembled in the balance, and then it was resolved to keep it. Ten battalions of the artillery and a company of Rangers were ordered to remain behind and through the long Canadian winter hold the ruins of Quebec against the efforts of Lévis and the French, for little more than ruins much of Quebec now was. It needed enormous labour to make the town secure against the enemy, or even habitable.

While Townsend sailed away to England, leaving General Murray in charge, many working parties of soldiers were distributed through the town to clear the streets of rubbish and to repair the buildings for occupation. The palace of the Intendant was turned into winter quarters for an English regiment, which found there quantities of unused firearms, iron-mongery, blankets, cloths and linen, trinkets and lace, furs, wine, sugar, moccasins, and other stores. These were seized upon with alacrity. Nearly 7000 English, with insufficient food and clothing, made ready to face the approaching winter. Outposts in the neighbourhood of Sillery, St. Foye, and Lorette were established in order to guard against a surprise and to cover the safety of the detachments sent out to gather fuel in the surrounding woods. Canadian winters are cold, and the English soldiers were not yet hardened to their severities, and this gathering of firewood became a very serious business. Each detachment could make only one trip a day to the forest, returning with a fair-sized load on a sled drawn by hand. The soldiers were obliged to go armed as they worked, and keep a sharp lookout for fear of attacks by the Indians, who were always skulking in the neighbourhood. Winter this year set in even earlier than usual, and the brave soldiers who had served in India and Europe were now face to face with an enemy more terrible than the French. Their faces, hands, and feet were often frost-bitten, and on some occasions half the force of a detachment would be borne back entirely disabled. As if this were not enough, fever and scurvy prevailed in the garrison the whole winter long, and the brave fellows perished by scores and hundreds. Those who died were buried in the deep snow to await interment in the spring, for the ground was fast locked by frost.

Meanwhile the inhabitants of the province were disarmed and required to take the oath of allegiance to King George. But they could not all be trusted. The English lived in constant insecurity, and during the winter many rumours came of a projected attack by the French, and several skirmishes took place. Once in November it was reported that Lévis was about to march upon Quebec with 15,000 men the next month, for had he not sworn an oath to eat his Christmas dinner under the French flag within the walls? So the half-frozen English, each man hugging his musket in his frost-bitten fingers, waited for the enemy. The enemy had a fine sense of humour. In February a party of French and Indians sent a message to the English officers that a large company of expert hairdressers were prepared to wait upon them whenever their services were required! Needless to say, the English took no notice of this handsome offer to deprive them of their scalps.

Not until April did the long-expected battle occur. For months Lévis had been gathering his forces, and now, with an army of 8000 men and many redskins, he set out to recover the lost city of Quebec. At the village of St. Foye, five or six miles away, he halted. So wary had been his approach, that Murray and his garrison were ignorant of danger. They might have learnt it too late but for a strange and fortunate accident. It so happened that a frigate called the *Racehorse* had wintered in the dock at Quebec Lower town. On board this frigate soon after midnight the watch heard a faint cry of distress proceeding from the river. He ran at once to the captain, who, believing that some one was drowning, ordered a boat to be put out to save him. Guided by the cries, the sailors found a man lying on a large cake of ice, wet through and half dead with cold. Carrying him to the ship and pouring hot cordials down his throat, the man at last found strength to mutter that he was a soldier in Lévis's army; he and his companions had been trying to land just about Cap Rouge, but the boat had overturned, and he was the sole survivor. His life had been saved by his clambering upon a cake of floating ice. "The army of Lévis?" echoed the puzzled ship captain. "Just so," answered the soldier; "there are 12,000 of us. We are coming to retake Quebec."

Although it was between two and three o'clock in the morning, the rescued soldier was wrapped up warmly, slung in a hammock, and carried straightway up the heights to the commander's quarters. General Murray was fast asleep, but, having risen and heard the man's story, he ordered the troops under arms on the instant. By daybreak half the English garrison, with ten pieces of cannon, were hurled on the French columns at St. Foye. But in his rashness and thirst for renown, Murray had not counted well the cost. The French had thrice as many soldiers, and although the English fought gallantly and doggedly, they were compelled at last to fall back. When the English columns withdrew again to the city, they had left 1000 dead and dying men on the field of St. Foye.

Then began what Murray dreaded most—a new siege of Quebec. Weak his men were with sickness, and feeble with toil, fighting, and hunger, but their spirit was as unquenchable as ever. While Lévis set up his siege guns in position and began a steady bombardment of the city, the English garrison worked unceasingly, officers and privates handling spade and pickaxe in the same trenches together. Not a man of them all was idle. Even the sick in hospital filled sandbags or made wadding for the cannons. The English fire grew hotter every day from the 150 cannon which had been planted upon the walls.

All depended now on the reinforcements of troops expected by both sides from England and from France. Whichever arrived first would settle the question of victory. It was on a bright May morning, as Murray sat pondering over his despatches at headquarters, that an officer burst in to tell him that a ship of war had been sighted far down the river. The news spread through the town; all were divided between hope and fear. Was this warship French or was she English? Every eye was strained on the approaching ship, which displayed no colours at her masthead. Slowly, slowly she drew near, and then hurrah! there unfurled to the wind the crimson flag of England, and the first boom of a salute of twenty-one guns reverberated across the mighty river. She turned out to be the *Lowestoft* bringing news that a British squadron was at the mouth of the St. Lawrence and would reach Quebec in a few days. "The gladness of the troops," wrote home one of the garrison, "is not to be expressed. Both officers and soldiers mounted the parapet in the face of the enemy and huzzaed, with their hats in the air, for almost an hour. The garrison, the enemy's camp, the bay resounded with our shouts and the thunder of our artillery, and the gunners were so elated that they did nothing but load and fire for a considerable time."

But if a French squadron had been first, what a shock to their spirits, what a test of their endurance, which they might not have overborne!

On the heart of the gallant Chevalier de Lévis this news fell, and brought a deadly chill. He withdrew his troops hastily, and it was soon seen that the French ships, which had wintered high up the river, were fated to destruction. Of these there were six altogether, two frigates, two small armed ships, and two schooners. Commanding them was a daring officer named Vauquelin. Although Vauquelin fought with dogged determination till all his powder and lead was spent, although he refused to lower his colours, the English mariners overpowered him and made him their prisoner. But the English knew a brave man when they saw one, and Vauquelin they treated with distinguished honour, inviting him to a banquet and toasting him loudly as a hero.

This was the deathblow to the hopes of Lévis. True, he had Montreal still in his hands, but what was Montreal without ammunition and provisions, with the enemy clamouring at the very gates? The Canadian Militia had deserted to their homes, and Vaudreuil and De Lévis had to defend the city with only 2000 disheartened troops; while against them was ranged a force of 17,000 English. Further resistance was useless, and so on the 8th of September Vaudreuil surrendered to General Murray, and Canada and all its dependencies passed to the British Crown.

Hopeless as the situation had been for a full year past, ever since Wolfe had laid down his life at the moment of victory on the Plains of Abraham, there were some amongst the French to whom the thought of defeat was unbearable pain. Invincible in spirit, we see emerging through the mist of a century and a half, the courtly, stalwart, chivalrous figure of the Chevalier de Lévis. To be conquered while his right arm could grip the handle of a sword was to him unutterable disgrace. When he heard that his superior, Vaudreuil, had agreed that the French troops should lay down their arms and serve no longer during the war, his manly cheek flushed and he insisted that the negotiations should be broken off. "If," he said, "the Marquis de Vaudreuil must surrender, let us at least withdraw with the troops to the Island of St. Helen in order to uphold there, on our own behalf, the honour of the King's army." But this step Vaudreuil could not, of course, permit, and the Chevalier could only grind his teeth in mortification and prepare to bid the Canada he loved an eternal farewell.

Canada was now a British colony, and those members of the old French Canadian families who were unwilling to become British subjects followed Vaudreuil and Lévis back to France. With them also went the rascally Bigot and the traitors and pilferers who had fattened on the distresses of their country. Nemesis awaited them! No sooner had they touched French soil than they were seized and flung into the Bastille. At first the brazen Cadet swore, when he faced his judges, he was innocent, but afterwards he confessed all. Bigot too denied his knavery, until the papers signed by himself put him to silence. His punishment was great, but far less than he deserved; he was banished from France for life, his property confiscated to the King, and he was made to pay a fine of 1,500,000 francs. Cadet was banished for nine years and fined 6,000,000 francs, while the rest were ordered to be imprisoned until their fines were paid, so that many who had betrayed New France languished in the gaols of Old France and died within those bare stone walls.

Canada, as you have seen, had now changed masters. But the red-man, so long the friend and ally of the French, standing at the door of his wigwam or stealing noiselessly in his war-paint through the forest, was puzzled and angered. He could not understand how it had happened; he could not understand why the flag of the lilies should be hauled down from every fort and trading-station, and the flag of the English or the "Boston men," as he called them, unfurled. His mind could not grasp the meek submission of the Canadian pale-faces—the farmers and traders—to the chiefs sent out by King George. "Why do you not," said one of their braves, "leave your towns and villages and set up your lodges in the forest? Then, when the English are lulled into security, return and fall upon and slay them? You can win battles by craft and cunning as well as by numbers and cannon." But although the French Canadians smiled and shook their heads at this plan, yet at the western settlements, such as Michilimackinac, Detroit, and Presqu'Isle, they did not scruple to tell the Indians that the English would soon drive them from their forest homes and hunting-grounds, and thereby to kindle hate in their hearts for the new conquerors. The French certainly understood the Indian character far better than the English, who treated them with contemptuous neglect. The vanity of the redskin chiefs was no longer fostered, and the tribes were told plainly that they were regarded as vassals and savages. For the English—the Boston men—could not forget the bloodthirsty cruelty which had been practised upon them and their wives and children for so long, and now that they felt that all power on the continent was in the hollow of their hands, they would not stoop to truckle to its aboriginal masters.

At first the haughty redskin chiefs were taken wholly by surprise at the contempt meted out to them; then all their hot savage blood mounted in their veins. All that they needed was a leader, and they had not long to wait. A leader of their own race, intelligent, daring, treacherous, and vain, suddenly appeared on the scene. Pontiac was a chieftain of the Ottawas, but so greatly had his fame spread that all the braves of the Hurons, the Ojibways, the Sacs, the Wyandots, the Delawares, and the Senecas looked to him as their guide and captain. In the strange drama which was now to thrill the Western world, Pontiac takes the stage as the central figure. In history this drama is called "The Conspiracy of Pontiac."

It was not many months after General Murray was ruling Canada in the name of his young master, King George III., that Pontiac, the chieftain of the Ottawas, saw with a keen eye the danger that threatened his people. Either the red-man and all the tribes would be crushed under the heel of the pale-faces, or else they must take up their dwellings and retreat farther into the western forests. "With the French," said Pontiac, "we can live in friendship, but with the restless English either we must flee afar or we or they must die!"

A plot grew and took shape in Pontiac's mind of uniting all the power of the red-men and driving the English for ever out of the whole country. He told his audacious plot to some of the Western French fur-traders, who expressed their joy, saying that the King of France would surely help him, and was even then sending out fresh hosts to slay the enemy. With the utmost care did Pontiac lay his plans. A day was chosen, a day in May 1763, when all the Indians who looked to Pontiac as their leader would rise in their might and fall with musket and tomahawk upon their unsuspecting victims. At this time the strongest of the western forts was Detroit, and this fort Pontiac had arranged to surprise and seize by strategy. A council of Indians arranged to meet Major Gladwin, the commander, and the other English officers within the fort on that day. They were supposed to be entirely unarmed, but beneath his blanket each conspirator concealed a musket, shortened by its barrel being filed in half. While they conversed pleasantly Pontiac was to give the signal which would sound the doom of the garrison. But the plot failed. To the love of an Indian maiden for Gladwin the English owed their lives. This young girl overheard the plot. She could not sleep the whole of one night, and in the morning stole hurriedly to Gladwin and told him of Pontiac's intended treachery. Altogether ignorant of how he had been betrayed, Pontiac and his fellow-conspirators, with faces calm and smiling, for the Indians can wear the most impenetrable mask, arrived at the fort to attend the proposed conference. To Pontiac's astonishment, he saw the English soldiers drawn up with loaded muskets as if for battle. Did he start back cringing and discomfited? Nay, not a change of expression passed his impassive features; he went on with the conference as if nothing had happened, and afterwards, without giving any signal, withdrew. Next morning Pontiac again came; this time he was ordered away from the gates of the fort. Fierce rage filled his heart; he knew then that his plot had been revealed to the English. Strategy had failed at Detroit, he must now fire the torch of Indian hatred and openly assault the stronghold. He attacked, and for months the red-men were kept at bay until succour could come to the heroic Gladwin and his men.

But if the devotion of one Indian maiden had spared Detroit, the treachery of another sacrificed Fort Miami and the garrison of the Maumee River. Captain Holmes, the commandant, had inspired the jealousy of a young squaw. She believed he loved another, and lent herself to Pontiac's schemes to encompass the English chiefs destruction. On the fatal morning she came to tell Holmes that her sister was seriously ill in one of the wigwams and desired to see him. All unsuspecting, he set out on his mission of charity, and was shot dead on the very threshold of the wigwam. As for his fort and company of soldiers, they fell into the hands of the watchful Indians. The same fate was reserved for the forts of De Boeuf, Presqu'Isle, and Sandusky. The blood of the colonists on the frontier of Pennsylvania flowed freely; the scalps of Pontiac's victims adorned many lodges.

It soon began to appear as if Pontiac's threat against the English had not been in vain. At Michilimackinac strategy carried the day for the red conspirators. On King George's birthday, the 4th June, Captain Etherington received an invitation from the Sacs and Ojibways to witness their favourite game of lacrosse by way of celebrating the day. Suspecting no danger, the gate of the fort was allowed to be left open, while the officers and soldiers, clustered in groups outside, became deeply interested in the progress of this most exciting game. The ball was passed and repassed skilfully between the goals, as, seizing their opportunity, a number of squaws, with muskets and tomahawks hidden under their blankets, stole unseen through the gates. Soon the ball bounced against the pallisade, and instantly a swarm of players dashed after it. In the twinkling of an eye they had darted through the open gates and snatched their weapons from the waiting squaws. Before the garrison could realise what had happened, fifteen of them lay weltering in their blood, and the rest were taken prisoners. Thus in only six weeks from the day of the first attack of Pontiac on Detroit, all the forts in the western country, except three, were seized and destroyed and the garrisons massacred or made prisoners.

To Pontiac and his men Fort Pitt bade defiance. After some weeks' delay Colonel Bouquet was sent out to reinforce it. Bouquet met and defeated the Delaware and Shawanoe tribes, and gave them so sound a beating that the tide against the English began to turn. The misguided chiefs slowly came to see that the power of

England was greater than they had supposed, and that of France extinguished for ever. In the following year several Indian tribes were defeated, and Pontiac, now deserted by many of his allies, was obliged to fall back farther into the west. Two years later the mighty chief's power was broken, and he was forced to submit. So ended the great conspiracy. The hundreds of prisoners whom Pontiac and his Indians had captured in their raids were at last restored to families which had, not without reason, supposed them to be dead. Parties of rescuers found that some of the young English girls had actually fallen in love with their savage captors and had wedded them in Indian fashion. Children had forgotten their parents. One girl only remembered her childhood when the strains of a lullaby fell from the lips of her rejoicing mother, whose face was strange to her.

Pontiac himself vanished with ignominy from history. Fallen from his high estate, defeated in his ambitious hopes, he engaged in a drunken bout with a warrior of the Illinois nation. From words the pair proceeded to blows, tomahawks flashed in the air, and the once powerful chieftain was laid low. Such was the ending to the career of a savage enemy whose name had caused the people in the English colonies to tremble for so long. But Pontiac and his conspiracy had taught the new conquerors a lesson. Justice and forbearance not only towards the French Canadians but towards the red-men was thenceforward the policy of English Canada.

All seemed now fair sailing for all the colonies under the rule of King George. But war-clouds were already mounting above the horizon which would gather in size and intensity as the years ran on. More blood would be spilt in Canada and on the great continent of which Canada forms so important a part.

CHAPTER XVI

THE COMING OF THE LOYALISTS

Fifteen years after Wolfe's victorious battle the restless American colonists were ready to revolt and cut themselves loose from the empire which had been won so painfully, so valiantly, and at such cost. Glad enough had they been of the protection of King George and King George's soldiers when the French menaced them from the north and the unsubdued tribes of fierce savages were threatening to drive them into the sea. But now that the power of both French and Indian had been crushed, when the thousands of brave English soldiers had been laid at rest amid the Canadian snows, the colonists felt a security they had never known before. They had now at their threshold no foe to fear, and as men dislike all authority which is not of their own choosing, demagogues and agitators quickly set to work to induce the Americans to throw off with violence what was called "the British yoke."

The British yoke consisted chiefly in a demand that the colonies should help to pay something of the cost the recent wars had entailed upon the mother-country. The mother-country asked to be helped to bear her burden, and in reply her daughterland—America—flew at her throat. But this is not the place in which to tell the story of the American Revolution. It was clear from the very first that Canada would be involved, and so certain were the American agitators and traitors to the King that Canada would join them, that they set up what was called "The Continental Congress" at Philadelphia. To their intense astonishment and chagrin Canada would have nothing to do with their designs. "The Continental Congress!" cried the loyal Governor, Sir Guy Carleton; "let me tell you that Canada on this continent will have none of your disloyalty!" So the Americans made up their minds to swoop down upon Canada and capture it before further English troops could come to its assistance.

Ticonderoga and Crown Point were surprised in rough-and-ready fashion by Ethan Allen and his "Green Mountain Boys." Through the old war-path leading into Canada, General Richard Montgomery, an Irish officer who had turned against his King, was sent to Montreal with an army of 3000 men. But as we have seen many times, to capture Montreal was not quite the same thing as capturing Quebec. Yet both might have succeeded if the Canadians had proved false.

For the mission to Quebec a strong, daring, even reckless character was needed, and such a one sprang up suddenly to notice in the American army. The name of this man was Benedict Arnold. It is a name which history has covered with infamy because of its owner's subsequent treason to the American cause. But nothing that he afterwards did can obliterate the fact that Arnold was fearless, enterprising, and generous-minded, and the equal in origin and manners of most of the American military officers of that day. Arnold had been successively druggist, bookseller, horse-dealer, shipowner, and shipmaster, and at thirty-five years of age found himself burning with military zeal and anxious to distinguish himself. He proposed to lead the 1100 men he had raised, by way of river and wilderness, over the mountains of Maine to Quebec and capture that city by surprise. His little force was composed of the roughest elements: ten companies of musketeers and three of riflemen, the latter hailed from the hills of Virginia and Pennsylvania, hunters and Indian fighters, wise in woodcraft, handy with the rifle, the hunting-knife, and birch-bark canoe, accustomed to hunger, exposure, and fatigue. They were armed each with a good rifle, a tomahawk, a long knife, a small axe, and dressed in a hunting-shirt of deer-skin, with moccasins and leggings of the same material. By the middle of September 1775 Arnold and his daring band were well on their way through the wilderness. When not paddling their canoes, the ground across the carrying-places was rough, rocky, and rugged, interspersed with bogs, into which the invaders sank often to their knees. New difficulties faced them daily, and their provisions grew scant, until at length they resolved to eat their pork raw and to make but two meals each day. Never was expedition undertaken more recklessly. Unacquainted with the distance they had to go, they were without map or chart; half a biscuit, half a square inch of raw pork formed their usual meal; but there were worse days to come, days when these invaders of Canada were called to kill the two faithful dogs which accompanied them, to make soup out of their old deer-skin moccasins, to devour roots and leaves greedily. But the thought of capturing Quebec fired every heart during the memorable six weeks' march. Thus it was that a camp at the French Canadian settlement was reached. Hearing of Arnold's arrival with his emaciated followers, the Indians of the country-side began flocking around, eager to know what had brought him hither. "Summon," said Arnold, "your braves in council, gather together your young men, and I will tell them why we are come."

Natanis, the principal chief, forthwith summoned an Indian conclave, and, boldly casting truth to one side, Benedict Arnold addressed it in these words: "Brothers, we are children of this English people who have now taken up the hatchet against us. More than a hundred years ago we were all as one family; we then differed in our religion and came over to this great country by consent of the King. Our fathers bought land of the red-men, and have grown a great people, even as the stars in the sky. We have planted the ground and by our labour grown rich. Now a new King and his wicked great man want to take our lands and money without our consent. The King would not hear our prayer, but sent a great army to Boston, and endeavoured to set our children against us in Canada. The King's army at Boston came out into the fields and houses, killed a great many women and children while they were peaceably at work. The Bostonians sent to their children in the country, and they came in unto their relief, and in six days raised an army of 50,000 men and drove the King's troops on board their ships, killing and wounding 1500 of their men. Since that they durst not come out of Boston. Now we hear the French and Indians in Canada have sent to us that the King's troops oppress them and make them pay a great price for their rum and other things, pressing them to take up arms against the Bostonians, their children, who have done them no hurt. By the desire of the French and Indians, our brethren, we have come to their assistance with an intent to drive out the King's soldiers. When driven off, we will return to our own country and leave this to the peaceable enjoyment of its proper inhabitants. Now, if the Indians, our brethren, will join us, we will be very much obliged to them, and will give them one Portuguese dollar per month, two dollars bounty, and find them their provisions and the liberty to choose their own officers."

Judge if, at this extraordinary speech, Natanis and his redskins looked their astonishment! But although they had never heard any of these terrible and unjust deeds on the part of King George before, their Indian cupidity and bloodthirstiness were excited, and little more persuasion was needed to induce some of them at least to tread the war-path. Natanis and his brother Sabatis, with about fifty warriors, joined the expedition on the spot.

Some days later Arnold and his men beheld the scene of their destined conquest spread out before them. The last leaves of the trees in the beautiful valley of the Chaudière had fluttered to the ground and the sunlight danced upon the hill-tops and on the waters of the St. Lawrence, lighting up in the distance the city and the fortress they coveted. The American general, George Washington, had beforehand written a manifesto to the Canadians which had been translated into French and printed before Arnold's departure. This manifesto Arnold now caused to be distributed, assuring them of American friendship and asking the assistance of the Canadians.

Luckily for the future of Canada under the British flag, a strong, brave man sat in the seat of authority. Sir Guy Carleton had been a friend of Wolfe, and had served with him before Quebec. He was as brave as Frontenac and as wise as the coming Haldimand. Carleton needed all his bravery and wisdom; he had only about 400 regulars and 600 French Canadian volunteers. The fortunes of Canada were in his hands! When Montgomery took possession of Montreal, Carleton retired to Quebec, escaping capture only by the most daring of stratagems. Before he could reach the fortress, the commandant he had left there had summoned all the loyal citizens together and prepared for battle. He dealt Arnold a blow by burning every boat on the river and sentinelling the channel with vessels of war. If Arnold could have crossed the St. Lawrence immediately on his arrival, he would have stood a far better chance of capturing Quebec, but his men had now to scour the country for birch-bark canoes. One dark night he succeeded in eluding a British frigate and sloop and landed 500 men at Wolfe's Cove. On the following morning, at daybreak, Benedict Arnold led his troops up the steep path and formed them in ranks on the Plains of Abraham above. His idea was to provoke a sally and attack the garrison as Wolfe had done. He believed that outside the walls were numerous sympathisers with the Americans who would rally to his assistance during a fight. So he marched his men up close to the battlements, as if daring the besieged to come out and fight. But the Commandant was not to be snared into the same trap which had proved the undoing of Montcalm. "If you want Quebec," he said, "you must come and take it!"

The news that Sir Guy Carleton was approaching with reinforcements from up the river quickly decided Benedict Arnold to retire from the Heights of Abraham. He withdrew his troops to a point some distance above Quebec, there to await the arrival of Montgomery, who was approaching with clothing and provisions. His failure to seduce the French Canadians to break their oath of loyalty to King George caused him the bitterest chagrin. If a siege dragged on till spring-time, the British fleet would surely relieve Quebec. Many of the American troops were sick, and their artillery was insufficient. Nothing remained to Montgomery and Arnold but an attempt to seize Quebec by a daring piece of strategy.

It was the last day of December. Snow had been falling heavily all day, and now, late at night, it was still falling. It had been planned that Montgomery should attack the Lower town on the side of Cape Diamond, and Arnold on the side of St. Roque. If once the streets near the river could be gained, they could scale the walls to the Upper town. To distract Carleton's attention from these two assaulting columns, two feigned attacks were made on other parts of the city. In order that they might recognise each other in the darkness, each of the American invaders wore on his cap a band of white paper on which was written "Liberty or Death." But Carleton was not to be taken by surprise, and the Quebec garrison was on the alert. Montgomery and Arnold were to meet in the Lower town and force a rough structure of pickets called Prescott gate. At the head of his men, Montgomery found himself intercepted by a party of British soldiers and seamen. "Come on, my brave boys, and Quebec is ours," he shouted. Flames of fire darted out from a log-house battery which barred his approach to the Lower town. Montgomery, his two aides, and ten others were struck down and killed on the spot.

On the other side of the Lower town Arnold was running forward with his men. Suddenly in the midst of the wild storm the bells of the city rang out the alarm, the beating of drums was heard, and the artillery began to belch forth shot and shell. Arnold was one of the first to be struck down, and, wounded in the leg, he retired to the rear. Those who did not follow his example of retreat were compelled to surrender. So ended this ambitious scheme for the conquest of Quebec! When morning came the bodies of Montgomery and others were carried into the city and given proper burial. Both Richard Montgomery, who had sought to tear down the Union Jack from the citadel, and Guy Carleton, who had defended the town and flag, had served under Wolfe in the campaign which made Britain mistress of Quebec.

The Americans, largely reinforced, continued for some time to hang about the city. British ships sailed up the St. Lawrence at last, and the invaders retired in haste. The coming of the warships was the signal to fall upon the Americans, seize their artillery, and turn them into a fleeing mob. The troops so long awaited from England arrived at last. Everywhere the invaders were routed. Benedict Arnold at Montreal found it prudent to leave that city, and it was at once entered and taken possession of by the English. Moreover, the forts on the lakes were retaken. The fleet which Arnold had gathered on Lake Champlain was destroyed, and the gates of Canada were again barred against the disloyal invader.

For many months the fate of the thirteen revolting colonies hung in the balance. Their troops were dispirited, ill-fed, ill-paid, ill-clad. Many thousands absolutely refused to serve or to obey their officers. A single great battle won by the King's soldiers might have sent them back to their homes willing to accept the terms of peace which the mother-country offered to the colonies. As it was, every third man you would have met, had you travelled from Boston to Savannah, was still a Loyalist or Tory openly or at heart. At the beginning of the conflict two-thirds of the entire population of America, which was then about 3,000,000, were Loyalists. But if you have read the history of the French Revolution, you know that peaceful majorities have little power when opposed by loud-voiced, vehement, energetic men, with a single object, and perpetually keeping that object in view. Thus we see as the war dragged on the numbers of Loyalists diminishing. Many had not dared to avow their fealty to King and Empire; many had not dared to express their opinion that America had been in the wrong from the first. They shrank from calling Samuel Adams a demagogue, and Tom Paine a wicked atheist, because this would have exposed them to the hatred of the lawless mob. For now that the King's authority had been overthrown, especially in the cities, the lives of peaceful, law-abiding men were at the mercy of the multitude. It was no time to be neutral. A man had to choose between his King and the Philadelphia Congress, and, moreover, he had to choose quickly. In many cases his choice was influenced by immediate fear. His house or shop might be broken into, his goods stolen, his chattels burned, even he himself, if he escaped stoning or the fanatic's bullet, might be tarred and feathered.

Under these circumstances, you see what a painful predicament they were in who in those distant colonies, proud of their imperial heritage as Englishmen, grateful for what England had done for them, convinced that the mother-country did not really wish to oppress them, stood firm for their sovereign, flag, and ancient Constitution.

History now shows that the Loyalists were, with a few striking exceptions, the best men in America. Their numbers embraced the most notable judges, the most eminent lawyers, most cultured clergy, most distinguished physicians, most educated and refined of the people, both north and south. Early in the war, nay, even long before the war broke out, the Boston mobs had set upon them for their loyalty. Any official or merchant suspected of sympathising with the British Army or British Government of the day became at once a target for their insults and persecution. They began by setting Governor Hutchinson's mansion in flames; sheriffs and judges were mobbed; feeble old men were driven into the woods, and innocent women insulted. As the war progressed the violence of the revolutionists grew in intensity. Thousands sought safety with the King's troops, thousands armed themselves and fought valiantly for the King. Any man accused of being a Loyalist was liable to have his estate confiscated and to be punished even with death. Now we can afford to look back on these things and to bear no ill-will to the good and wise Americans who built up the United States. It happened long ago; we have long forgiven. But Canadians can never forget.

What the Loyalists had suffered during the war, when the issue of the contest still wavered, was far, far less than that which they had to endure when the Revolutionists at last triumphed.

The British Empire had been badly served by the officers England had sent out to America. If she had had a soldier of the stamp of Washington to direct her armies, there would have been a different conclusion; but all was mismanaged, and her Generals, Gage, Burgoyne, and Cornwallis, planned feebly and fought half-heartedly. If there was any doubt as to the result, that doubt was speedily set at rest when England's hereditary enemy, France, espoused the cause of the American insurgents. French money, ships, and men poured into America. The Americans fought with French muskets, they were clad in French clothing, and they were paid with gold which the impoverished people of France could ill spare. Great is the debt America owes to the French King and statesmen of that time.

Then came the day when Cornwallis found himself shut up at Yorktown by the French and American armies under Rochambeau and Washington, four times greater than his own forces. The French fleet turned its guns upon him from the sea; retreat was cut off, and Cornwallis surrendered. To the hopes of the Loyalists this was the last blow, and indeed to the hopes of British King and Parliament.

The war was all but over, but not yet over was the terrible ordeal which the men who had stood staunch and faithful to the United Empire were destined to undergo. They were termed "traitors"; they were pursued through the streets; their families were driven into the woods; they were shot down remorselessly. Rows of them were hung up like felons. At the battle of King's Mountains in North Carolina ten of the prisoners, men of character and influence, were hanged in cold blood. There were many other instances when prisoners were ferociously executed.

New York remained in British hands a year or two longer. There came one morning tidings that a Loyalist named Philip White had been hanged. The Loyalists, led by William, the able, stout-hearted son of Benjamin Franklin, now resolved to retaliate. For every Loyalist, they proclaimed, who was murdered they would hang a Congress officer falling into their hands. Accordingly one Joshua Huddy, who had been taken prisoner by them, was hanged. On his corpse was fastened this notice: "We determine to hang man for man, while there is a refugee living." Verily, an eye for an eye, and a tooth for a tooth! Naturally Washington and the Congress were very angry at this, and by way of further retaliation condemned a young officer, nineteen years of age, Captain Asgill, to die on the gibbet. Lady Asgill, the mother of the young officer, failing to obtain mercy from Congress, applied to the French, and De Vergennes requested that young Asgill should be set at liberty, saying: "Captain Asgill is doubtless your prisoner, but he is among those whom the armies of the King, my master, contributed to place in your hands at Yorktown." Such a request Congress did not dare refuse, and the destined victim was set at liberty.

Canada proper during the war had not again been molested. But far to the north let us turn our eyes for a moment to witness a scene occurring there.

All this time the vast country bordering upon Hudson's Bay remained in undisputed possession of the English Hudson's Bay Company. Their forts and factories, though capable of offering a strong defence, were built of logs, with bastions of stone. Only one really noble fort lifted its crest in the sub-Arctic region. Fifty years before the remembrance of their former posts destroyed by fire and the cannon of the redoubtable Iberville induced the Company to fortify its best harbour on a splendid scale, and erect in the northern wilderness, in the hushed solitudes of the moose, the bear, and the wolf, a mighty fortress which would evoke the admiration of Europe. A massive 30-feet-wide foundation was begun from the plans of the military engineers who had served under the Duke of Marlborough, and, after some years, in 1734, Fort Prince of Wales, a rival to the French stronghold of Louisburg, 2000 miles away, was reared at the mouth of Churchill River. The walls were 42 feet thick at their foundation; three of the bastions had arches for store-houses, and in the fourth was built a magazine 34 feet long and 10 wide. For fifty years Fort Prince of Wales stood undisturbed, none daring to offer it insult or attack. The remote Chippewas and far-off tribes from Athabasca and the Great Slave Lake travelling to Hudson's Bay gazed with wonder at its masonry and formidable artillery. The great cannon whose muzzles stared grimly from the battlements had been woven into Indian legends.

So strong did the Company deem it, that no thought of any conquest seems to have entered their minds. The garrison was allowed to wane in numbers, until on an August evening 1782 only thirty-nine defenders within its walls witnessed the arrival of three strange ships in the Bay. Word ran from mouth to mouth that they were French men-of-war. All was consternation and anxiety at first, quickly succeeded by dread. Two score pair of English eyes watched the strangers, as pinnace, gig, and long-boat were lowered, and a number of swarthy sailors began busily to sound the approaches to the harbour. Anxious indeed was the night passed in the fort by Governor Samuel Hearne and his men. Daybreak came and showed the strangers already disembarking in their boats, and as the morning sun waxed stronger, an array of 400 troops was seen drawn up on the shore of Churchill Bay, at a place called Hare Point. Orders were given to march, and with the flag of France once more unfurled on these distant northern shores, the French attacking party approached Fort Prince of Wales, the Company's stronghold.

Four hundred yards from the walls they halted; two officers were sent on in advance to summon the Governor to surrender. The French ships turned out to be the *Sceptre*, seventy-four guns, the *Astarte*, and the *Engageante*, of thirty-six guns each; they had, besides, four field-guns, two mortars, and 300 bomb-shells.

It appears that Admiral la Pérouse, who commanded this hostile fleet, had counted on arriving just in time to secure a handsome prize in the shape of the Company's ships, for which he had lain in wait in the Bay. But these luckily eluded him. At the spectacle of the French attacking force, the Governor of Prince of Wales Fort, Samuel Hearne, seems to have become panic-stricken. Believing resistance useless, he snatched up a table-cloth which, to the surprise of the French, was soon seen waving from the parapet of the fort. Without a shot being fired on either side, Fort Prince of Wales had yielded to the foe.

The delighted French admiral lost no time in transporting what guns he could find in the fort to his ships, as well as in replenishing his depleted commissariat from its well-filled provision stores.

Afterwards came much noisy rioting on the part of the French soldiers and the utter looting of the fort. An attempt was made, occupying two days, to demolish it; but although French gunpowder as well as English was freely used, yet the walls were of such solid masonry as to resist their best efforts. The artillerymen of the enemy could only displace the upper rows of the massive granite stones, dismount its guns, and blow up the gateway, together with the stone outwork protecting it.

Then La Pérouse sailed away for York Factory, which at this time was garrisoned by sixty English and twelve Indians. Its defence consisted of thirteen cannon, twelve and nine pounders, which formed a half-moon battery in front; and it being thought probable that the enemy would arrive in the night and turn these guns against the fort, they were overturned into the ditch. On the ramparts were twelve swivel guns mounted on carriages, and within was abundance of small arms and ammunition. A rivulet of fresh water ran within the stockades to quench the thirst of the besieged; and there were also thirty head of cattle and as many hogs, to keep them from hunger.

Two Indian scouts, sent out to obtain intelligence, returned in about three hours with the information that the enemy were less than a league distant. Several guns had been heard firing in the neighbourhood; and at sunset of that day all could plainly discern a large bonfire, presumably kindled by the French, about a mile and a half to the west. A night of anxiety was passed, and by ten o'clock the next morning the enemy appeared before the gates. "During their approach," says one of those in the fort at the time, "a most inviting opportunity offered itself to be revenged on our invaders by discharging the guns on the ramparts, which must have done great execution."

But here also the Governor was not the man for such an emergency. He knew nothing of war, and had a wholesome dread of all armed and equipped soldiery. Trembling so that he could scarcely stand, he begged the surgeon, "for God's sake to give him a glass of liquor to steady his nerves." There being none at hand, he swallowed a tumbler of raw spirits of wine, and this so far infused courage and determination into his blood, that he peremptorily declared he would shoot the first man who offered to fire a gun. Dismay filled the bosoms of many of the fur Company's servants. The second in command and the surgeon endeavoured to expostulate, and to silence them the Governor caught up a white sheet with his own hand and waved it from a window of the fort. This was answered by the French officer displaying his pocket-handkerchief.

Under the sanction of this flag of truce a parley took place. The Governor was ordered to surrender within two hours. But no such time was needed; the fort was most ingloriously yielded in ten minutes. In vain did some of the English council plead that the fort might have withstood the united efforts of double the number of those by whom it was assailed. Vainly they showed that, from the nature of the enemy's attack by way of Nelson River, they could not use their mortars or artillery, the ground being very bad and full of woods, thickets, and bogs. The miserable Governor was resolved to yield the place, and he carried out his intention, much to the astonishment and satisfaction of the French.

The fur-trading company never rebuilt Fort Prince of Wales. The distant traveller may behold its ruins to-day standing to mark the most northern stronghold on the North American continent, a reminder of bygone strife, useful now only as a beacon and a resting-place for flocks of Arctic birds.

Peace was declared between Britain and America in 1783, but there was no peace for the American Loyalists. When the King's armies sailed away from Charleston, the last spectacle they saw was the bodies of twenty-four Loyalists swinging from a row of gibbets. Of no crime were these men guilty but that of refusing to disunite the glorious Empire, of refusing to fight against him whom they regarded as their lawful sovereign, and an honest and benevolent prince.

By the Treaty of Versailles they had been abandoned by the mother-country, left to the tender mercies of the American conquerors. No wonder there were men in both Houses of Parliament who were shocked at this treatment.

"When I consider the case of the colonists," cried Wilberforce, "I confess I there feel myself conquered; I there see my country humiliated; I there see her at the feet of America!" "A peace founded on the sacrifice of these unhappy subjects," declared one noble lord, "must be accursed in the sight of God and man."

Months before the peace was actually signed Canada itself, which was to be the Canaan of the Loyalists, was almost lost to the Empire. A French fleet of thirty-five ships were assembled at Martinique in the West Indies and about to sail northward for the reconquest of New France. America would not have dared to gainsay the wishes of her French allies to possess Canada, yet there was nothing that the Americans dreaded more. They knew that the time would come, were France once again entrenched in Canada, when they would be obliged to fight her future Frontenacs and Montcalms for the possession of Quebec and the security of their northern frontier.

But the fears of the Americans were never realised. The gallant sea-dog Rodney fell upon De Grasse in West Indian waters, inflicting upon him a crushing defeat, and so Canada was providentially preserved to the British flag.

It was now time for the Loyalists to journey forth from the new republic they despised and distrusted. Somewhere—for most of them knew it but vaguely—in the northern wilds, in the virgin forests of pine and maple and hemlock, in the solitudes of lakes and rivers, which no man of English blood had ever seen, was the refuge the Loyalists sought. No longer could they hope that their confiscated property would be restored or even that the little they had left would be secured to them.

In the month of November 1783 New York was evacuated by the King's troops under Sir Guy Carleton. With him went all the stores belonging to the Crown, all the baggage and artillery and 40,000 souls. New York was the stronghold of the Loyalists; Pennsylvania had been equally divided between Loyalists and Revolutionists; there were more Loyalists in Virginia than adherents of Congress; and Georgia had at least three Loyalists for every rebel. Thousands had perished; thousands had sought refuge in England; thousands had recanted. Fifty thousand now set out with their wives and children and such belongings as were left to them to traverse the hundreds of miles which lay between them and their new homesteads in Canada. These United Empire Loyalists were the fathers of English Canada. Comfort came to them in a proclamation that England would not think of deserting them.

Seated on the throne at Westminster, King George had addressed to Parliament these words: "I trust you will agree with me that a due and generous attention ought to be shown to those who have relinquished their property or their possessions from motives of loyalty to me, or attachment to the mother-country."

Delay, alas, occurred; commissioners had to be appointed to consider Loyalists' claims, yet in the end England was not ungrateful; land and money were bestowed upon them freely. Albeit there was a long period of suffering and privation, of cold and hunger and hardship. There are few tales which history has to tell so stirring and noble as the exodus of the Loyalists. Most of them had been brought up in comfort, and even luxury; their women were tenderly nurtured and unaccustomed to hardship. But one spirit animated them all, one hope fired all their bosoms, one faith drove them out of the American republic into the wilderness.

The exodus was divided into two main streams, one moving eastward to Nova Scotia and the country where a century and a half before Poutraincourt and De la Tour had fought and flourished. The other moved westward to the region north of Lake Ontario, which had witnessed the labours of Frontenac and Lasalle and the sufferings of Brébeuf and his brother Jesuits. These came in by Lake Champlain and ascended the St. Lawrence in open boats, bivouacking at night, resuming their journey by day. They crossed from Oswego on Lake Ontario to Kingston and York, and began at once felling trees and erecting rude cabins. Many had travelled by waggons from North Carolina and Georgia, exposed to insult and danger all the way. Those who followed the eastern course landed at the mouth of the St. John River, New Brunswick, on the 18th May 1783, a day still celebrated in the city of St. John's. They took up settlements in the meadows of the Bay of Fundy and at Port Rasoir in Nova Scotia. There, like the city in the Arabian tale, there sprang up, as if by magic, the town of Shelburne, with 12,000 inhabitants, where yesterday had been but solitude.

All eastern Canada, all the country indeed which lay between Detroit and the ocean, became dotted with the settlements of the Loyalists. By them Canada had been little known. They found, to their surprise and their infinite gratitude to God, that instead of the bleak, inhospitable wilderness, they had come into a smiling, sun-kissed, fertile land. Only patience and industry were needed to fell the timber, plough the soil, and reap a harvest. Many difficulties and much self-denial there were to undergo, but the United Empire Loyalists felt amply repaid when they gazed round in years to come at their snug and tidy homesteads, at the little church set by the foot of the green-clad hill, and saw the flag of their ancestors, rudely wrought by loving hands maybe, but oh, how cherished! floating in the crisp, pure air.

One year was called the Year of Famine in the Lake region, for in that year the crops had failed, and many families had to live on roots and beech-nuts. A sack of flour then, it was said, would have purchased an entire farm. In that year some of the old and feeble perished, but none of the living lost courage, none would have exchanged their new lot with its prospects for even luxury under the flag of the Republic across the border.

No one will know, because none has told, all that these brave pioneers underwent for their devotion and fidelity. You will see to-day on the outskirts of the older settlements little mounds, moss-covered tombstones which record the last resting-places of the forefathers of the hamlet. They do not tell you of the brave hearts laid low by hunger and exposure, of the girlish forms wasted away, of the babes and little children who perished for want of proper food and raiment. They have nothing to tell of the courageous, high-minded mothers, wives, and daughters who bore themselves as bravely as men, complaining never, toiling with the men in the fields, banishing all regrets for the life they might have led had they sacrificed their loyalty.

No distinction that the Congress could give them equalled to their minds the distinction which their King accorded them of affixing to their names the letters U.E.L. To-day the Canadians who can trace their descent from the U.E.L. dwell upon it as proudly as if there flowed in their veins the blood of the Howards, Vernons, and Montmorencys. No great monument has been raised to their memory; none is needed; it is enshrined for ever in the hearts of every true Canadian, and of every one who admires fidelity to principle, devotion, and self-sacrifice.

CHAPTER XVII

HOW CANADA'S ENEMY WAS FOILED

Slowly under the labour of the Loyalists and their children did the forests of Canada give way to civilisation. Smiling fields, trim homesteads, and flourishing gardens replaced the rude and solitary wigwams of the red-men of Ontario, Quebec, and the maritime provinces to the east. English, Scotch, and Irish emigrants found their way in shiploads to Prince Edward Island, which you may remember as the Isle St. Jean of the French. Lord Selkirk, the founder of the Red River Settlement, of which we shall soon hear, brought whole colonies of thrifty Scotch families; the name of the island was changed and that of the father of the future Queen Victoria bestowed upon it. For Prince Edward, Duke of Kent, was now commander of the British forces in Quebec.

In the midst of the increasing prosperity of the New Empire which was growing up for Britain in the west, an empire compounded of both French and English, a war-cloud began to loom upon the Southern horizon. The American Republic, after thirty-five years of independence, quarrelled once more with the mother-country. Once again England was, in 1812, as she had been in the days of the American Revolution, engaged in a terrible struggle with France. The ambition of Napoleon Bonaparte had rendered him an appalling danger to the whole of Europe. It was to quell Napoleon that Britain put forth all her strength. On land she met with alternate victories and defeats, but there was none to gainsay her on the sea. The embargo on British goods pronounced by Napoleon in the Continental blockade was America's great opportunity. A great ship industry, a splendid carrying trade sprang up between America and France. England insisted on a right of searching any vessels suspected of bringing "aid and comfort" to the enemy or of harbouring English deserters. Dozens of times was it shown that the cargoes the American vessels carried were not American products, but had been bought at a French colony and were on their way to France. Even many of the vessels flying the American flag were foreigners or English blockade-runners. This act of self-preservation was all the excuse the Americans wanted to declare war and pounce once more upon Canada, in the sure hope this time of success attending their plans. They declared that their object in taking up arms was to uphold the honour of the Stars and Stripes. "The flag," they said, "covers the cargo; you have no right to search for seamen who have deserted or for contraband goods. If you persist, we will fight you."

Wherefore, in June 1812, Congress declared war. It was not so stated in the declaration, but its real object was to snatch Canada from Britain, and, with the help of Napoleon, extinguish King George's maritime and colonial Empire. True, there were many opponents of this war in America. The people of New England in particular denounced it as wicked and senseless, and in Boston the flags were hung at half-mast. Yet the temptation was too strong for the masses led by Thomas Jefferson. "France," he said, "should be the mistress of Europe, America should be mistress of the New World!"

It seemed natural to expect that 400,000 people could not stand out against 8,000,000. The Stars and Stripes must be planted forthwith at Quebec, York (Toronto), Montreal, and Kingston. "On to Canada" was the cry of the war-party. So while Napoleon, at the head of a vast army, was marching on to Moscow, and Wellington in Spain was holding Napoleon's marshals at bay, the American army set out once more to conquer Canada.

Innocent of having given any cause of offence to their neighbours, the Canadian people, farmers, lawyers, doctors, school-teachers, shouldered their arms to a man and steadfastly waited the foe. Enough it was for them to know that the enemy had declared war against Britain, and that their portion of the Empire was threatened with invasion. A long frontier it was to guard, 1700 miles, and there were only 5000 regular troops. But Canada had a host unto herself in the gallant, dauntless person of General Isaac Brock, commander in Upper Canada. Brock had scarce need to call for volunteer battalions before they were already formed. More men flocked to his banners than there were arms with which to equip them. The Indians, too, well content with British policy and fair play, came tribe after tribe and offered their services. Chief amongst them stands the noble figure of Tecumseh, leader of the Shawanoes. His tribe had already fought the Americans, and been defeated by them at the battle of Tippecanoe. After the battle the red-men, like the Loyalists, had refused to live under the flag of the Republic and had migrated northward to Canada. Three distinct American armies began the attack. The leader of one of these, General Hull, crossed the Detroit River and, landing in Canada, issued a proclamation offering peace, liberty, and security to all who would accept American rule. To those who refused, all the horrors of war would descend upon their heads. Instantly another proclamation was issued by General Brock. "Britain," it ran, "will defend her subjects!" Canada, well knowing her duty to herself and her sovereign, was not to be bribed nor bullied. A little band of Canadian soldiers and voyageurs appeared before the American fort of Michilimackinac, which commanded Lake Michigan, and compelled it to surrender. Another small body of 350 Canadians, accompanied by Tecumseh and his zealous Shawanoes, cut off Hull's supplies and checked his progress. This prompt action greatly astonished the bombastic American general. He set out at once upon a retreat to Detroit, and there was quickly followed by Brock. The Canadian leader commanded but little more than half the number of men his adversary could boast, but nevertheless Brock was bent on storming the enemy's fort. He was on the point of giving the signal for assault when, to his amazement, a white flag was raised aloft and Hull offered to capitulate. The result was that 2500 troops and 33 cannon and the whole territory of Michigan was surrendered to Canada. No wonder that Brock became a hero, and that the heart of every Canadian who heard the tidings was fired with patriotic enthusiasm.

Meanwhile how fared it with the other American armies? General van Rensselaer brought his clamorous, eager followers to Niagara, where the mighty torrent of waters scarce could drown their huzzas of expected victory when they sighted from afar Canadian soil. The woods flamed with crimson and yellow, vineyards were thick with their purple harvests when Van Rensselaer led his army to the attack on Queenston heights. The Canadian shore of the Niagara River rose sheer and splendid from the foaming rapids below. At a spot where the river's course is somewhat checked the embarkation took place. The sound of oars caught the ear of a sentinel, and a Canadian battery opened fire. Too late! The Americans also had their batteries planted, and they were far more numerous. Thirteen hundred Americans, led by Captain Wool, moved slowly up the slope and gained the summit.

The sound of the firing reached Fort George, where General Brock then was. No time was to be lost; he flew to the fray. The Americans must be dislodged at the point of the bayonet. "Scale the heights!" rang out as the battle-cry. Waving his sword at the head of the charging lines, Brock's voice could be heard shouting, "Push on, ye brave York volunteers!" The words had scarce left his lips ere the brave Brock sank down shot through the breast.

Under the hot fire from the summit on Queenston heights the ranks of his followers were fast mowed down—so fast, that at length the Canadians were fain to halt awhile to gather breath. They had not suffered without inflicting suffering on the foe. The American general was disabled, many of his troops killed, and his position on the crest far from secure. Although he still had several hundred more men than the Canadians could bring against him, and 4000 more American soldiers were at hand on the other side of the river, the fate of the invaders was sealed. Brock's successor, Roger Sheaffe, stormed them on three sides, while on the fourth side was a precipice, 200 feet deep, its base washed by the angry river. They fought madly, but nothing could stop the fury of the Canadian charge. Back, back they fell until the very edge of the precipice was reached. There was nothing now but death or surrender, and 1100 Americans laid down their arms and became prisoners of war.

When the first year's campaign came to an end Canadian soil had been freed from the invader.

Next year, however, the enemy attacked with even greater vigour. They had met with several successes against the English at sea, for England could not always spare her best ships for the American conflict, and America thus felt the late defeats of her generals more than atoned for. York, afterwards Toronto, was captured, its public buildings burned, the church pillaged, and the public library sacked. A number of private houses were also looted and destroyed. But all this was not to go unavenged. Before the war was over a British general in the very capital city of the enemy had exacted terrible retribution. The capitol at Washington was burned and several other public buildings destroyed by way of retaliation.

With this campaign is associated in Canadian annals the story of a brave woman, Laura Secord. It shows the qualities which the womanhood of Canada possessed at a time of storm and stress, when their country was invaded by the foe. The American general-in-chief despatched one of his officers, Colonel Boerstler, to capture by surprise two of the Canadian outposts. Two valiant Canadians held these posts, Fitzgibbon at De Ceu's farm and De Harren at Twelve Mile Creek. On a clear June night the Americans set out from Fort George. In advance of their main body a strong picket roamed the country to capture all the male inhabitants they met, so that no tidings of the American approach could reach the threatened garrison. But although they captured many, there were some they were constrained to spare. Of these was a wounded militiaman, named James Secord. He had lately been fighting for his country and flag at Queenston heights when an American bullet had brought him low. Deeming him helpless, the pickets of the enemy spoke freely. Secord overheard them speaking of the projected attack on De Ceu's farm, where Fitzgibbon's thirty picked men slept ignorant of danger. A pang shot through the hapless Secord's breast. How to warn Fitzgibbon? How to apprise him of the certain doom which awaited him? He spoke of the matter to his true-hearted wife, Laura. She too came of sterling Loyalist stock. The parents of both had suffered much at the hands of the American revolutionists. They had lost all they possessed and had fled to Canada for refuge from persecution. She saw instantly the danger, and said quietly to her husband, "Fitzgibbon must be warned, and I will warn him." Secord stared at his wife in amazement. Did she realise the magnitude of such a task? The roads were swollen with rain and almost impassable by reason of the mud. The woods were deep in swamp. American and Indian marauders abounded. Twenty miles of wilderness had to be traversed, not by a strong, lusty man in the pride of youth, but by a frail woman, nearly forty years of age, and the mother of five children. Yet Laura Secord did not shrink. Seeing her resolution, her husband bade her God-speed, and she set off dauntlessly at daybreak. After struggling along through unfrequented paths for nineteen miles, subject to constant alarms, she came to a branch of a river. For want of a bridge to cross it, she reached the opposite bank by the aid of a fallen tree-trunk. At nightfall she suddenly found herself in an Indian camp. The moonlight shone on her figure, and the Indians, seeing her, burst into fearful war-yells. Laura Secord was almost slain before she could give an account of herself to the chief. The Indians were friendly and conducted her to Fitzgibbon; to him she quickly imparted her tidings. The Indians suggested that the Canadians should wait in ambush for the American column. Fitzgibbon was a brave, intelligent officer and made his plans swiftly. Sending word to his fellow-officer, De Harren, he distributed his dusky allies through the woods and waited.

At daybreak Boerstler's advance-guard was received with a murderous, unseen fire, accompanied by terrific yells. Then came the column of the enemy, which was similarly greeted. Boerstler's men began to drop in their tracks. Judging by the noise and vigour of the invisible enemy, Boerstler fancied he was being attacked by an overpowering force. He sent back for reinforcements to Fort George, and ordered his men to press on with what speed and courage they could. At this juncture Fitzgibbon, with admirable presence of mind, took advantage of the situation. Emerging suddenly from the thicket with his little handful of men, he greeted

Boerstler with a flag of truce. It was a white handkerchief which he had tied hastily to his sword. At the sight of the redcoats and their commander the fire stopped, "I wish to avoid bloodshed," said Fitzgibbon to the enemy. "In the name of the King, I call upon you to surrender!"

Laura Secord intercepted by the Mohawk scouts

By this time Boerstler was greatly alarmed, but he summoned up enough courage to mutter that he was not accustomed to surrender to a force which he had not seen. But Fitzgibbon was obdurate. He knew that Major de Harren with 200 men would soon join him, and he again pressed for instant surrender. At the time he made this lofty demand he had scarce forty men at his back! "I will give you five minutes," he said to Boerstler; "I have no longer power to control my Indians." Boerstler believed he had fallen into a trap. He had received two wounds in the skirmish. His mind was greatly agitated, and he put his hand to the articles of surrender. While he was penning his name De Harren arrived with his 200 bayonets.

By this surrender 25 officers, 519 non-commissioned officers and men, 2 field-guns, 2 ammunition cars, and a large number of horses were captured by the British.

As for Laura Secord, she soon recovered the fatigues of her thrilling adventure, and lived to be an old lady of ninety-three, greatly honoured by Canadians for her heroism and fidelity to her country's cause.

But the glory and honour of the campaign was offset by a disgraceful British reverse.

At Detroit the general, Proctor, was cut off from his supplies, and, recognising his position, resolved to evacuate and fall back on Burlington Heights. In order that the fort at Detroit might be of little use to the enemy, he dismantled it as much as he could, carried the guns away with him, and beat a retreat up the valley. With his garrison of 900 Canadians went the valiant Tecumseh and 500 Indian braves. In the footsteps of this retreating force followed 3000 of the enemy. At Moravian Town, on the banks of the river Thames, Proctor halted. It was a capital spot for a defence. On his right was a thick cedar swamp which was quickly occupied by Tecumseh and his 500 warriors. Between the swamp and river only about 300 yards intervened. But Proctor had made a terrible blunder. He had not dreamed the enemy were so nearly upon him. His scouts and skirmishers told him nothing. He felled no trees, he threw up no ramparts. In this fancied security, never thinking they would dare to attack him until he had time to make preparations, the hardy riflemen of Kentucky were swiftly upon him. They were led by the American general, Harrison, who afterwards became President of the United States. When they appeared Proctor and his men trembled. There was a momentary indecision. Perhaps the troops felt that if they had had a brave, wise commander to lead them they might still give battle to the enemy. A moment later their indecision yielded, their ranks broke, and the Canadians fled. Not so, however, Tecumseh and his redmen. Deserted by their white allies, they still held the Cedar Swamp for the British flag. But they were six times outnumbered; fight as they might, their defeat was a foregone conclusion. Amongst those who fell was the stalwart hero, Tecumseh, whose loss was mourned not more by the Indians than by the white men of Canada. Not even his heroism could save his dead body from the disgrace of mutilation by the foe. But in so doing the disgrace of the latter was greater than that they inflicted. In all his battles, as in all his life, Tecumseh had ever been humane, just, and moderate. As for the incompetent general, Proctor, he was court-martialled for his conduct and dismissed by the King from his service.

In the autumn of this year (1813) Lower Canada was threatened by a force of 7000 Americans, commanded by General Hampton. This army advanced from Lake Champlain to the Chateauguay River, designing to reach the head of Montreal Island. At this spot they expected to be joined by 8000 men under General Wilkinson, coming down the St. Lawrence in boats from Lake Ontario. To oppose the troops led by Hampton and prevent them from joining their comrades near Montreal, was a little force of 1600 men, commanded by one of the old French Canadian noblesse, Colonel de Salaberry, who had already fought for Britain in foreign climes. He was an experienced soldier; he knew that courage and endurance in the cause of patriotism more than atoned for want of numbers. He determined to throw himself in Hampton's path in the forest, and so prevent his reaching Chateauguay. Accordingly he threw up his trenches and waited for the oncoming of the Americans.

In due time they came; the battle began, and the first ranks of the foe were mowed down like grass. De Salaberry had taken the precaution to scatter a dozen buglers through the woods, who sounded the advance at intervals through the fray. The invaders, hearing the repeated trumpet blasts, thought a vast Canadian army opposed them. Nevertheless they pressed forward, the defenders purposely giving way a little. The hidden buglers blew harder than ever, panic seized the enemy at last, and they fled back into the bushes, dropping their knapsacks, drums, and muskets as they ran. Their comrades behind took them for victorious Canadians advancing to a charge, and fired upon them. Discovering their mistake too late, they in turn fled, and soon the victory of 380 Canadians over ten times that number of the enemy was complete. Miraculous to relate, the Canadian loss was only two killed and sixteen wounded; that of the Americans will never be known. But on the day following the battle nearly 100 graves were dug on their bank of the river.

Chateauguay was a blow to American pride which required many battles and more than one victory on the sea and the Great Lakes to atone for.

Meanwhile what of Wilkinson and his army which was to join Hampton at Montreal? Of the defeat and retreat of Hampton they knew nothing. They supposed him to be advancing triumphantly from the south to join them. Wilkinson and his Americans could not understand why the Canadians took such trouble to oppose him. For did he not tell them he was come to release them from their fetters? that they would no longer be slaves under the monarchy of King George, but henceforward as free as the air under a splendid republic? He could not understand it. He complained bitterly of the "active, universal hostility" of the male inhabitants of the country; he had come, he said plainly, to "subdue the forces of His Britannic Majesty, not to war against his unoffending subjects."

The answer to this kind of talk was supplied by the Canadians at the battle of Chrysler's Farm. It happened in this wise. While the American general descended the St. Lawrence by water, some 3000 of his troops marched abreast by land on the way to Montreal. In their rear a force of 800 Canadians from Kingston followed them day and night, attacking whenever they had the chance. At last the invaders received their General's command to set upon these Canadian skirmishers and "brush away the annoyance."

On a November afternoon a little force under Colonel Morrison drew up at a spot called Chrysler's Farm to receive the foe, three or four times outnumbering them. They fought fiercely, and when the struggle was over the Americans had received signal defeat; their general had fallen mortally wounded, they had lost several hundred men, and the British took more than a hundred prisoners. Thus, completely routed, Wilkinson's sole hope lay in joining Hampton at Lachine. But, alas, the news of the defeat at Chateauguay caused him to change his plans; the attack on Montreal was given up, and the army of the invaders retired for the winter.

One of the most hotly-fought contests of this war occurred in the following year at Lundy's Lane. Here 3000 British faced 4600 Americans, and this again was a British victory of which Canada has reason to be proud. In the following year the war was over, and an American statesman, Quincey, could say in Congress: "Since the invasion of the Buccaneers, there is nothing in history more disgraceful than this war."

As far as Canada was concerned the enemy had gained nothing. They had been repeatedly defeated by people fighting against many odds, whose territory they had wantonly invaded. To retaliate for their destruction of York, the capital of Upper Canada, the American capitol and other public buildings at Washington had been burned, 3000 of their ships had been captured by Britain, and two-thirds of their merchants were bankrupt at the close of the war. But Canada, baptized by fire, came out of the ordeal with a new spirit, a new self-reliance and pride in her achievements and destiny.

While the forces of America and Canada were eyeing each other angrily across the border, in the far west a new colony which would some day form a great and vigorous portion of the Dominion was born. You may remember that all these lands between the Red River in the north and Hudson's Bay were claimed by the Hudson's Bay Company. But it seemed to many an unfair thing that this large and fertile district should be given up as haunts for the fox and the beaver, the moose and the buffalo.

Accordingly a benevolent Scottish nobleman, the Earl of Selkirk, struck by the poverty of his peasant countrymen, obtained a grant of land from the Company and resolved to begin a settlement on a large scale at Red River. Now, at this time the Hudson's Bay Company, as a fur-trading enterprise, had a rival in Canada. This rival was known as the North-West Company of Montreal. The "Nor'-Westers," as they were called, objected to having the solitudes of the north-west invaded by farmers and shepherds, and no pains and misrepresentations were spared to prejudice the public against Lord Selkirk's scheme. They went up and down telling everybody that the country was cold and barren, half waste, half forest, unfit to be the abode of white men. "If you plant a colony out there," they told Lord Selkirk, "your colonists will either freeze to death or be massacred by the savages." Nevertheless Selkirk sent out his emigrants in ships across Hudson's Bay, and they made their way from thence slowly southward to Red River.

There was, besides the Hudson's Bay traders and their rivals the Nor'-Westers, another class which bitterly resented this invasion into their hunting haunts. These were the half-breed bushrangers, who were commonly called the Métis or Bois-Brulés. These men, rough and untractable, were chiefly the descendants of the French fur-hunters and trappers who had married Indian women and settled down on the shore of some distant lake or stream. In the midst of these French half-breeds there grew up also a number of Englishmen and Scotchmen hardly less fond of the wild life of the wilderness than themselves. These also took Indian wives, and when they or their children were asked whether they were English, Scotch, or Indian, they declared they were not one or the other: "We belong to the New Nation."

It was only natural that amongst this rude race there should arise a leader, a half-breed to whose superior ability and natural advantages was added an education in Montreal, the seat of the co-partnery. Cuthbert Grant, which was the name this individual bore, was known far and wide amongst the hunters and trappers of Rupert's Land, and everywhere commanded homage and respect. He had risen to be one of the most enterprising and valued agents of the Nor'-Westers, and was constantly admitted to their councils.

At the beginning of spring the "first brigade" of immigrants resumed its journey to the Red River Valley, arriving at what is now known as Point Douglas late in August 1812. Hardly had they reached this spot than they were immediately thrown into the greatest fright and disorder. A band of armed men, painted, disfigured, and apparelled like savages, confronted the little trembling band of colonists and bade them halt. They were told briefly that they were unwelcome visitors in that region, and must depart. The colonists might have been urged to make a stand, but to the terrors of hostile Indian and half-breed was added that of prospective starvation, for none would sell them provisions thereabouts. The painted warriors, who were North-West Company Métis in disguise, urged them to proceed to Pembina, across the American border, where they would be unharmed, and offered to conduct them thither. They acquiesced, and the pilgrimage was resumed for seventy miles farther on. At Pembina they passed the winter in tents, according to the Indian fashion, subsisting on the products of the chase, in common with the natives.

Spring came, and it was decided to venture again to plant the colony on the banks of the Red River. Means were found to mollify their opponents, and log-houses were built and patches of prairie sown with corn. A small quantity of seed wheat, obtained at Fort Alexander, yielded them handsome returns at harvest time, and the lot of the settlers seemed brighter. Nevertheless they decided to repair to Pembina for the winter, and, carefully saving their corn, live by hunting until the spring.

While affairs were thus proceeding with the colonists, Lord Selkirk, in 1813, paid a visit to Ireland, where he secured a large number of people as servants for the fur trade and the colony, in addition to those engaged in the Highlands.

His colonists spent a winter rendered miserable by the unfriendliness of the

Indians and half-breeds. But the Nor'-Westers were not yet satisfied. They met at their great post of Fort William in the spring, and set about planning for the complete destruction of the colony. It excited the greatest indignation and bitterness. They now determined to seduce and inveigle away as many of the colonists as could be induced to join the North-West standard, and after they should have thus diminished their means of defence, to exhort the Indians of Lac Rouge, Fond du Lac, and other places to rise and destroy the settlement. It was likewise their avowed intention to seize the Governor of Red River and carry him to Montreal as a prisoner, and so degrade the authority under which the colony was established in the eyes of the natives of that country.

Gradually a number of the settlers were seduced and instigated to disloyalty against their benefactors and the Company. A large band of the Bois-Brulés were, for two years, maintained and paraded in arms. Now that the preparatory measures had reached this stage the time seemed ripe for more decisive measures.

The ruling spirit amongst the half-breed hordes, Cuthbert Grant, appeared on the scene, and with him some of his choice dare-devil crew. The return of the settlers to Red River had filled the minds of the Bois-Brulés with rage. The contempt of the wild hunters of the plains for the peaceful tillers of the soil was great. They scorned them for their manual labour; they reproachfully termed them "the workers in gardens," and the phrase "pork-eaters," formerly applied to the voyageurs east of Fort William, was now used derisively towards the Scotch settlers. All was now ready for a final blow to the infant colony.

In June 1815, after the colony at Red River had been deprived of the means of defence and was in great measure surrounded by its enemies, a large force of Nor'-Westers, consisting of half-breeds, servants, and clerks, sallied forth to make a combined attack on the settlement. A sharp fire of musketry was kept up for some time on the Governor's house and adjacent buildings. After a series of attacks and skirmishes, Governor M'Donnell was obliged to surrender himself as a prisoner, and under a warrant from a partner in the North-West Company, sent to Montreal, charged with an undue arrogance of authority, to the detriment of the fur trade.

Great joy filled the breasts of the North-Westers assembled at Fort William when these brave tidings were conveyed to their ear. The news was accompanied by convincing proofs of the great victory gained over the enemy in the persons of 134 settlers, including men, women, and children!

Deep were the potations, turbulent was the revelry when the flushed Nor'-Westers returned from Red River and took their places at the board. They had gained a victory over the miserable colonists despatched by Lord Selkirk to begin the peopling of the West. The war between Britain and America was ended, and so further relieved their dread of punishment. But decisive as their triumph seemed, it was short-lived. Even as they rejoiced and made merry, the despised settlers had returned, and affairs at Red River were shaping for a tragedy. A new brigade of immigrants from Scotland also arrived at Red River only to gaze upon the embers of the burnt settlement. With them came a new Governor for the colony, Robert Semple by name. Governor Semple had been appointed to the chief control of all the Hudson's Bay Company's factories at Rupert's Land.

Lord Selkirk himself arrived in Canada and began engaging a number of disbanded troops to help him quell the outrages of the Nor'-Westers and inflict vengeance upon them for their murders and misdeeds. The Nor'-Westers had not thought of this.

The war with America being over, the hired European regiments of De Meuron, Watteville, and the Glengarry Fencibles in Canada were out of employment. The privates, as well as their officers, were entitled on their discharge to grants of lands in Canada, and in the event of their accepting them, the members of the two first-mentioned regiments were not to be sent back to Europe. Selkirk perceived in them an instrument ready to his hand, and, mustering them together, he travelled towards the stronghold of the Nor'-Westers, Fort William.

Meanwhile Cuthbert Grant and his Bois-Brulés began final hostilities against the Red River settlement. One large post of the Hudson's Bay Company was seized and pillaged, not only of all the English goods, furs, and provisions, but also of the private property of the servants. The Bois-Brulés then set out to wipe the colony of Red River from the face of the earth.

On a bright June day Governor Semple, on the way from York factory, learnt that he was to be attacked in two days by the Bois-Brulés, who were determined to take the fort. If any resistance were made, neither men, women, nor children should be spared. Two days later, while he was still gathering the friendly Indians about him, a man in the watch-house called out that the half-breeds were coming. Semple and his officers surveyed the neighbouring plains through their telescopes, and made out the approach of some men on horseback.

Semple, ever a man of peace, said, "We must go out and meet these people; let twenty men follow me." So they proceeded by the frequented path leading to the settlement. As they went along they met many of the colonists, who were running towards them, crying: "The half-breeds! The half-breeds!" An advance was made of about one mile, when some persons on horseback were discerned close at hand, and the Governor, somewhat uneasy at the signs of their numbers, had just decided to send for a cannon, when a fearful clamour pierced the air, and he saw it was too late. The half-breeds galloped forward, their faces painted in the most hideous manner. All were dressed in the Indian fashion, and surrounded the Hudson's Bay people in the form of a half-moon. As they advanced, the latter party retreated, and a North-West hunter named Boucher rode up close to Governor Semple and asked what he wanted there? Semple replied by demanding of Boucher what he and his party wanted? Boucher said, "We want our fort," and the Governor's answer was, "Well, go to your fort." "You rascal," shrieked Boucher, "you have destroyed our fort." Semple, a man of extremely mild manners and cultivated mind, flushed with indignation at such an address. Incautiously he laid hand upon the bridle of Boucher's horse. A few high words passed. Two shots rang out in quick succession, by the first of which an aide fell, and by the second Semple was wounded. In a few minutes the field was covered with bleeding forms; almost all Semple's men were either killed or wounded. Save in a single instance, no quarter was given; the injured were summarily despatched, and on the bodies of the dead were practised all the revolting horrors which characterise the inhuman heart of the savage.

To Lord Selkirk, on his way westward with a party of about eighty soldiers, the first intelligence of the massacre and destruction of the colony was received when Sault Ste. Marie was reached. They told him that the settlers and a large part of the property of Red River had been transported to Fort William.

Filled with indignation, and determined to demand an explanation of this further bloody deed, the Earl pressed on with all haste to the rendezvous of the North-West Company. There, all unconscious of his approach, no plan had been made either to defend themselves or to arrest Selkirk's progress.

Let us peep in at Fort William. On the night preceding the Earl's arrival the Nor'-West partners and their servants are seated at a rude banquet, at which rum and brandy flow like water. Haunches of beef and venison repose on the board, flanked by many kinds of forest game. Laughter and toasting deafen the ear.

But if the scene within was noisy and animated, that without beggars description. Hundreds of voyageurs, soldiers, Indians, and half-breeds were encamped together in the open, holding high revel. They hailed from all over the globe, England, Ireland, Scotland, France, Germany, Italy, Denmark, Sweden, Holland, Switzerland, America, the African Gold Coast, the Sandwich Islands, Bengal, Canada, with Creoles, various tribes of Indians, and a mixed progeny of Bois-Brulés or half-breeds. "Here," wrote one trader, "were congregated on the shores of the inland sea, within the walls of Fort William, Episcopalians, Presbyterians, Methodists, Sun worshippers, men from all parts of the world whose creeds were 'wide as poles asunder,' united in one common object, and bowing down before the same idol." Women, soldiers, voyageurs, and Indians, in ever-moving medley, danced, sang, drank, and gambolled about the fort this night.

But Nemesis was at hand. The Earl approached the fur-trading stronghold swiftly and silently. He was on them before they realised it. An attempt was made to shut the gate and prevent the troops from entering. The fort people had succeeded in shutting one half of the gate, and had almost closed the other by force, when thirty soldiers forthwith rushed to the spot and forced their way into the stronghold of the Northmen.

The notes of a bugle rang out across the river. A fresh force of about thirty other veterans of European battlefields hurried quickly over the stream to join their comrades. Awed by the apparition of so many arms and uniforms, the North-Westers abandoned further resistance, and bloodshed was happily averted. Those who had refused obedience to the Earl's commands were seized and taken forcibly to the boats, the others submitting peaceably to arrest.

Fort William and the Nor'-Westers, together with about two hundred French Canadians and half-breeds, and sixty or seventy Iroquois Indians in and about the fort, had been captured by Lord Selkirk. He had become possessed, to use his own words, "of a fort which had served, the last of any in the British dominions, as an asylum for banditti and murderers, and the receptacle for their plunder; a fort which nothing less than the express and special licence of his Majesty could authorise subjects to hold; a fort which had served as the capital and seat of government to the traitorously assumed sovereignty of the North-West; a fort whose possession could have enabled the North-West Company to have kept back all evidence of their crimes."

Meeting of the Nor'-Westers at Fort William, 1816

The heads of the evil-doing were summoned to stand their trial in the east. But the Nor'-Westers were bitter against the Earl who had dared to plant a colony in the midst of their hunting grounds.

"That canting rascal and hypocritical villain, Lord Selkirk, has got possession of our post at Fort William," wrote one of the aggrieved partners. "Well, we will have him out of that fort," he pursued amiably, "as the Hudson's Bay knaves shall be cleared, bag and baggage, out of the North-West."

But although no man was destined to see this part of their prophecy fulfilled, yet Lord Selkirk, a few weeks later, evacuated Fort William. No sooner had the Earl and his forces left this great post than the sheriff of Upper Canada arrived, took possession of the fort and the Nor'-Westers, and restored it to its original owners. Afterwards Imperial commissioners appointed in the name of the Prince Regent to restore law and order to the region went on to Red River, whither Lord Selkirk had repaired. Law and order were, however, not so easily restored. The rivalry between the fur-traders was too strong, the memory of bloodshed too recent for perfect peace to be established in a few weeks or months.

In the meantime Lord Selkirk left the matter of retribution upon the murderers of Governor Semple to the law and returned to England. Punishment was duly meted out to the wrongdoers. The Red River colony struggled manfully against adversity for several winters, and it was not until 1822 that it at last surmounted the evils which threatened to starve it out of existence. But the heart of its founder was not to be gladdened by the tidings of its growing prosperity. The Earl had reached England disheartened; his health was shattered by the long and anxious struggle to found a colony at Red River, and in April 1820 he breathed his last. Selkirk may be truly called the founder and father of the prosperous North-West of to-day.

Soon after his death the Hudson's Bay and North-West Companies, for so long such fierce competitors in the fur trade, joined hands in friendly partnership.

Gone now for ever were the old free days of the hunters and trappers, the bushrangers and voyageurs. The whole fur trade was placed on a strictly commercial basis. The Nor'-Westers, rough, enterprising adventurers, found themselves part of a huge machine operated by a governor and committee in far-away England. Smaller and more remote grew the regions where they could roam free and undisturbed. Rupert's Land extended from the American border to the Pole, and from the Great Lakes to the Pacific, and the officers of the Hudson's Bay Company ruled it and most of those who dwelt there with a rod of iron for the next fifty years.

Trouble, however, was still in store for Red River. Blood was yet to flow before the Bois-Brulé could adapt himself to the new order of things.

CHAPTER XVIII

TRAITORS, REDCOATS, AND REDSKINS

When on that memorable morning in June 1837 the young Princess Victoria was awakened from her slumber and told that she had become mistress of the British Empire, far away, in one part of the Empire, two men were plotting to overthrow the new Queen's authority. Canada was again beset by disloyalty and rebellion. By this time that portion of the country which Champlain had founded and Frontenac ruled, now called Lower Canada, was filled with industrious, God-fearing peasantry, tilling their farms, pursuing the peaceful, wholesome life of the village and countryside. Westward to them lay Upper Canada and the towns and homesteads of the Loyalists, into which many more thousands of settlers had poured since the days of King George III. Amongst both these people a host of agitators arose, restless lawyer-politicians for the most part, who cried out for liberty and a republic. We have seen these crafty-eyed men, with their loud voices and sardonic smile, stalking all through the pages of New World history. They were the successors of the renegades who revolted against Champlain, just as 150 years before that there were the jealous malcontents who revolted against Christopher Columbus and brought him in sorrow to the grave. Frontenac faced them, and with an effort he put them down; the gallant Lasalle met his death at their hands; under Samuel Adams they achieved a triumph in New England which led to the loss of the thirteen American colonies. A noisy, reckless faction of this kind it was which had forced America into the shameful, useless war of 1812. Now the revolutionists stalked rampant in Canada, and it was high time their leaders were overthrown and crushed. In the English part of Canada, the Upper Provinces, the revolutionaries were led by a rash and impulsive Scotchmen named William Mackenzie. In Lower Canada, which was chiefly peopled by French Canadians, the rebels looked to Louis Papineau as their leader. When Lord Gosford, the Governor, warned the people of the peril they ran in listening to the counsels of the demagogues who would ruin them, they only met in the streets shouting "Long live Papineau, our deliverer!" Daring bands of rebels, called "Sons of Liberty," tore down the Governor's proclamation. In a few weeks Papineau gave the signal and his followers flew to arms. It was the time of harvest; the grain had ripened and was ready for the reaper, but the English settlers in Lower Canada, loyal to their young Queen, dared not use their scythes and sickles for fear of the loaded muskets of the French Canadian rebels. They fled for refuge to Montreal, where the first skirmish in the rebellion took place. Then the rebels set upon a small body of loyal cavalry marching from St. John's, on the Richelieu River. Amongst them was a young officer, Lieutenant Weir, the bearer of despatches from Colonel Gore. He was made prisoner and placed in the custody of some of the insurgents, who, regardless of mercy and decency, butchered him in barbarous fashion. While Weir was being hacked to pieces by Papineau's men, the rebel leader learned from the captured despatches that Gore and his soldiers were marching upon them. At St. Denis, therefore, they entrenched themselves, and for some hours held the post, keeping up a deadly fire upon the troops.

Fortunately for the English flag in Canada, there was an able man to defend it in the person of Sir John Colborne, one of the generals of the Duke of Wellington. He sent Colonel Wetherell to take the rebel post at St. Charles. Here a weak and foolish American, who called himself "General" Brown, abandoned his men almost at the first artillery discharge. Though they fought on for a time, none the worse for their leader's absence, they were soon dispersed by assault. Colborne himself, with a force of regulars and militia, marched to the villages of St. Eustache and St. Benoit. The parish church at St. Eustache, built of stone, was turned into a fort, and here, in the sacred edifice, the rebels bade defiance to the soldiers of the Queen. Their fate was a terrible one. Flames shot through the roof and steeple, and the walls began to fall in. The rebels continuing to make a stand until escape was too late, almost the whole number of those who thus held St. Eustache were burnt to ashes.

When Colborne marched his men on to St. Benoit the rebels, now thoroughly frightened at their misdeeds, sued for peace. They surrendered ignominiously, but this did not prevent the British settlers, whose homes and harvests they had destroyed, from venting their anger upon them, so that this village and many houses round about fell a prey to their wrath. That night the countryside was lit up by a terrible glow. On the morrow it was seen how few amongst the vast body of French Canadians were really disloyal to the Government which had given them political and religious liberty. In one of the districts which had been claimed by Papineau, 1500 militiamen put themselves under the French Canadian, Colonel de Hertel, and declared themselves staunch in their allegiance and ready to help in quelling the rebellion. Although Papineau's men had fled cravenly across the border at the first outbreak of trouble, others still continued to foment war and bloodshed. Two unhappy brothers named Nelson gained an unenviable notoriety. One of them boldly proclaimed the "Republic" of Canada; but all they gained for their pains was the melancholy pleasure of seeing their countrymen, of both French and English origin, in distress, gaols filled with their deluded followers, many of whom were afterwards hanged for treason.

While this was happening in Lower Canada to cause the young Queen and her ministers anxiety, in Upper Canada William Mackenzie and his followers revelled in riot. Mackenzie fancied he was another Washington; he wrote bombastic letters to his fellow-traitor, Papineau, and busied himself with designing a flag for his new Republic, on which were two stars, one for each province. At last Mackenzie considered the time had come for war, and he and his friends decided to capture Toronto.

One bright, cold December day 1000 rebels were entrenched at their rendezvous, Montgomery's tavern, a few miles outside Toronto. An old soldier, who had fought under Napoleon, Van Egmond, undertook to drill them; Sam Lount, a beetle-browed blacksmith, was their commander-in-chief. To nip their schemes in the bud, against them marched the royal Governor, Sir Francis Head, with 500 militia. The Governor called upon them to surrender and lay down their arms; they refused, and an exchange of fire took place. Then the courage of the insurgents oozed out, and they fled, the ringleader, Mackenzie, being among the first who took to his heels. He retired to a little spot in the middle of the Niagara River called Navy Island, and proceeded to establish what he called a Provisional Government. Overhead, greatly to his own satisfaction, floated the two-starred flag of the Canadian Republic. Here Mackenzie impudently issued grants of land to all who would take up arms in his cause, and despatched them in a steamboat called the *Caroline*. One dark night a dashing young British lieutenant seized the rebel *Caroline*, which his American sympathisers had lent to "President" Mackenzie, set her on fire, and dropped her, a burning mass, over the Niagara Falls.

A time soon came when the American sympathisers felt that they had gone too far, and their President issued a proclamation warning his people against attacking a friendly power. In spite of this, however, several American filibustering expeditions took place before they realised the hopelessness of endeavouring to seize Canada, as they had seized Texas from a friendly nation like Mexico and make it a part of their Republic.

Mackenzie was arrested by the Americans themselves and sentenced to eighteen months in gaol. Had he been caught in Canada, he would have suffered the fate of his companions and been hanged, as he richly deserved, for treason.

The disaffection all came to an end when Queen Victoria's Government, acting on the advice of Lord Durham, who had been sent to Canada to inquire into the disturbances, united Upper Canada and Lower Canada into one province, and granted the people the power to manage their own affairs in a Parliament of their own. After a time, when the Canadian people could not agree upon a spot to be chosen for a capital town for their now united Provinces of Ontario and Quebec, they called upon Queen Victoria to select one for them. It so happened that there was on the banks of the Ottawa a little village named Bytown, not far from two beautiful falls, the Rideau and Chaudière. It was the scene of a prosperous lumbering camp, and several sawmills throve there; it was far removed from the stress and the struggle of the French and English parties, and from bitter political feeling. So the young Queen, who had seen some sketches of the village, chose it for the meeting-place of Parliament and the residence of her Governor-General. All parties were pleased, and so it came about that Bytown was rechristened Ottawa, and it in course of a few years became filled with magnificent buildings and beautiful homes.

Ottawa was destined to be still more important and famous as the capital of the entire DOMINION OF CANADA. For as time went on all the British provinces, both of the east and the west, that begun by Poutraincourt 250 years before in Acadia, and that founded by Selkirk on the Red River, all the colonies between the Atlantic and the Pacific north of the American border, had grown and flourished and sought to be welded into a single nation under the British flag. Thirty years after Papineau's rebellion, therefore, the desired union took place, and in 1867 the Canadian Dominion, under Sir John Macdonald's leadership, began its career.

The new order of things involved many changes. Amongst others it was time in the Far West that the power of the Hudson's Bay Company over the vast region of Rupert's Land should come to a close. No longer was it meet and proper that a body of fur-traders should be lords paramount over all this territory. Yet neither the Company nor its dependents, the voyageurs, trappers, and hunters, were eager for any change. The Métis or Bois-Brulés, of whom we spoke in the last chapter, had grown accustomed to the Company's rule. "If," said they, "the Company is no longer to govern us, then we should govern ourselves." When they saw the first advance guard of Canadians from the east coming in to take their land for farms, to lay out roads and townships, the Bois-Bruits met in angry protest; they defied the Canadians to take their country without their consent. They were joined by a number of American immigrants, who regarded any political trouble with pleasure as hastening the annexation which was the object of their desire.

Again did a leader step quickly forth from their ranks. His name was Louis Riel. Half-educated, fanatical, this young man dreamed dreams of future power and glory. In person he was short and stout, with a large head, a high forehead, and an intelligent eye; above his brow a mass of long and thick black hair clustered. No sooner was it clear that the authority of the Hudson's Bay Company had been sold for Canadian gold, than Riel proclaimed himself Dictator of the new province of Rupert's Land; he issued a bombastic proclamation to his people refusing to recognise the authority of Canada "coming to rule us with a rod of despotism," and declaring a Provisional Government, as so many agitators had done before him. A new flag, comprised of the fleur-de-lys and a shamrock, out of compliment to the Irish Fenians, was hoisted over Fort Garry, a strong stone fortress which the Company had built on the Red River, not far from where the city of Winnipeg now stands.

When the Canadian Government heard of the trouble that was brewing in its newly-acquired territory of Rupert's Land, the greatest alarm was felt, for at that very moment Governor MacDougall was on his way to Fort Garry to take charge of the new territory. The Governor had just set foot across the border when he was met by Riel and three or four thousand followers at a barrier built across the roadway. Two courses were open to him: to fight or retreat. As he had no desire to shed blood, he returned quietly across the border.

Riel could not now keep his hot-headed followers in hand. Sixty prisoners, all who dared to oppose his schemes, were seized and locked up in the fort. A commissioner was sent from Canada, Donald Smith, afterwards Lord Strathcona and Mount Royal, to allay the excitement, but his mission had no immediate effect, for Louis Riel was resolved to play a heroic part in the eyes of Indians and Métis. Several of the leading men of the Company were put in irons. So overwhelmed was the Company's governor, that he took to his bed and never recovered. While he lay in the shadow of death, the pitiless Riel stood over him heaping him with abuse. As for Donald Smith, Riel gave orders to his guard, "Shoot that man," said he, "if he makes an attempt at escape or disobeys my orders." But Donald Smith survived the ordeal, living to be governor of the territory, and afterwards to be known all over the Empire as one of the chief builders of the Canadian Pacific Railway.

The Defeat of Louis Riel, Fish Creek, 1885

Amongst the prisoners who had dared to defy Riel's power was a resolute young Canadian named Thomas Scott. Scott had refused to bow the knee to the Dictator, and Riel resolved that he should die. So on the 4th March 1870 Scott was led outside the gate of the fort, with a white handkerchief bound across his brow; his coffin, with a white sheet thrown upon it, was carried with him; his eyes were then bandaged, he was allowed a few minutes for prayer, and then told to kneel in the snow. Six half-breeds, who had been plied heavily with drink, then raised their muskets; their shots rang out, and Scott immediately fell back, pierced by three bullets. He had not been executed; he had been brutally murdered. Like wild-fire through the east flew the news of the death of Scott. Volunteers and regulars were hastily summoned. At that time there was in Canada an able Colonel of the British Army, by name Garnet Wolseley. Very few knew his name then, but he, too, was destined to be world-famous. He instantly put himself at the head of the Red River brigade and pressed on to Fort Garry to punish the impudent traitor who had dared to set Canada at defiance. The Red River brigade pressed on through bad roads, dense forests; they crossed lakes and turbulent rivers in leaky boats. A number of accidents occurred and many narrow escapes from rock and rapid. But at last through the 600 miles of wilderness Colonel Wolseley and his men of the brigade came to the neighbourhood of Fort Garry. A line of skirmishers was thrown out in advance; it was not yet known what defence "the little Napoleon," as his adherents were fond of calling Riel, would offer. To Wolseley's surprise, no banner floated from the flagstaff and the gates of the fort were open. Through the portals the Colonel and his brigade marched, angry that they had been balked of their prey. Louis Riel's courage had oozed out at the last moment, and he had fled across the Assiniboine River.

But Canada was not yet done with Louis Riel. Fifteen years passed away—years of stirring change. Thousands of colonists had poured into the new and fertile province now called Manitoba, and a flourishing city arose on the site of Fort Garry. In sullenness the half-breeds still further withdrew into the heart of the wilderness and settled on the banks of the Saskatchewan and the far Saskatchewan Valley. Silently they nourished hate against the settlers, looking to their leader Riel, who lived in exile across the American border, to come some day and avenge their wrongs.

Slowly but surely the farmers and ranchers pushed the half-breeds and hunters farther and farther, until they felt the forests slip from them. When they could bear it no longer, they sent a message to Riel to free them from the tyranny of the Canadian immigrants. Riel answered the call; he rejoiced this time in the title of Liberator, for he told the Indians and Bois-Brulés he would liberate their lands from the harvesters and ranchmen. Gathering together not only the half-breeds, but many of the red-men as well, the rebels advanced on the Canadian militia at Duck Lake and inflicted upon them a defeat. Flushed with this triumph, Riel sought the chiefs of the Cree and Black Feet tribes; he showed them how the Canadians could be driven out of the country, and the old happy, careless, prosperous days of the Indians would return. Amongst those who listened was Big Bear, chieftain of the Crees, and Crow Foot of the warlike Black Feet, besides Poundmaker and other chiefs. War and butchery ensued; helpless settlers were shot down without mercy. But Nemesis was at hand. Canada was pouring an army of redcoats into the turbulent North-West, and the fate of Riel and his deluded half-breeds and redskin followers was sealed. He himself was seized, found guilty of treason, and hanged at last for his folly and his crimes.

We have now in the pages of this book marked the Romance of Canada from that summer day nearly four centuries ago when the adventurous Cartier sailed into the Gulf of St. Lawrence and marvelled at the red-men and the beauty of the Canadian forests; we have marked the gallant Poutraincourt plan his picturesque little colony in Acadia; noted the deeds of the valiant Champlain and his loyal trust in the land for which he spent and suffered so much. Can you forget the fortitude and unquenchable heroism of the ill-fated Jesuits? The picturesque fidelity and thrilling adventures of Charles de la Tour and his brave wife; the heroic achievements of Frontenac; the fierce struggle against fate of hapless Montcalm; the glorious victory of Wolfe; the zeal and sufferings of the United Empire Loyalists, pass in a succession of pictures as we compass those three centuries of time since Canada became the settled habitation of lion-hearted men.

Gradually the ferocious red-man with his musket and tomahawk has been driven from his lodges and wigwams in the east, to make way for bustling cities and thriving towns and villages. The lakes and rivers, where the birch-bark canoes of the savage, where the daring fur-hunters once thronged, laden with the spoils of the forest, now bear on their bosoms hundreds of busy steam-boats, freighted with the produce of farm and orchard and factory. The lonely, dangerous trails along which Champlain, Frontenac, Lasalle, and Verendrye led their men have given way to steel highroads which traverse the entire Continent. Everywhere the spirit of progress has smiled upon the land, and the farms, orchards, and homesteads of Canada smile upward to the clear heavens in return.

Do not forget that Romance, though unseen by the bodily eye, never dies. It is as beautiful as the landscape or the setting sun. Search for it in the annals of the past, and each grey lake, every simple river, both hill and dale, have their stirring story to tell of valour and heroic sacrifice, of noble endurance, of patriotic deed.

Canada was not easy in the making; much blood flowed and many loyal hearts were broken before the Great Dominion arose.

INDEX

A

B

C

D

E

F

G

S

T

V

W

Y

Lector House believes that a society develops through a two-fold approach of continuous learning and adaptation, which is derived from the study of classic literary works spread across the historic timeline of literature records. Therefore, we aim at reviving, repairing and redeveloping all those inaccessible or damaged but historically as well as culturally important literature across subjects so that the future generations may have an opportunity to study and learn from past works to embark upon a journey of creating a better future.

This book is a result of an effort made by Lector House towards making a contribution to the preservation and repair of original ancient works which might hold historical significance to the approach of continuous learning across subjects.

HAPPY READING & LEARNING!

LECTOR HOUSE LLP
E-MAIL: info@lectorhouse.com

Printed by Libri Plureos GmbH in Hamburg,
Germany